GOOD COP
BAD COP

GOOD COP
BAD COP

Rebecca H. Dartt
with David McElligott

Expanding Horizons
An imprint of New Horizon Press
Far Hills, New Jersey

Expanding Horizons books are published by

New Horizon Press
P.O. Box 669
Far Hills, NJ 07931

All Kensington titles, imprints, and distributed lines are available at special quantity discounts for bulk purchases for sales promotions, premiums, fund-raising, and educational or institutional use. Special book excerpts or customized printings can also be created to fit specific needs. For details, write or phone the office of the Kensington special sales manager: Kensington Publishing Corp., 850 Third Avenue, New York, NY 10022, attn: Special Sales Department, Phone: 1-800-221-2647.

ISBN-13: 978-1-933893-05-1
ISBN-10: 1-933893-05-2

First New Horizon Press Hardcover Printing: 1994
First Expanding Horizons Mass Market Printing: July 2007

10 9 8 7 6 5 4 3 2 1

Printed in the United States of America

Dedicated to the Memory
of
Tony, Dodie, Shelby and Marc Harris
and
the efforts of
The New York State Police,
The City of Ithaca Police Department,
and the *Tompkins County Sheriff's Department*

ACKNOWLEDGMENTS

My deepest thanks goes to Senior Investigator David McElligott for his unusually patient and generous part in supplying information concerning the investigation of the Harris murders and David L. Harding. In many instances, the details he was able to provide had never before been made public.

I am also indebted to the many investigators and troopers with the New York State Police and to local police officers who talked with me with unfailing courtesy and openness during almost three years of my research and writing. Their input was crucial to telling the story of this investigation.

Also, I am grateful to Tompkins County District Attorney George Dentes, to Senior Investigator Karl Chandler, to New York State Police Chief Inspector Francis DeFrancesco, to defense attorney Bill Sullivan, and to the special prosecutor Nelson Roth for their valuable contributions.

I would like to thank Mary Harris, Don and Patricia Lake and other Syracuse family members and friends for sharing with me their remembrances of Tony, Dodie, Shelby and Marc. I am also grateful to the Harrises' friends in Marietta, Georgia, who talked with me about the Harrises they knew and loved.

Though there were some Harris friends and neighbors in Ellis Hollow who wished not to be interviewed for reasons of privacy or because they were still pained by the tragedy, I am extremely grateful to those who came forward. Dennis and Elizabeth Regan not only were willing to talk with me, but made me feel the project was worthwhile from the very beginning. Without people like the Regans, I may not have persevered.

My sincere thanks to Ed Reynolds and Doris Rosenblum of Manhattan's Westside Alternate High School for their cooperation.

I am grateful to Dr. Charles Bahn, a forensic psychologist at John Jay College of Criminal Justice in New York City, and to Dr. Murray Miron, a sociologist at Syracuse University, for helping me gain a better understanding of the psychopathic personality.

Others who made a real difference with their personal support were Robin Cofer, Carolyn Lindquist, Maureen Aung-Thwin, and Louis Kraar. And many thanks to my husband, Bob, for his computer assistance and for believing I could do it.

In addition to interviews and court transcripts, written accounts of the story which were valuable appeared in *The Ithaca Journal, The Syracuse Post-Standard, The Binghamton Sun-Bulletin,* and in Tompkins County court records. Other important written sources included *The Harris Family; Ellis Hollow Lore* by Zelle Middaugh Pritchard, 1962; *The Peopling of Tompkins County* by Carol Kammen, 1985; and *A Short History of Tompkins County* by Jane Dieckman, 1986.

CONTENTS

Preface		11
One	The Last Day Begins	13
Two	Michael Anthony Kinge a/k/a Tony Turner	29
Three	Their Last Day Ends	41
Four	Two Days Before Christmas	47
Five	Aftershock	61
Six	A Country Paradise	67
Seven	McElligott and His Team	75
Eight	Christmas in Ithaca	100
Nine	A Lost Bicyclist	103
Ten	Running Hot and Cold	109
Eleven	Coping	117
Twelve	The Young Tipster	129
Thirteen	Stakeout	137
Fourteen	A Straightjacket	151
Fifteen	The Peregrine House	158
Sixteen	Getting the Evidence	179
Seventeen	Firefight	192
Eighteen	In Custody	206
Nineteen	The Lineup	225
Twenty	Preliminaries	230

Twenty-one   Advance Maneuvers   247

Twenty-two   The People Decide   251

Twenty-three Mistaken Notion   268

Twenty-four   Lies and Truth   280

Twenty-five   Shelling Paradise   292

Twenty-six   Vainglory   297

Twenty-seven The Last Straw   313

Twenty-eight The Real David Harding   323

Afterword   332

Addendum: What Happened That Night   335

Epilogue   345

Preface

The Harris family tragedy and its aftermath takes us beyond the edge of evil into the heart of darkness that shows us how a depraved man can act and how that brand of wanton terror can leave us with permanent scars of suspicion and vulnerability. The story and all its horror reflects many of contemporary society's problems—racist attitudes, friction between the poor and wealthy, as well as humanity's oldest sins of mendacity, lust, and revenge.

When I started gathering material, this was to be the story of the Harris family murders, how they sent terror through our quiet college town in upstate New York two days before Christmas in 1989, and how the crimes were solved by the state police in only six and a half weeks. But just as I finished my first draft of the manuscript, a completely unexpected revelation came to light which dramatically changed the thrust of the story. The case was catapulted into widespread notoriety, exposing the deception of one primary police investigator and his partner. Their duplicity put the Harris investigation and the practices of police everywhere into question.

GOOD COP/BAD COP is a primarily factual account of events as they evolved from December 1989 to December 1992. The incidents and dialogue are based upon over fifty interviews with police, lawyers, educators and the neighbors, friends and family of the characters, as well as input from numerous court records and newspaper articles.

Shirley Kinge, Sallie Reese, and Joanna White refused requests for interviews. Since Michael Kinge was dead, information was obtained from those willing to talk with me, officials, and public documents.

Only in a few instances have the names of individuals been changed to protect their privacy. Additional incidents and dialogue have been deduced from known facts, interviews with police, lawyers, educators and neighbors, friends and family of the characters, as well as input from numerous court records and newspaper articles.

The randomness and brutality of the murders plunged Ithaca into a new era. No longer do we leave our doors unlocked or freely offer help to strangers. The Kinge case, the Harding case, and their aftermath have changed our assumptions about the criminal justice system. The lies of police officers are a firm reminder that individual integrity forms the core of our faith in any law enforcement organization and when it is corrupted, faith fails.

Real justice finally prevailed only after a torturous journey through specious justice, public cynicism, racism, mass disillusionment, and private burdens. We witnessed an example of clumsy democracy in slow-motion. Not pretty, but better than the alternatives.

Rebecca H. Dartt

One

The Last Day Begins

Tony Harris woke up Friday, December 22, to the loud scraping of a snow plow's blades as it roared along Ellis Hollow Road. It was a familiar early morning sound in the winter that could be heard for miles around. Tony strained to hear the 6:45 weather report coming over WHCU: "Currently five degrees in Ithaca with more snow predicted for today and tonight. Fifteen below zero tonight. Snow flurries on Saturday with a high of six degrees."

That meant it was probably colder in Ellis Hollow, because the temperature dropped lower in the outlying valleys. Tony was accustomed to getting up early, preferring not to hurry. During the week he left the house around 7:30 in order to be at the office by 8:00, unless he had to drive to the branch office in Gaithersburg, Maryland, or catch a plane for Raleigh or Atlanta, in which case he left earlier. He slept a half-hour later this morning, having retired later than usual, about 12:30, after watching the Syracuse-Georgetown basketball game. Marc, their eleven-year-old son, had taped the game for him earlier, but he hadn't found time to sit down and watch it until then.

As he shaved, Tony reviewed his plans. This should be an easy, relaxing day, and he was even going in a little later. Not much going on the day before Christmas break except the scheduled afternoon office party. Dodie usually stayed in bed a few minutes longer than Tony, rising in time to set breakfast on the table before Shelby, their fifteen-year-old daughter, and Marc came downstairs.

Tony was a family man. He never let getting ahead in business interfere with what he considered the most important part of his life. Filled with ambition, he wanted to excel in his career yet maintain a solid family life. Now, at thirty-nine, Tony had achieved both. He was near the top of his company as director of marketing and sales on the East Coast for the Deanco Corporation, an electronics distributor based in Ithaca. Jim Felton, the Deanco manager who had hired him in 1974, had lured him away from an insurance firm in Syracuse after Tony sold him a million dollars of business and personal insurance. Felton knew that anyone who could sell him that much insurance would be an asset to Deanco. Tony started as a salesman in charge of the Syracuse area and in three years had expanded his territory to cover New York state.

Growing up in Mattydale, a predominately Catholic, blue-collar neighborhood in North Syracuse, Tony's family lived in a modest, one-story frame house, like many that cluster together on the orderly grid of streets off Route 11, a commercial district near the airport. It was the kind of place where folks regularly displayed the American flag in their front yards or on their porches.

His father, an industrial pattern maker, abandoned the family when Tony and his brother and sister were preschoolers, forcing his mother to support the family on the low wages she earned as a cook in the school cafeteria. Mary

Harris, a strong, perceptive woman, made sure her children knew what the important things in life were and how to stick to them—keeping their religious faith, helping others whenever they could, and staying in school. She believed strongly that education was the way to get ahead and to better themselves.

Tony learned the lessons well. Very soon he also figured out that in order to get ahead he had to use his head and his will. That determination was coupled with a strong sense of responsibility. As the eldest boy, he thought of himself as the man of the family. At twelve, Tony started a neighborhood paper route, getting up before 6:00 A.M. to deliver the *Syracuse Post-Standard*. In a few months he had doubled his route, partly as a result of close attention to customers. Each morning Tony placed the paper at their doorstep, rang the bell, and wished them good morning. A week before Christmas in his first year as a paperboy, Tony politely requested customers to give him tips early enough for him to buy presents for his family; the extra hundred dollars bought jackets for the children and a lined raincoat for his mother.

A short while later he convinced his mother of the idea first and then a local merchant—to sell him a snowblower on time. Tony would put some money down and then pay the rest off week by week, allowing him to expand the snow removal business he'd started in the neighborhood. The blower paid for itself before the winter was over, and Tony made a small profit.

By the time he was a teenager, people who knew Tony Harris assumed he had a bright future; he had all the attributes which contribute to success. For instance, Tony's self-confidence enabled him to tackle new tasks and to be inventive in transforming mundane ones. Tony convinced his tenth-grade English teacher that making an oral report about Walt Whitman was as acceptable as writing a composition about him. He loved speaking in front of people, but writing was another matter. Other students who preferred talking to writing followed suit and the teacher was pleased too; it meant fewer papers to grade.

Tony intended to become a math teacher, having been encouraged by his instructors at North Syracuse High School before entering Onondaga Community College. But Tony was so turned off by the unruly and lackadaisical students he saw on a visit back to his old high school during his senior year, that he changed his career plan. Taking a course in public relations and marketing was exciting. Tony discovered he had a natural bent toward public relations and in a sense had been practicing the art of persuasion for years. Before graduation in May 1971, he landed a job selling insurance for Mutual of Syracuse. The same summer Tony married Dodie Lake, who had grown up on the east side of Syracuse; a pretty brunette with a sensitive nature that he appreciated. Tony felt he was a lucky man.

This morning, dressing in jeans, the cream-colored sweater Dodie had given him last Christmas, and his tan dockside shoes that felt so comfortable on his feet, Tony felt relaxed. His casual personality had never fully meshed with a business suit and tie. He liked the feel of comfortable clothes and they matched his unpretentious nature.

Just under six feet, Tony had always been a little overweight. After years of eating on the road—conference dinners, whiling away lonely evenings in restaurants—he had put on more pounds then his frame could hide. He grew tired of seeing himself in the mirror with a double chin that was getting more prominent every day. The pounds had accumulated to the point where Tony decided to do something drastic. In February he'd joined a Weight Watchers group, and lost fifty-three pounds in nine months. On Tuesday nights, he'd even started playing basketball with a group of guys and running a bit to get in better shape and to keep his weight down. The suit worn to his interview with Deanco was too tight for him at the time, but now it was too loose.

Dodie had begun to change Tony's ideas about food when they lived in Atlanta in the mid-1980s. After Dodie was afflicted with breast cancer, she made changes in the family's diet, cutting down on fatty foods and serving more fresh fruits and vegetables. The crisis brought on a sudden urgency to be serious about a healthy lifestyle. Tony stopped smoking and tried to eat more chicken, but being a meat and potatoes man, he found it hard to stick to the lighter fare. It was not until he tried Weight Watchers that he found a plan to which he could stick and with which he'd found success.

In six days Tony would turn forty—he felt it the demarcation line between being young and middle-aged—but except for a slight hair loss in the front and a few age lines on his face, he could still pass for a man in his thirties. A family ski trip to Greek Peak, a popular ski area thirty miles north of Ithaca, was planned for the following Thursday to celebrate his birthday.

Tony liked the early morning, even these cold winter ones when he looked out over the white fields and the hills to the south in back of the dream house that Dodie's father had built for them three and a half years before. When they moved to Ithaca in 1985 from Marietta, Georgia, where he was branch manager for Deanco, they searched for enough land to build a large house, and an antique and country gift store that Dodie had wanted for a long time. They needed enough space for children and animals; their long-range plans included raising geese and maybe a horse or two.

Ellis Hollow fit their priorities. The location offered an independent country life in a community that held traditional family values. The Harris's could enjoy their privacy, yet join in community activities when they chose. Seeing the empty pond a few hundred yards to the east of the house reminded Tony of one project that had failed. It was to be a farm pond, very common on the rural landscape, used for fishing, perhaps swimming, and during the winter when it froze over Marc and his friends would practice skating. Ice hockey was Marc's passion. But the pond did not fill up, apparently due to the rocky soil. Tony and Dodie laughed about it with friends and neighbors, but he felt sorry for Marc's sake.

It was a lively breakfast scene in the Harrises' kitchen that morning. Marc's dog Annie, a German shepherd and collie mix, barked loudly at the newcomer, a six-month-old tabby cat named Shadow, sending her running out of the room. Annie was a stray they had found while living in Marietta. She was a peaceful family fixture who slept with Marc and followed Dodie around all day, even riding in the van when she went shopping.

"Calm your dog down, Marc, for gosh sakes, the poor cat is scared to death," yelled Shelby, as she wrapped up the cookies she had baked the night before to take to her friends at school.

"Mom, remember about going over to Jim's house tonight at seven, okay?"

Shelby knew her mother never forgot anything. *Why did she ask?* But the reminder just popped out of Shelby's mouth as she sat down to eat a toasted raisin bagel and drink a mug of hot cocoa at the kitchen table. Her mother was a near-perfect mother, and Shelby loved her deeply. They had become even closer during Dodie's bout with cancer. After the first mastectomy the doctor said he had gotten it all, but a few months later found a malignant tumor on Dodie's other breast. Shaken by these threats to her life and convinced she might have limited time to live, Dodie decided she had to return to New York to be closer to her family in Syracuse. The Harrises planned their move back north even though Tony didn't know if Deanco had anything open for him in the Syracuse area. He rejected Dodie's desperate suggestion that in order to keep his job he might have to live in a condo in Atlanta and commute to New York on the weekends. He was willing to resign from the company in order to keep the family together.

"Shelby, I'll drop you at Jim's tonight around seven. I have a few things to pick up at the mall, so I'll do that and come back for you in an hour or so. All right?" Dodie said to her daughter as she poured her a small glass of orange juice.

Jim Ciolek was Shelby's first serious boyfriend. They'd known each other since DeWitt Middle School, but started going out in the fall after finding themselves in the same tenth-grade English class.

Ithaca High School was intimidating to many students, but not to Shelby. She thought the school with twelve hundred students was exciting; she liked the range of activities she could try and opportunities to make new friends. Most of the kids Shelby ran around with were active in school sports and ski club and were tracked either in the honors program or regents classes.

Shelby played second doubles on the girls' tennis team and planned to go out for lacrosse in the spring. She didn't like the high school cliques that jammed everybody into rigid categories: athletes, nerds, the popular crowd, and so forth. She chose friends on her own terms.

Those around Shelby were attracted to her easygoing, friendly nature, but her outward appearance could be misleading. Underneath a frivolous teenager veneer lay a serious streak not usually associated with a fifteen-year-old. She shared her simple faith without hesitation in a Catholic confirmation class, saying that belief in God meant that you were sure that if you died at that moment, you would go to heaven. Her close friends appreciated the sound advice she gave them about boyfriends, getting along with their parents, and what social choices to make, such as laying off drugs and alcohol. She was active in the high school's Students Against Drunk Driving group.

Despite her serious side, like most teenagers, Shelby loved clothes and spent plenty of time in front of the mirror getting her hair and makeup on just right and talking endlessly on the phone. She and her mother loved to shop. She usually liked her mother's taste in clothes but also had her own ideas. One school day a week before the winter formal, they drove to Syracuse to pick out a dress for the occasion. Shelby persuaded her mother to buy her a long, strapless taffeta gown in emerald green, modeling it for Dodie at the store. Shelby was physically well developed for her age and popular with boys, which made Dodie uneasy at times. It was such a grown-up kind of dress that Dodie hesitated, not sure the strapless part wasn't a bit too much, but Shelby's enthusiasm won her over.

Unfortunately a snowstorm canceled the formal, but her dad's Deanco dinner dance went on as scheduled; so Shelby and Jim's plans were not completely scrapped. Seeing the grown-up Shelby dressed in a formal was a lovely family moment, one Dodie wanted to look back upon. Jim in his tuxedo and Shelby in her taffeta gown stood in front of the Christmas tree as Dodie clicked photographs of the couple before they all left for Deanco's party at the Ramada Inn.

Tony and Dodie Harris had the kind of rapport with their two children that many admired and some envied. Shelby, now almost sixteen, hadn't shown signs of the kind of rebellion endemic to teenagers. But Dodie thought she was growing up too fast, and she hated the idea of letting her go. Dodie was very emotional, especially when it came to her children. She couldn't imagine living without them.

Even though her physical looks were maturing Shelby still had the easygoing, affectionate ways of her childhood. She hugged and kissed her parents in front of friends, and it pleased her that Dodie watched every tennis match she played for the high school team. Her mother was the kind of person who cheered for everyone, made sure they had team sweatshirts, and brought cookies for the players after matches.

The Harrises believed that staying involved with their children and providing wholesome opportunities for the kids to express themselves kept the family close. Marc and Shelby often had friends to sleep over, and Dodie cooked the customary waffles or pancakes the next morning. They had staged an elaborate party the previous June for Shelby's birthday, with a band set up in the garage and a crowd of friends dancing on the driveway.

With their son they were a bit stricter. Tony disciplined Marc with a firm hand, insisting he behave, and although it was not a buddy-buddy relationship, they shared many interests. Both were avid baseball card collectors; Tony went on weekend outings with Marc's Boy Scout troop; they put model rockets together and fired them from a hill in back of the house. Tony couldn't forget the gap left when his own father had deserted his family, but instead of harboring resentment, Tony worked to be the kind of father he wished he'd had.

Shelby, on the other hand, was her father's girl, and there was little discipline involved. Like her mother she had a sweet disposition. She was a pretty child who had blossomed into a beautiful creature that her father adored. Occasionally Shelby called her father at work to check in and to let him know she loved him. During Dodie's illness Shelby had taken on many responsibilities around the house and developed a seriousness and sensitivity unusual at such a young age.

Tony got downstairs just in time for Shelby to kiss him on the cheek and call, "love you," directed at all of them as she went out the door to catch the school bus, which stopped in front of their house.

"You want to take some Christmas cookies for your friends, Marc?" Dodie had baked dozens of fancy bars and cookies for the neighborhood cookie exchange she hosted on Monday night. Marc asked for the plain sugar ones. She wrapped up a bunch of cookies and put them inside his knapsack.

Marc was a kid who liked to be neat. He wore the usual jeans with preppy shirts, not the neon-colored sweatshirts that were the latest rage at school. And he liked his hair cut short. This morning he was more keyed up than usual. He and his friend Michael Mazza had written a skit for their sixth-grade English project and were performing and video-taping it that day. He hurried out the kitchen door to the garage to find some rope they planned to use as a prop for "The Grammar Round-up." He and Michael met while on the same hockey team the previous year and had become good friends since landing in the same homeroom at DeWitt Middle School in September. Both ran in the election to represent their homeroom at student council. Marc won (giving "the speech of my life," he later told his mother) and Michael came in second. Marc, however, decided they would share the responsibility equally.

That morning Marc had just enough time to take Annie for her walk—more like a run—around the house before the school bus came. This was a regular chore for Marc twice a day in the winter, when it was too cold to keep Annie out-side. Annie pulled on the leash that morning as she always did; the invigorating cold air made her run like a pup.

Walking back inside the house, his cheeks pink from the cold, Marc gave his mother a quick hug, patted his father on the shoulder as he sat at the table, and ate a bit of cereal. Too excited to finish, he said, "See you guys later." He ran out the front door to catch the bus.

Dodie sat down at the kitchen table with her cup of tea. Although she never drank coffee, she made a two-cup pot of brewed coffee for Tony every morning. That morning he sat sipping it slowly. It was one pleasure he had no intention of giving up. His breakfast of a high-fiber cereal and wheat toast or bagel was a far cry from what he really liked and used to eat for breakfast—bacon or sausage and eggs sunny-side up. On the weekends he splurged a bit with waffles or pancakes—no longer soaked in butter.

"I'm going to deposit all this cash I have from the shop when I'm out on errands today. The Grey Goose will just have to operate on its own for a little while," Dodie said as she refilled Tony's mug.

Tony tried not to worry about the huge amount of money they had put into Dodie's shop. The Grey Goose had cost them twenty-three thousand dollars to build; it would be a long time before they would recoup their investment, if ever. Their assets had always been tied up in real estate, so much so that only recently they bought their first new living room furniture. They had lived with used pieces that Dodie refinished or antiques she bought at a bargain because he felt so anxious about having invested so much cash in the store.

Keeping financial records wasn't something Dodie liked to do or did very well, so Tony kept track of the money. He usually gave her a check for two or three hundred dollars on Monday for household expenses, the amount depending on what was coming up that week. This eliminated the need for a checkbook and spared Dodie the temptation to spend the shop's income. At the beginning of each week she carried a wad of bills in her wallet or pants' pocket. By week's end she was cash poor. That morning Tony made out a six-hundred-dollar check and gave it to her to cover the weekend's holiday expenses.

It was a busy time of year at the Grey Goose. Many shoppers came for her country-style gifts: straw wreaths and wood-cut wall ornaments that she made, decorative mailboxes and tree ornaments. The shop was filled with items on consignment from friends or crafts people Dodie met at fairs or through contacts at other shops in the area.

Dodie's father had built the two-level shop in the same saltbox style in wood clapboard that Dodie designed for the house after she studied design magazines and got ideas from visits to gift shops around central New York. It was important to her that she do the thing right, so there was no detail left to chance. Dodie wanted the shop to be a short walking distance to the house, but not close enough to disturb the peaceful ambiance she carefully planned for their dream home. Fifty yards separated the two buildings.

Flair and talent were attributes Dodie had—her house resembling a Norman Rockwell painting, inside and out. She used geese as her decorating theme; a white wooden goose that she had designed and painted stood next to the mailbox to advertise her shop, and other cutouts of geese in various sizes and colors were on the wall or on kitchen shelves among her pewter mug collection. Country antiques and other home-made decorative items filled the house. Rusty old kitchen utensils and an ancient frying pan hung on the family room wall.

She fell in love with the country style when they lived in a Marietta subdivision. The dark wood-frame houses, modernized log or mountain cabins set in pine woods landscaping, looked like the country in an area a few miles from interstate highways and metropolitan Atlanta. This was the time when decorative, "homemade" country items were starting to be popular.

Although the shop was important to Dodie, she refused to be a slave to it. Occasionally the door to the Grey Goose was left unlocked with a note on the door inviting guests to browse and stating the approximate time she would return.

"I'm just going over to the store for a few minutes, Tony wait for me," she said smiling at Tony. He nodded. She quickly walked to the store.

Dodie wanted to keep the shop open for last-minute shoppers that day, but with the cold weather, she knew the wood stove wouldn't keep the rooms warm enough to stay in there for long stretches. She decided to leave the door unlocked in the morning while she was home. She had so many things to do. She wanted to make phone calls to Tony's old friends in Syracuse and invite them for his fortieth birthday party next week, and she needed to start getting ready for all their Syracuse relatives, who were spending Christmas day with them. There was major food shopping to do, and she had to clean the house and do more baking, not to mention picking up some last-minute gifts and finishing the present wrapping.

Getting back home she opened the front door and called, "Hello." Her husband returned the greeting. The wreath she had made with evergreen branches and red ribbon hung on the door, and shiny wrapped boxes lay in an antique sleigh on the snow-covered lawn. As she stepped inside, she smiled. The spruce Christmas tree they had cut down from the woods in back was decorated with ornaments that she and the children had made; a red velvet bow was tied with green sprays to the staircase. Dodie's decorations were meaningful expressions of her dedication to family life. They gave the children the feeling of having contributed to the holiday. As she sat down again with Tony, she looked around at the lived-in house where kids and their friends ran in and out or messed up the kitchen making cookies, where dogs, cats, and gerbils were welcome, and where she frequently had someone over for an impromptu lunch. At the slightest chill, she built a wood fire in the kitchen fireplace.

Dodie thought about playing tennis but realized she didn't have time and sighed. Tennis was Dodie's big passion outside her home and family. She had started playing in a neighborhood doubles league while they lived in Marietta, and it became an absorbing part of her life. After her breast surgery, she returned to the court as soon as the doctor allowed, and she perfected the lob she used to outwit her opponents. She lost some strength in her arms after the surgeries, which made it harder to hit ground strokes with power, but she still loved playing.

Tennis brought out a competitive spirit in her unseen in other aspects of her life. If it was her time to play a match in league competition, she wanted to play even if another doubles team had a better record and was more likely to win. Dodie played in a women's morning league in Cornell University's indoor tennis facility and was in charge of maintaining the Ellis Hollow community courts in the summer. Cindy Desmond, who was in the Marietta league with Dodie, tried to reason with her that sometimes you had to be realistic even if it didn't seem fair, but Dodie disagreed. Fair was fair. She was convinced that if she treated others fairly, they would do the same with her.

Tony wasn't as serious about tennis as Dodie. To him it was an outdoor sport and more social than anything else, but with his recent push to get into better shape, he had agreed to play doubles during the winter on Sunday nights with Barbara and Kevin White at the new indoor courts in town.

Dodie grew up in a close family, grounded in old-fashioned values and the Catholic tradition. However, like Tony's, hers was not an easy childhood. Her mother, who suffered a serious heart ailment from having rheumatic fever as a child, ran a strict household to keep confusion and disorder to a minimum. Not being physically strong and with three children close in age, and a husband away from home a lot starting a construction business, she had to be a firm manager. Money was not plentiful, so extras in treats, toys, and visits with friends were rare.

Giving her children all the missed opportunities of her youth was the benefit of being financially well-off. Not only did Dodie and Tony indulge Shelby and Marc, but they also liked to share their good fortune with friends and family. To them, success wasn't spending a lot of money; it was having enough time to do what they wanted with the people they cared about.

Dodie's flair for design emerged in childhood when she drew clothes for the paper dolls that she and her sister, Sharon, played. After taking a sewing class in high school, she often made her own clothes. An art teacher suggested she develop her drawing talent: perhaps she should look into the Fashion Institute of Technology in New York City. Dodie didn't know anything about the prestigious school, but with encouragement from her family and friends, she applied and was accepted.

As part of Dodie's interview, the young woman was asked to sketch a Queen Anne chair that stood in the admissions office. She performed well under pressure (the drawing received high praise from the interviewer). This gave her the confidence needed to spread her wings in unknown territory. Going to New York—the fast, sophisticated big city—was a complete departure from life as Dodie had known it in Syracuse. And it was the first time she'd been away from home.

Dodie stuck it out at FIT for one semester, but she didn't like the city. The fast pace, the dirt and grime of the streets and subways, and the unfriendly people turned her off. Classes were okay, but she felt uncomfortable around the students who were so different from those in Syracuse. She was hurt by the blunt remarks they and the teachers made about her work; the criticism seemed more cruel than helpful. Dodie had a soft shell when it came to others judging her work; it was as though they were attacking her personally, and she needed to be well-liked.

Moreover, Dodie was driven more by a desire to get married and have a family than to concentrate on a successful career. When she met Tony Harris, he was in his junior year at Brockport State and she was working in Syracuse's major furniture store as an interior decorator. She fell in love with the gregarious, easygoing Tony, not knowing at the time how driven he was to succeed. They became engaged less than a year later. However Dodie's happiness was interrupted by her mother's death from a heart seizure a few days after the couple announced their engagement.

Her mother's untimely death hit Dodie hard, and she often thought about it when her own life was threatened with cancer at thirty-one. By 1989, though, Dodie could feel more relaxed about her health. The cancer had been in remission for over five years by then, and the prognosis looked good. The news seemed a blessing from on high. It made her feel grateful for every day and filled her with a determination not to fritter time away on unimportant things.

After a last sip of coffee, Tony kissed his wife goodbye, said he loved her, and took the plate of cookies she had wrapped in foil for his office party.

Putting on a jacket, he walked from the mud room and into the garage. His breath formed smoke rings. Tony appreciated garages on mornings like that one. It was nice not having to scrape the windshields or brush off snow. Tony remembered many cold mornings in Syracuse, trying to start the older model cars he had then, parked on the street or driveway. Each day he had struggled to scrape the ice off the windows. His New Yorker sedan, although two years old, looked new because of Tony's gentle care. The luxurious leather interior was wonderful plus the ease and comfort of driving such a car. By the time he backed out of the garage onto Ellis Hollow Road, the heater had taken off the chill. Tony began to think of the day ahead.

Two

Michael Anthony Kinge a/k/a Tony Turner

That afternoon Joanna White got out of bed around two o'clock, her normal routine after working the night shift at Ithacare, a nursing home in downtown Ithaca. It felt chilly in the apartment in spite of the kerosene heater that her boyfriend, Tony Turner, had put in because they were so far behind on their gas and electric bills. The landlady, Mary Tilley, didn't allow kerosene, but they figured what she didn't know wouldn't hurt her.

They had an arrangement with Tilley to help pay their monthly rent of $396; every time Tony cleaned her rental apartments, she deducted the rent they owed her from his pay check.

He had signed an agreement with New York State Electric and Gas Company that morning, stating he would make twenty-eight dollar monthly payments for three months to catch up on unpaid bills. Otherwise, the electricity in their apartment would be disconnected. But he didn't have enough cash in the bank yet to mail a check with the agreement.

Tony's last steady job, cleaning movie theaters at the Pyramid Mall, had ended several months earlier after he refused to pick off chewing gum stuck to the back of theater seats. He had been working for his friend Ron Callee, a neighbor he hung out with when he lived in Locke, a rural hamlet north of Ithaca. Callee told him he couldn't take his slipshod work any longer. Refusing to clean up the gum was the last straw.

As Joanna boiled water for coffee, Tony gave her their one-year-old son to hold and said he wanted her to give him a ride in a little while, so he could "go to work." By work Tony meant going out to rob somebody. He always described those excursions as work. She never asked any questions.

Joanna had met Tony Turner, an assumed name he used after moving upstate, at a downtown bar in 1980. He was ready for a new start. Tony was on parole from Fishkill State Prison, having served one year of a three-year sentence for armed robbery (a fact in the beginning he kept from Joanna). Tony's looks appealed to her: His five foot, eight inches tall lean, lanky expressible body, Afro hairstyle, glowing ebony skin was very different from the small town guys she knew. His deep-set black eyes seemed to look through her. He came from New York City and flaunted an arrogant, "I've seen and done it all" attitude. He was a mix of soft-spoken charm with an explosive fuse that went off abruptly. There was a magnetic wildness about him that both scared and excited her.

In those days there was no doubt Tony was a charmer whose mild mannered ways made people want to help him.

Tony was originally named Michael Anthony Kinge and called Michael until he started using an alias when he moved upstate to escape the law. As a kid, Michael had been fastidious about his appearance. When he was twelve, he asked his mother to teach him how to sew his own clothes. He learned the craft and from then on made most of his clothes. In addition to his handiness with a needle, Tony liked to read and take small household objects apart and put them back together. His mother marveled at her son's abilities and since a toddler, Michael could smile his way out of trouble. His sister wasn't so fortunate; from early on a rivalry existed between brother and sister that developed into full blown hostility by the time they were adolescents.

With no man in the household and no financial support from her ex-husband, Shirley was away from home working to support the family a good deal of the day and night while her kids were growing up. She had met her husband, Robert Kinge, at a lunch counter in Newark while she was working for the government as a key punch operator in 1954. They got married when she was four months pregnant and after their daughter, Gabrielle, was born, the marriage began to sour. Shirley went home to her mother after Robert slapped her for something she said that he felt insulted his manhood. Her mother said he wasn't any good anyway. They got back together for a few months until Michael was born a year after Gabrielle. The next time Shirley left it was for good. She couldn't stand to be bossed around. Shirley went home to her mother, Sally Reese. Shirley and the children lived with her until 1963 when she moved to New York City.

While they lived there Shirley worked hard but she barely earned enough as a bus information clerk at New York City's Port Authority Building to pay the rent for their apartment on the Upper West Side of Manhattan. It was an integrated, middle-class neighborhood when they moved there and Shirley liked it that way. She wanted to move up the social and economic ladder. She was an independent, articulate woman with a hard edge who was always getting a raw deal, she felt. Boyfriends stayed around for as long as they got what they wanted. At least, she ended up with some nice clothes and fur coats. She was taken in by Manhattan's penchant for fashion. Having expensive clothes and jewelry became important to her.

Shirley was used to lying about her son Michael. She'd been covering up for him since he first told her he didn't feel like going to school when he was nine or ten years old. It was easier to give in. The kid was a real charmer and she didn't have any man around to show authority, so she had to just glide through and try to rock the boat as little as possible. There was enough friction between Michael and his sister already. She didn't want any more problems to deal with.

Michael didn't know his father as he was growing up. He came around a few times while they lived in Newark, but Shirley and her mother put up such a fuss when they saw him that he stopped coming.

One day Michael bumped into his father on a Newark city bus. He wouldn't have known him, but Robert Kinge recognized his son. It was the last time they saw each other.

The neighborhood had changed; the more affluent moved out and poorer blacks and Hispanics moved in. Street crime was on the rise. It became tougher for Shirley to cope. She was tired of a job that wasn't going anywhere; she was often late or absent from work.

Later Shirley tried to forget those years in the city. Gabrielle started running away from home when she was barely a teenager, Michael was always in trouble, and the neighborhood was rotting with crime. Their apartment was broken into three times.

By the time Michael reached junior high school he missed as many days as he attended. School absence was a well-entrenched pattern by then. School work didn't interest him; he considered teachers and school kids dumb; his mother was the only smart one. Occasionally he'd put on his charm and help with after-school projects. But more frequently he was an unresponsive loner who could lose his temper when things didn't go his way. His short fuse was noted in elementary school by a teacher who reported that Michael lacked self-control. He was the last to finish class assignments, an underachiever who routinely performed below his scores on aptitude and intelligence tests. Michael was fifteen when he entered the new alternative Westside High School designed for kids at risk.

Michael was adept at using his charm to flirt with girls. He often got his way. At sixteen he fell for a white girl from a rich family. Her parents scorned her for going out with a black boy, but she defied them and continued to see Michael. When she discovered she was pregnant, the situation overwhelmed her. She couldn't face her family with that kind of news. In desperation she killed herself.

The following January, Michael was arrested for burglary and sent to Rikers Island for sixty days. Westside High's secretary, who was as much a social worker as an administrator, was concerned that no one was visiting him in prison. She arranged for a school volunteer to see him several times during his incarceration.

Michael dropped out of school at seventeen and joined the Marine Corps with his mother's blessing. After his girlfriend's suicide, Michael wouldn't even look at black girls. No one was going to dictate to him who he would see and what he did. His girlfriend's suicide seemed to harden his determination to defy the rules. And he began to wear his anger as a badge of honor.

At the time he met Joanna in 1980, he was out on parole from Fishkill prison, having served one year of the three-year sentence for a crime he committed in New York City in 1975. He had skipped town when convicted in 1975 on an armed robbery charge and not until 1978 when he applied for a $1,300 bank loan using a bogus name and social security number in Auburn, New York, did the law catch up with him. After he served eight months in Cayuga County jail for the loan fraud, he was moved to Fishkill prison in Clinton, New York.

Tony liked Joanna well enough to make an effort at trying to do something that could lead to a good paying job. He attended Cayuga County Community College in Auburn, graduating with a business degree in 1982. He had lied on the college application form about his "honorable discharge" from the Marines; he was actually court-martialed in July 1974 when stationed at Okinawa, Japan, for refusing to obey his commanding officer to clean latrines and for stealing four cartons of Winston cigarettes worth about $5. He was ordered to forfeit $400 in pay and was given thirty-five days at hard labor. He'd been trained as a mortarman during his brief tenure in the Marines.

It was against New York State law to ask about an applicant's criminal record on the college admissions form.

Tony applied to large and small business firms in the area. He dressed in a business suit and imagined he was going somewhere, now that he had a degree. But he was rejected wherever he applied. This was a time, during an economic recession, when many firms had a hiring freeze on, but Tony took it personally. He felt they didn't hire him because he was black and he was convinced that companies would investigate and find out about his criminal record.

Five months after graduation, he was arrested in New York City with a loaded firearm.

Like his mother, Tony also aspired to material things, good things, and attractive companions. In his case he seemed to care little about how he got them.

Joanna found out later that Tony only went out with white women. He was proud of his success with them; they enhanced his self-image and gave him a sense of power. Joanna turned him on with her petite good looks and long, light brown hair. And she liked a good time. Soon he convinced her to drive to New York. It was an exciting adventure for a rural girl whose idea of wild up to then was getting drunk and smoking a little pot. They slept in the car most of the day and at night.

Joanna worked as a go-go girl in a striptease joint. Tony was doing stickups at grocery and liquor stores. After Tony had robbed enough cash and loot to last a while, he'd buy drugs at a good price on the street. The big city capers ended when Tony was arrested in the city on an armed robbery charge one night. He didn't appear in court the next day, so a bench warrant was issued in the name of Michael Kinge.

Joanna's father disowned her when she started dating Tony. He was a proud redneck who didn't like blacks; the idea of his daughter going out with one infuriated him.

It was not too surprising that Joanna went against the taboo so strongly held by her father. It was her way of saying, "I am me and I'll run my own life." After her parent's divorce, she had lived with her mother and sisters in West Village, a low-income housing project on Ithaca's west hill. They didn't approve of Joanna going out with a black man either. The relationship eventually caused so much dissension in the family that Joanna moved out and got a room of her own downtown.

Not long afterward, she and Tony moved in together. She was game for almost anything during the first years they were together and had little to do with her family.

But then five years later, her son James was born. Having a child changed Joanna, who wanted a calmer more secure life. And Tony, never a patient man, yelled at her in a swearing rage these days when nothing was going right.

By now Tony was always looking for a quick hit for cash. Sometimes he got grandiose about it. He talked of ripping off a money-rich drug dealer or a Mafia bookie. Then he wouldn't have to worry about cops. He hated cops. He told Joanna he wouldn't go back in—he'd shoot it out first. His dream was to wear a bulletproof vest and goggles and ride a motorcycle with a headset in the helmet, so he could track police movements on scanners. Sometimes he dressed in his black Ninja costume and practiced sneaking around the neighborhood, just to see if he could creep around and not be detected.

Tony couldn't stand the feeling of being controlled by other people. That's why he couldn't hold down a job for long. He thought he was smarter than everybody else, so he decided the only way to get what he wanted was to operate outside the system. He had formed a fantasy world where he could control others (the women in his life who did his bidding) and exert a kind of power that made him feel powerful. To keep control, he made sure his women knew that violence or the threat of it was close at hand. Tony had been a student of violence for years.

His favorite movies were packed with violence. He never tired of watching "Lethal Weapon." He dreamed about owning a Beretta because that was the weapon of choice Clint Eastwood had made so famous. He read paperback accounts of vigilante heroes, like *The Executioner* series, where the hero takes the law in his own hands and guns down drug dealers with powerful weapons. Books like *Improvised Weapons of the American Underground* gave him ideas for his workshop. He bought hard-core pornographic magazines, especially ones that covered bizarre and violent sex.

Although her father still refused to see her, Joanne reestablished contact with her mother after the birth of her son. Two months earlier Joanna had told her mother she wanted to move out. Tony was depressed, couldn't sleep, had migraine headaches, and he exploded in anger at the slightest thing; she was walking a tightrope with him.

It was nervous energy and worry about her son that kept

Joanna going. She raced around all day before leaving for work at the nursing home, and on the job she kept going with few breaks. Being able to smoke was one of the advantages of working the night shift. Because of anxiety she chain-smoked. She couldn't go long without a cigarette. Thelma Thomas, the aide who shared the midnight shift with her, a grandmotherly older woman, noticed how thin Joanna was getting and said, "Just look at you, you'd better slow down and eat more."

Joanna nodded but hadn't replied.

As for Tony, even smoking pot didn't relieve his jitters for long now. He was hooked on grass and no matter how strapped he was for funds, he found enough to buy a nickel bag, often borrowing from his mother Shirley or grandmother. He tried to grow marijuana plants in the apartment, but gave up when their electric bills nearly doubled. It had been a while since Tony used acid. The local supply fluctuated and when it was scarce, the dealer marked the drug up to the point Tony thought it wasn't worth it. Drug busts were on the increase in the area.

Because Joanna was alarmed by Tony's behavior, she frequently left the baby with Tony's grandmother Sallie Reese when she went to work at night. Mrs. Reese, an independent woman, had few attachments. The reason she took care of Tony's child had more to do with her own daughter Shirley than her interest in the baby. She was committed to her daughter and did anything to help her. Sallie had decided to retire and moved from Newark, New Jersey, where she had lived most of her life, and bought an old farmhouse on a two and a half acre property for $13,500 in Cayuga County. She wanted to escape the city's noise and crime and live an easy life. But she discovered it was expensive living in an old country house. To make ends meet she had to go back to work as a live-in nanny and housekeeper with an Ithaca family. She sold the property two years later and moved closer to her daughter.

Now that she was finally retired, her biggest pleasure was watching television in peace and quiet. She made sure baby-sitting her great-grandson didn't get in the way of that. The baby slept or played in the crib in the bedroom next to hers while she reclined in bed and looked at television movies and her favorite programs.

Meanwhile things for Tony and Joanna went from bad to worse. They were behind in their rent and hadn't paid gas and electric bills for two months. The landlady had just served them their third eviction notice. Finally Joanna asked her mother if she and Jimmy could stay with her for a little while. The situation had to be pretty bad, because Joanna would rather walk through fire than ask for help from her family. She hated to admit she couldn't go it alone. Her mother said no, it wouldn't work out at their house because her husband (Joanna's new stepfather) couldn't stand the noise that babies made. She gave Joanna four hundred dollars to pay the rent.

On the Friday afternoon of December 22 Tony and Joanna took their son over to Tony's mother and grandmother who lived on the other side of the duplex. The house they shared was on the dirt and gravel stretch of Etna Road that ran close to Tompkins County Airport and parallel to Route 13, the north-south highway out of Ithaca. They liked the isolation of the place. The few scattered houses were situated among thick woods on both sides of the road. A ranch house and a collapsing barn were across from them and around the corner on the other side were two more frame duplexes of the same design, also owned by Mary Tilley.

Farther down the road was an old logging trail. A stripped-down, yellow flatbed truck sat on cinder blocks in their front yard. The mixture of well-kept and shabby properties on one road was common in the area, where zoning laws either didn't exist or weren't enforced. The location fit their unsociable lives and their shaky finances; although on rare occasions a friend of Tony's stopped by, the women never had company. They let Tony's lifestyle set the tone for all of them.

The duplex looked cheap and rundown. It was made with gray, vertical board and baton siding, a flat roof, aluminum storm doors, and no windows on either side of the building. Each apartment in the duplex had three bedrooms upstairs with two rooms and a kitchen downstairs. But with so little square footage to each room, the place seemed crowded.

Walking outside they couldn't help but notice the bad weather. Neither said anything about it. Joanna had to get to work and Tony was intent on leaving as quickly as possible and didn't care about ice and snow.

Joanna got in the driver's seat of the 1977 blue Ford pick-up while Tony put a bicycle in the back. A few months before, he had gone downtown and had come home with the black Nasbar. Joanna didn't ask him what had happened. She knew he'd say it wasn't any of her business, and she really didn't want to know anyway.

Then Tony told Joanna to drive to Turkey Hill Road. He didn't say what his destination was. She took his silence for granted. He was in one of his dark moods and that meant the only talking he did was when he barked out orders and she did as she was told. She had to drive slowly, because of the snow buildup on the road. They took back roads as they generally did. Tony insisted they stay off the main highways when he was in the truck or in his mother's car. There was less chance of meeting cops on secondary roads.

They passed a few houses and long stretches of cut-down cornfields frozen to the ground. When they reached the bottom of Turkey Hill, he told her to turn left. She didn't know the name of the road. They went a few miles and turned right. After a short distance Tony told her to stop before a bridge. They were on Genung Road. He got the bicycle out of the back and slung a knapsack over his shoulder. He usually had a gun in it since he always wanted to protect himself. He had on a dark blue parka with a fur-lined hood.

Joanna turned the truck around and as she drove away, she saw Tony in the rearview mirror, standing up as he pedaled the bike uphill toward Ellis Hollow Road. It was 3:20 P.M. and the temperature was ten degrees above zero and falling.

Three
Their Last Day Ends

A boisterous crowd of students filed out of Ithaca High School late that afternoon. Excitement and relief were in the air as students looked forward to a long winter break. Shelby Harris and Jim Ciolek talked about their plans to exchange gifts that night as they walked to the school bus stop. He watched her board the bus with Meghan Long.

Shelby and Meghan had become good friends after they started high school the previous year and rode the same bus. Today they ate some of the leftover cookies Shelby had brought to class while they talked about a lot of things coming up—what Shelby had gotten Jim for Christmas, plans they had for the holidays. Shelby invited Meghan to go skiing with them when Jan Colbert came to visit from Ohio the following week. Jan and Shelby were close friends as middle school classmates and neighbors in Ellis Hollow. Shelby said her family would be celebrating her father's fortieth birthday on a ski trip to Greek Peak on the Thursday after Christmas. Meghan was welcome to join them. Meghan got off the bus at Eagles Head Road. Shelby called, "I'll call you next week. Have a great Christmas."

Shelby got off two minutes later in front of her house.

When Shelby walked in the side door through the mud room, Dodie was on the phone with Rita Demerest, a Grey Goose customer who had shopped at the store earlier that day, finding the note on the door that welcomed customers to browse and then ring the house next door to make purchases. Rita explained to Dodie that she didn't come over to the house because her child was cold and she was afraid of getting stuck in the snowy driveway. Dodie assured Rita she would deliver the wooden Christmas trees and Santas, along with the antique tool chest Rita had arranged to buy earlier, that evening around 7:00 or 7:30 after Dodie dropped Shelby off at her boyfriend's house.

It had been a frantic day for Dodie. She'd been on the road half the day, going to the bank, picking up gifts, doing a huge grocery shopping for Christmas, and leaving space heaters on Barb White's doorstep, thinking they could use the extra heat in their high-ceilinged kitchen during this frigid weather.

While her mother talked on the phone, Shelby smiled and gave her a little wave. Then she poured a mug of cider and took it upstairs to her bedroom. She was thirsty after all the cookies she and Meghan had eaten on the bus. Thoughts ran through her mind about meeting Jim that night. She wondered what his reaction would be to the long-sleeved sport shirt she'd bought for him at the mall. And she tried to imagine what he would give her. Then her mind turned to the evening ahead. What should she wear? Probably her dark blue wool pants (it was so cold) and the white angora sweater. Once she decided, she had to find the wrapping paper and scissors. Shelby liked wrapping gifts and for Jim she wanted to take her time and make the package look especially nice. She would make a card for him, too.

*   *   *

Marc Harris had a long trip on the school bus from De-Witt Middle School to Ellis Hollow, but he didn't mind the ride. He was a sociable kid who liked to joke around with his friends, so the time went by quickly for him. Everyone on the bus was excited and loud that Friday afternoon before winter break. Several of Marc's friends got off a stop before him and started a snowball fight at the corner of Hunt Hill Road and Ellis Hollow Road.

Marc wanted to get on home. He didn't plan to do much for the rest of the day since he had to play in a hockey game in Geneva the next morning at five o'clock. They'd have to leave the house by four o'clock. His dad would be one of the drivers as he often was.

Marc loved to play defense. He knew he wasn't good enough to skate front line, but he loved the sport and had practiced so he could skate backwards and do crossovers pretty well. It bolstered his confidence when he found out that his coach he'd had the previous year traded a player for him after Marc hadn't come up in his draw.

Annie, the family dog, was excited when Marc came home. She yelped and jumped up on him, following him around the house until he got the leash and took her outside. Doris Snyder, the Ellis Hollow mail carrier, saw Marc come out of the front door with his dog shortly after four. About thirty minutes later on her route, she noticed a bicyclist in a hooded parka who looked like he was having trouble riding on the snow-covered shoulders of Ellis Hollow Road. He was headed east—in the direction of the Harris home.

About 4:15 Ann Parziale called Dodie to discuss the previous night's meeting of the Parents' Advisory Committee on high school athletics. Ann and Dodie were good friends. They invited each other over for lunch often and talked about their kids. Dodie told Ann she would be taking Shelby over to her boyfriend's house that night to exchange gifts. They said they would talk after all the holiday confusion was over.

After she got off the phone, Dodie slipped on her parka and told Marc she had a few things to pick up for a customer at the shop before it got completely dark. She thought about asking Marc to help her, but the tool chest and other items Rita Demerest had selected weren't heavy. Dodie went out the front door, yelling to Marc that she'd be back in a minute and would he please bring in the rest of the groceries from the van? As Marc passed the kitchen window he decided to flip on the outside Christmas lights. He saw his mother standing with someone in the driveway facing the shop. *Who could that be?* He didn't see a car parked anywhere. It was probably a neighbor who wanted to buy something at the Grey Goose.

Marc left the window and walked through the kitchen to the door that led to the garage, the unknown figure turned from Dodie and started walking toward the house.

One garage bay was open, the side next to the house where Dodie usually parked the van. She hadn't moved it inside yet, so Marc walked through the garage, and as he slid the van door open to get a bag of groceries out, a figure in a hooded parka and ski mask walked toward him.

"Your Mom said you had an air pump I could use. My bicycle's back tire is flat."

"Sure, it's in the garage on one of the shelves," Marc told him. Marc was glad he wasn't riding a bike on a cold night like this.

Marc Walker, a friend of the Harrises who lived nearby on Eagles Head Road, drove by their house on his way to pick up his son at Caroline School about 4:45 that December afternoon and noticed two people standing in the driveway, facing the Grey Goose. He thought one person must be Dodie and the other he wasn't sure about—not Marc, because the figure had a ragamuffin appearance.

* * *

The sales and marketing departments at Deanco where Tony worked traditionally got together for an office lunch party at holiday time. Everyone brought a dish-to-pass and exchanged gifts. Normally Tony left the office during lunch and picked up a quick sandwich to eat so he could spend his time doing other things. A few days before he had made a trip to a Dryden card dealer to pick up 1990 baseball cards to give to an employee's children as well as a set to give Marc.

The party began promptly. It was a merry and lively scene (only nonalcoholic drinks served) as presents were opened, plates were filled and refilled with good homemade food, and people laughed and talked until quitting time. Cathy Carpenter had drawn Tony's name for the gift exchange. She gave him a Syracuse University basketball, knowing what an avid fan he was. They were an easygoing group who got along well with each other.

About 5:15 Tony left the gathering and walked out to the parking lot with Bob Morazzi, the product manager, and Tony's secretary, Teresa Morehouse. Tony helped Teresa carry out gift boxes and a coffee urn. He put them in her car. They all wished each other a Merry Christmas. "And a Happy New Year," Tony added, "Remember, I'll be on vacation for a week." Then he got in his car and headed home.

Kathleen Martin came by the Grey Goose from Brooktondale around 5:45, hoping to stop and buy some Christmas ornaments, but the shop was closed. The Harris house looked dark too.

As Jim Raponi drove by the Harris house about 7:15 on his way home to Brooktondale, he noticed a figure, illuminated from behind, walk by a downstairs window. He saw a light on in an upstairs window. Raponi was in the habit of looking at the house as he drove by. He had watched it go up three years before.

When Shelby didn't show up at her boyfriend Jim Ciolek's house by 7:30 that night, he called her, letting the phone ring and ring. He thought, *This isn't like Shelby not to show up or at least call. Maybe her family went to dinner on the spur of the moment.* He hoped she hadn't had a car accident. The road conditions were very bad. He called every half hour until eleven and then gave up.

Four

Two Days Before Christmas

Bruce Miller awoke to a loud, high-pitched sound just before daybreak. It had to be some kind of siren going off, but where was it coming from? Somewhere outside. He shivered as his feet hit the cold floor. He rose and walked to the window. Maybe he should investigate. His wife, who was still half-asleep, mumbled that it wasn't a good idea and told him to come on back to bed—which he did.

Elizabeth Regan was awakened by the same shrill, penetrating noise at 6:35 that cold December morning. She woke her husband, Dennis, who realized in his half-awake state that it had to be looked into. The sound was so loud that he thought it was coming from somewhere in their two-story house. Perhaps the severe cold had caused an electrical malfunction in the furnace. Elizabeth remembered hearing something similar a few years before during the winter, when a neighbor's car horn malfunctioned and went off continuously for twenty minutes.

Getting up, he trudged down to the cellar, searched it, and then began looking all over the house. He opened the door of his daughter Lisa's bedroom. She was sound asleep. He went to the back of the house and opened the kitchen door. The noise seemed louder, but he didn't think it was coming from that direction. He walked to the front entrance and opened the door. Then he knew. It was coming from their next-door neighbor's house about thirty-five yards to the east of them. He saw that one of the garage doors was open and wondered why.

Around 6:40 Bob Armstrong heard an alarm as he put Saturday's *Ithaca Journal* in the Harrises' paper tube that stood next to their mailbox on Ellis Hollow Road. He thought about calling the police, but by the time he finished his route, he had forgotten about it.

Meanwhile, Dennis Regan had walked back to his bedroom. He still was sleepy and now baffled. "It's over at the Harrises," Dennis said to his wife. "It's some kind of alarm."

Dennis and Elizabeth hadn't known that the Harrises had an alarm system, but obviously they did. Why weren't they shutting it off? Elizabeth assumed they were not home. The family probably had gone to Syracuse to pick up Dodie Harris's father for the holidays. She had overheard Dodie at her cookie exchange party last Monday night, talking about having him spend Christmas with them. The Regans surmised that the cold weather had caused a water line to freeze and break, setting off the alarm.

But just to be sure, Dennis called the Harrises to make sure they weren't sleeping through this noise. He let the phone ring about ten times and then called the State Police barracks in the town of Dryden on Route 366, about six miles from Ellis Hollow.

"I don't know if I should be calling you or the Sheriff's Department, but the next-door neighbors must have a burglar alarm and it's going off really loud. I called them and their telephone doesn't answer."

The soft-voiced police dispatcher asked Regan for his name and address and the neighbors'.

"It's next door, further out Ellis Hollow Road toward

Route 79 on the same side of the street," Regan told the dispatcher. "Probably something shorted out, but I don't know. Their outside lights are on, but no inside lights."

"Okay, I'll have a patrol check on that."

Regan felt better now. The police would handle it.

Fifteen minutes passed. The Regans didn't hear any car wheels crunch on the Harrises' gravel driveway, but suddenly the alarm stopped. They were puzzled. Regan called the Harrises a second time. Still no answer. He called the police again and told the dispatcher the alarm had stopped, no one answered the phone, and he'd noticed earlier one of their garage doors was open. The dispatcher replied, "We're checking it out."

It was now about 7:10 A.M. The alarm was silent, the cops would be there soon, and everything seemed okay. Dennis went back to bed and fell asleep. He and his wife Elizabeth were exceptionally tired, as they had stayed up late the night before, celebrating their daughter Lisa's early acceptance to Cornell University by having dinner at her favorite restaurant on the outskirts of town. When they got home, Dennis had built a fire in the living room fireplace. He and Elizabeth had some brandy and talked until late.

Sleeping soundly once again as the darkness outside turned to light, the Regans awoke suddenly when they heard more noise. This time it was the sound of cars moving in and out of the gravel driveway next door. They opened the bedroom blinds a bit, peeked out and saw a lot of commotion at the end of the Harrises' driveway. Police cars and other vehicles were parked along Ellis Hollow Road, men were hurrying up the driveway to the house, and some were in groups near the road. Then they noticed smoke coming out of the far side of the Harrises' house. They knew the house was new and well-built and the Harrises were careful people. If the Harrises had gone away, they were not the kind to leave ovens or irons on. How could a fire have started? The Regans decided to throw on some warm clothes as fast as they could and go see for themselves. In the upstairs bedroom that faced the Harris home, Lisa was still asleep.

State Trooper John Beno came on duty earlier than his regular shift. December 23 was his wife's birthday and they had planned to celebrate it with an afternoon Christmas party at a friend's restaurant in town. After patrolling in his car, Beno stopped off at the police barracks to have coffee with some other officers. Another trooper, Scott Hendershott, asked if Beno would mind going to check an EID (electronic intrusion device) over on Ellis Hollow Road. It wasn't Beno's assigned post for the day, but he was up and ready to walk out the door, so he said he'd go over.

The roads in Tompkins County were slippery—a light snow had fallen during the night—and the back roads still had an icy undercrust which loudly crunched as the patrol car's tires rolled over it. It was just before daybreak as Trooper Beno proceeded slowly on Route 366, turning onto Turkey Hill Road, which intersects Ellis Hollow after three and a half miles. Beno was glad it wasn't a real emergency with these terrible driving conditions. He passed Ellis Hollow Creek Road and Peaceful Drive, then crept along behind a Town of Dryden snow plow. He thought Hendershott had said the alarm was at the house after the one with lights on, but when he passed it, there were no other houses on the right-hand side. Beno knew he'd gone too far. He turned around, drove back to the house with the outside lights on, and radioed the barracks for clarification. A new dispatcher verified the address.

Beno parked on the road by a circular driveway. He saw a gray New England saltbox house standing far back from the road in an open field. The house carved a towering presence on the barren, white landscape. There were no trees to soften the sharp edges; only Christmas lights strung along a split-rail fence that bordered the road brought relief to the deserted scene.

It was now 7:20 and a pale gray dawn was finally breaking after the longest night of the year.

Beno walked up to the house beside a set of fresh tire tracks, which he noticed were cut through the lawn. His boots made a crunching noise in the snow, the only sound to break the winter silence. The tracks missed the driveway by ten or fifteen feet and he could see they had swung wide out of the garage. By now, the faint stream of light was growing, penetrating the dull gray sky. As Beno turned from the front of the house and started walking around to the back, looking for footprints, he felt a gust of cold wind hit his face and the brim of his hat moved up and down. All he could see were deer tracks etched in the snow.

Beno rang the front doorbell, then walked to the side door and yelled, "Anybody home?" After he found the front and side doors locked, he entered the garage through an open bay and noticed a power tool on top of a dark sedan. Searching the area, he discovered an unlocked door inside the garage and entered the mud room, connected by a narrow hallway to the kitchen. Smoke was in the air, a panel of red lights was flashing on the right-hand wall, and he heard the beeping sound of smoke detectors in the background. He yelled out, "State Police," as he walked into the kitchen.

It didn't feel hot inside. Beno thought a chimney damper might have been shut and had trapped the smoke in the house. He stuck his hand next to the fireplace where there were burned logs and ashes, but they were cold. He walked into what he assumed was the family room, passing a Christmas tree. Haphazard boxes lay open underneath, and about them was strewn red and green wrapping paper. He saw a man's jacket hanging on the staircase banister. Family photographs were displayed on the fireplace mantel. He kept calling out, "State Police, anybody here?" as he moved from room to room. He saw a gas can lying on its side on the carpet in the living room. The room smelled of gasoline, but nothing seemed burned.

Trying to hold his breath, Beno opened the front door and then some kitchen windows to let the smoke out. He lifted the receiver on the kitchen wall phone to call for assistance, but the line was dead. He looked down; the wires had been ripped out.

"Jesus, what have I got here?" he asked himself out loud. Beno's ten years' experience as a trooper had been routine up to then—giving out speeding tickets, making DWI arrests, handling traffic accidents. With a heavy feeling in his chest, he hurried outside to his car and radioed for help. It was 7:30 A.M.

While waiting for his backups, Beno went back inside to see if anyone was still in the house and needed help. He raced up the stairs to the interior balcony that looked down on the family room. He opened the bedroom door at the top of the landing, but couldn't see anything in the dark, smoke-filled room. He flipped on the light switch and the bulb blew out. Thick smoke hung over the balcony, making it difficult to breathe. He continued to call out, "State Police, anybody home?" He continued to call out as he opened doors to closets and looked into a room and bath down a short hall off the balcony. His eyes stung and watered from the smoke. Again and again he tried to catch his breath, finally having to go downstairs for air. A few minutes later back on the second floor, he noticed light coming from the room at the end of the hall. Walking toward it, he saw a demolished telephone and another gasoline can lying to the side of the door.

By this time he heard other cars. Three other troopers had arrived at the scene: Scott Hendershott, who had just gotten off the graveyard shift, and Michael Simmons in one car and William Standinger in another. Beno went downstairs, gave

them a fast rundown on the scene, and grabbed Simmons'
flashlight. He returned to the room at the top of the stairs
with Hendershott and Simmons. Beno opened the door and
pointed the beam into the dark room. Slowly he moved the
light around to the right as he took a step inside. "What in
the hell's going on here," he mumbled.

Blackened mattress coils were protruding from a double
bed, and drawers and clothes were strewn around on the
floor. He took another step inside, directing the beam to his
left. On the floor between a dresser and the bed, he saw the
lower part of a human body; the rest of the torso was either
covered with something or had burned up. The sight of
charred, white flesh of human legs made Beno gasp. A mus-
cle in his throat started to quiver as he screamed to Simmons, standing in the doorway, "Jesus, we've got a body in
here!"

Beno thought it was a woman's body they'd discovered.
Remembering the family photographs he'd seen on the mantel downstairs, a morbid scenario went through his mind. He
pictured the husband leaving in a hurry after he murdered
the wife and kids, whom they'd probably find in another
room. Domestic violence around the holidays was all too
common. There was no sign anyone had been outside the
house, and he couldn't see any indication of a break-in.

Going on ahead, Standinger started to open the door at
the end of the hall but quickly closed it after seeing a red
glow.

The state troopers taped off the south side of the Harrises' house before the firefighters arrived. They marked a
route through the front door into the foyer, right through a
passage in the kitchen, and up the stairs. This was the most
direct route for the firefighters to bring equipment and would
not destroy evidence downstairs. The troopers helped lay the
hoses out. The object was to have as few people as possible
inside. It helped to have Simmons on duty. As chief of the
Berkshire Volunteer Fire Department, Simmons knew how

to work with other firefighters. This saved time and prevented misunderstandings.

In his car on the way to his office to clear up a mountain of paperwork that sat on his desk, Investigator Charlie Porter clicked into the station's radio service as he headed toward Route 13. Soon he heard John Beno over one of the frequencies going out to check an EID. A little later, Porter heard Beno say something about a fire.

"This can't be," he mumbled. "I've got too much work to do." By the time he passed the Cayuga Heights exit, he heard over the radio about the ripped telephone cords and the gasoline can in the living room. Porter was well experienced and a twenty-year police veteran who had transferred to Ithaca in 1988 after a six-year stint with the narcotic unit in Binghamton. *Damn,* he thought. *There's no way I'm not involved now.* An empty gas can made it obvious this was not an accidental fire.

Porter got off at the next exit, Triphammer Road, and headed for Ellis Hollow. He drove through the Cornell campus, still worrying about the desk work he had planned to do that day.

When he arrived at the scene, he pulled up next to Scott Hendershott, who was standing at the end of the driveway.

"What the hell have we got here, Scott?" he barked at Hendershott.

The trooper shook his head. "We found one body and fire engines are on the way." Porter could see the property was already taped off. He had to make sure the troopers kept as much as they could of the inside scene undisturbed. He could see his own smokey breath as he walked up the driveway and met John Beno outside the front door. It was ten degrees, but with the wind chill factor it felt below zero. Snow had drifted against the doors and windows, and it had started snowing again.

"Well, you better tell me what you found, John. This is one hell of a way to start the day," Porter complained, still hoping they could tie up the thing quickly. It ran through his mind that this was probably a family affair—people did crazy things at Christmas.

Ron Flynn walked out of the Bangs Ambulance building on Albany Street. He and his brother, both Emergency Medical Technicians, had just gotten off duty. They were trying to decide where to go for breakfast when Flynn's pager beeped. It was Dryden's Volunteer Fire and Rescue Squad: "We got a possible 1070 out Ellis Hollow Road, the number is 1886. We've been alerted to respond immediately."

"1070," Flynn repeated.

The Dryden chief's assistant didn't waste any time getting in his car and heading out to the east side of town when he heard about a body. Then a message came over his pager that the Varna Fire Department was to respond to a possible structure fire at the same address. "Okay," he mumbled, "I'll have to wait to eat." He was glad they'd stopped by the donut shop for coffee before their shift ended.

Flynn was the first firefighter at the scene. Firefighters from Varna and Dryden were on the way.

The Harrises' place was taped off along the split-rail fence that separated the property from the road, stopping at the far side of the driveway next to the Grey Goose gift shop. Trooper Simmons, his eyes reddened from the smoke, met him there and told him hoarsely, "Trooper Beno has found one body. We don't know if there are more. It's black fog upstairs. We can hardly breathe in there," Simmons said coughing. He added, "We gotta keep everybody off the other side of the drive where we found some tire tracks."

Flynn could see smoke coming out near the peak of the roof on the south side. Radioing Tompkins County Fire Patrol, he reported the visible smoke. He stood on the road a few minutes, waiting to direct the fire trucks to the side. Police wanted them to go in. The first to arrive was a Dryden pumper truck driven by the fire chief.

The fire in the master bedroom smoldered and went out. No water was needed there. Marc's bedroom at the end of the hallway only took a few minutes to hose down. The firefighters were surprised the fires hadn't spread further, but on closer analysis, they realized the arsonist either wasn't too smart or he panicked when he shut the doors. Fires need oxygen to burn. In Marc's room there was a small trap door leading to the attic, which may have let enough air in to feed that fire.

Gasoline dumped on the living room carpet, on the furniture, and in the fireplace had not been lighted, and what was spread on the floor outside Marc's room caused little damage. The solid construction of high-grade sheetrock-lined walls and ceiling helped to keep fires contained. Despite this, if whoever spread the huge quantity of fuel in the living room had torched it, the fire would have been uncontainable.

Flynn relayed to the chief what he'd heard from the state police: "They've confirmed one body and don't know if there are others inside." The pumper drove up to the house and the men immediately set up their portable pond, the supply of water that firefighters carry with them when there are no fire hydrants available.

The chief divided his firefighters into two teams—search and back-up crews. The guys who already had their air packs on formed the first crew and went inside. Flynn grabbed a fireproof jacket and high boots, put those on and then his air pack. He and his partner were part of the back-up crew. They followed the hose line in through the front door and around to the right and to the bottom of the stairs. Beno told Flynn the fire was in the room at the end of the hall upstairs. "Standinger said there's a red glow."

Flynn could barely see the advance team at the top of the stairs. They couldn't hear each other speak through their air masks, so Flynn started pointing toward the doors, asking if they'd finished searching the rooms. They pointed to the room at the top of the stairs to indicate they hadn't completed the search as their air bells were going off. While the first crew went downstairs to refill their air bottles, Flynn and his partner searched the master bedroom with a flashlight and saw the partially burned body that Beno had told them about.

Flynn's body shook slightly. The scene gave him the chills. He noticed that some kind of cloth material hung over the windows, keeping out the daylight. "Someone created havoc in this room," he murmured. He spotted a dog on the floor near the bath; looked like a small collie. He could see it was dead, probably from smoke inhalation. Searching the adjoining bathroom and closets, he looked for possible survivors. He turned left out of the master bedroom and went down a short hall off the balcony, searching a bathroom and another bedroom at the end of the hall. They came back to the balcony and faced the room where Standinger said he saw the glow. All they could see was smoke coming from under and around the closed door.

Flynn turned to his partner. "Grab the firehose and be ready to use it when I open the door." He was afraid of a possible backdraft. He pushed the door back as far as it would go. About three quarters open it hit something solid—a piece of furniture, Flynn assumed. There were no flames inside, but thick smoke forced him down on all fours. As he crept inside he bumped into a body. He stretched out his hand, felt the length of it, and knew it was an adult. Crawling a little further, he felt another body, which he decided was also an adult. At that moment his low air signal went off. As he crawled out of the room and shut the door behind him he radioed the Varna fire chief that they had two more bodies. He met the attack crew on the balcony, their fresh air replenished, and pointed to the end room, signaling for them to go in and finish the search.

Downstairs, getting another air bottle, Flynn could not shake off the eerie unreality of the scene. A strange thought struck him. He decided he'd better verify that those were real bodies he felt in there and not stuffed animals. He'd feel like a damned fool if it turned out those were just a child's toys. When he reentered the end bedroom, two men were trying to open the window; they finally smashed the glass with a crowbar and sprayed water out the window to suck the smoke out. Inching closer he still found it diffcult to see clearly, but it looked as if there was some type of material covering the heads of the adults' bodies. He saw another smaller body away from the adults, which the attack crew had discovered earlier. He bit his lip to push back his uneasy feeling. There was no doubt the carnage was real.

One firefighter with the attack crew who, like the others, found himself on his hands and knees in the room because of the heavy smoke, suddenly wanted to vomit when he realized he was crawling over one body and then another one. He couldn't take it and got out of the room, clutching his stomach. He lurched through the kitchen hallway, tearing his mask off, his face pale.

"You guys are paid to do this. I'm not," he said as he hurried out the front door.

After the firefighters were gone, Beno took Charlie Porter upstairs; first he showed him the scene inside the master bedroom. Then they investigated the end room. Beno hadn't gone in there yet. Most of the smoke had escaped through the broken window panes and now outside light streamed into the room. The men saw two charred humps, slouched forward on the floor, one directly behind the other; they were bound with some kind of wire and cord to the bedposts. The larger body with loafers on was hog-tied. The burned shroud over his head made Beno think of fish net torn apart. A child's body lay along the left wall, attached to another bed.

The child's head was covered as the adult's were. Porter assumed they had been shot. He stared at the grisly sight unable to look away. Beno couldn't get the scene out of his mind for days afterwards.

In another neighborhood across town, Tony had arrived with his bicycle at Ithacare to ride home with his companion Joanna. He told her he had burned people, by which she thought he meant robbed them. He got the car keys from her and waited in the truck until she got off work. On the way home they stopped off at several banks, where Tony said he wanted to get some cash. Joanna saw Tony dump a bunch of credit cards on the kitchen table when they arrived at the apartment around 8:00 A.M. She noticed the name Warren Harris was on one of the cards but said nothing.

Elizabeth and Dennis Regan had moved into their "modern Victorian" house in Ellis Hollow in November 1988. They found the design in a magazine and had the builder adapt it to their specifications. The Regan property was located down a gradual slope from the Harrises' and on a slight downward grade from Ellis Hollow Road, which added to its feeling of privacy. The Regans were so involved with their busy lives at Cornell that neighbors were not a high priority with them; in fact in other houses they'd lived in, they barely knew who lived next door to them. But the Harrises were too nice to ignore. They were their own "welcome wagon." Dodie brought a greeting card and a small wall plaque of a miniature Victorian house over to them soon after the Regans had moved in, and she invited them to dinner to meet other Ellis Hollow neighbors.

Now the Regans dressed quickly and rushed next door. Billows of smoke were coming out of the Harris house as they approached the circular driveway. Pink police tape extended around the perimeter of the property. Trooper Hendershott, dressed in street clothes, was guarding the entrance and ordered them to go back. Dennis nodded, explaining they lived next door and he was the one who had called in the alarm.

"Something very bad happened here," Hendershott said soberly. "We'll be down there to talk to you in a few minutes."

Dennis looked into the open garage door and saw their van was missing. He mentioned this to the police. It was clear now that someone had been in the house. Walking home, both the Regans felt badly. They told each other they should have called the police sooner about the alarm, or gone over to the Harrises to investigate in spite of the frigid weather, still under the assumption it was only a fire they were dealing with next door.

When a police investigator knocked on the Regans' door a short while later asking to use their telephone, they overheard him say, "Homicide," and request the coroner and an ID person.

Their daughter Lisa came downstairs, awakened by the doorbell and voices in the kitchen.

"What's going on?" she asked.

Elizabeth Regan put on a large pot of coffee before she answered her daughter. She knew it was going to be a long day.

Five

Aftershock

A short while later at the crime scene, Investigator Porter's face appeared puzzled. He had gone over everything with John Beno, the first trooper at the scene. They had walked around the Harris house, and Beno had showed Porter the tire tracks, the open garage bay, and the empty gas cans on the floor. "This is going to be a snap," Porter mumbled to himself. "Pressure on the husband, so he killed his wife and took off." Beno looked as if he'd heard.

"We don't know the full story yet, sir, of what happened over here."

"I have to use a phone right away," Porter said hurriedly and trudged over to the nearby Regan house.

Thoughts of the Harrises were churning in Elizabeth Regan's mind after she discussed the awful news with her daughter. Elizabeth told her daughter that the police had sent them back to the house and that someone would be down to speak with them later.

A few minutes later, after Lisa went upstairs to her room,

the doorbell rang. Dennis looked out the window and noticed a car parked on their driveway next to the front porch. He walked over and opened the door.

"I'm Investigator Porter with the state police. Could I use your phone, please?" The tall, graying investigator showed Dennis his badge.

Dennis nodded and said politely, "Yes, Officer, come on in."

Dennis walked him down the hall to the kitchen to the nearest phone. "I have to look into the missing vehicle," Porter said. He chose not to explain that he didn't want to take a chance and call over his car radio because messages could be picked up by anyone monitoring a police scanner. He turned to Dennis. "Would you mind leaving me alone to make the call, sir?" Dennis nodded and walked back to Elizabeth. Porter wanted privacy. He had to notify the station to alert his superiors as to what was happening and to run a vehicle check.

Speaking softly, Porter first asked the dispatcher, "Could you pull up the data on the black Chrysler sedan we found in the garage?" He gave her the license plate number.

In a matter of seconds the dispatcher replied, "The registration is listed to a Warren A. Harris, 1886 Ellis Hollow Road, and a GM van to the same individual." She gave Porter the van's registration number. "Hold on a minute," Porter said.

Porter found Regan. "Do you know what color their van is?" Porter asked him.

"It's brown, I think. Isn't it, Elizabeth?"

"Brown, of course," she replied. "We've seen it enough times parked outside the garage, and Dodie drove Lisa to Ithaca High with Shelby several times when they missed the bus."

Porter went back to the phone.

"The van is brown," Porter told the dispatcher. "Put an APB out looking for that vehicle in connection with a homi-

cide in the town of Dryden. Get the coroner over here, too."
He hung up and rejoined the Regans.

"Can you tell me about the make-up of the family next door?"

Dennis told him that Tony and Dodie Harris had two kids, Shelby and Marc. It ran through Porter's mind that the killer didn't have to be the husband—maybe it was the wife's boyfriend. He wanted something simple they could wrap up in a hurry.

"Excuse me again," Porter said and went back to the phone.

Then Porter called Carl Shaver, the Bureau of Criminal Investigation Captain in Troop C of the state police, who was in nearby Windsor that morning concerning another homicide case. Shaver ran down the checklist with Porter: Had he made sure the evidence was taped off (we don't want the firefighters screwing it up)? What about outside the house, have you made sure it's secured from the public? And so on. Porter knew it was the captain's job to ask these procedural questions, but it irritated him to be wasting time on what he considered to be bureaucratic bullshit.

"We need an ID man over here right away, Captain," Porter said and gave him the Harris address and the Regans' phone number.

"I agree," Shaver replied. "I'll get McElligott to come up right away and take over."

Porter walked back to where the Regans were waiting.

"Can you tell us what happened?" Dennis asked anxiously.

Porter repeated what he knew. "One body was found in the Harris house, and there was a fire." The Regans had so many questions they didn't know what to ask first.

"We feel like we're in the middle of a storm raging outside with no one telling us how bad it is or what we can do about it."

"I wish I could tell you more, but we're just finding out

the complete story ourselves." Porter grimaced. "I'm going back there now, and I'll try to keep you posted."

The full horror of what had occurred next door began to sink in when Investigator Porter returned a while later to use their phone. He said, "There are four homicides."

While Elizabeth Regan walked around the house, trying to cope with the shock of the Harris murders, she found a list she'd made of things to do that weekend: go over to Dodie's shop for stocking-stuffers, borrow Tony's saw to cut down the Christmas tree. She had borrowed the saw the previous year too, Elizabeth remembered. Tears came to her eyes.

Dennis and Elizabeth kept focused by answering questions the police asked about their neighbors; it made them feel they were doing something to help. They desperately wanted to believe that the murders weren't random, but who would want to kill the Harrises? They knew robberies were common near Christmas when people needed extra cash. "If it was a random choice," Elizabeth said, "it could have been our house just as well." She shivered. They checked the locks on their doors, and for hours they kept watching out the window, suspicious of anyone coming into their driveway. Finally, Dennis decided he had to keep busy with his usual routine; if not, his anxiety would be too great. He decided to meet his regular running partner at noon and run their usual six miles in Ellis Hollow.

The wire services had already picked up the story and by the next day it appeared on the front page as far away as North Carolina and the Midwest.

David Long walked down his driveway on Eagles Head Road in Ellis Hollow to get the Saturday newspaper from the tube next to their mailbox. His neighbor yelled over to him. "Have you heard about what happened over at the Harrises?" Long shook his head. She went on, "I heard sirens earlier and asked my husband—he went into his office early—to check it out and let me know. He just called me with the news."

Kathy and David Long dreaded telling their daughter, Meghan. She was still in bed, and they decided to wait a while until they could hear her get up. Memories of Dodie rushed through Kathy's mind. "She was the friend who encouraged me to go back to full-time teaching," she sighed. "She was so happy for me when I found out I'd be assigned to Caroline School." She thought about the time Tony drove Meghan to school on a snowy ski day and left a meeting that night to pick her up while Shelby, his own daughter, was sick at home all day.

After Meghan heard the story from her mother and it began to sink in, she became terrified that the killer might have seen her telephone number in Shelby's room and somehow would come after her.

Ron Daily, one of Tony Harris's old friends in Syracuse, received a phone call while he was washing his wife's hair. She still had trouble using her arms as a result of a near-fatal car accident that she and her daughter had been in six months before. It was Steve Seleway on the line. Steve was another pal of Tony's from Mattydale.

"I'm afraid I have very bad news about the Harrises," he said. Ron's first thought was that the family had been in a terrible car crash. Steve took a deep breath and continued. "The Harrises were all shot and killed in their home last night."

Ron put the phone down in a daze, wondering if this could be a bad dream. Dodie Harris had called the Dailys the day before to invite them to Tony's fortieth birthday the following week, asking them to bring something that was popular forty years ago as a gag type of gift. Ron considered Tony to be a close friend, and although they didn't see each other frequently, they'd spent their formative years together in high school.

Marc and Melanie Walker, who lived two blocks away

from the Harrises, had made plans to attend a party that Saturday night. Their neighbors' daughter, Meghan Long, was scheduled to sit with their two boys. Kathy Long phoned the Walkers to say that Meghan could not sit that night because she was too upset. "I hope it isn't anything serious," Melanie said. That was when she learned about the Harrises. Melanie felt sick from the shock. She remembered how much her son, Joshua, looked up to Marc Harris. Marc was three years older than Joshua, and he had often sat and kidded with him on the school bus the year before when he was still in Caroline Elementary School.

Don Lake, Dodie Harris's brother, was drinking a mug of coffee at the kitchen table Saturday morning when the doorbell rang. He and his family lived in Manlius, a suburb on the east side of Syracuse. His wife, Pat, went to the door and found two men standing outside. The older, gray-haired man began, "We're state police investigators." Both men pulled out their badges. Immediately, Pat wondered if their daughter had had a problem the previous night while taking out the family car for the first time.

As soon as Pat escorted the police officers back to her husband, the younger, brown-haired officer said soberly, "Could we speak with you privately?" Don nodded, and Pat walked back to the kitchen. The older man stepped forward. "There's been a terrible tragedy in Ithaca, sir." From then on the story emerged as Lake, close to tears, asked question after question about his sister and her family's deaths.

Six

A Country Paradise

News that the Harris family had been murdered descended on Ellis Hollow that December morning like a snowball going downhill—slowly at first, gathering momentum, and then out of control as rumors passed from house to house. It was two days before Christmas, a Saturday, when folks woke up to thoughts of last-minute shopping or cutting down a Christmas tree.

Suddenly the people of Ithaca were confronted with their worst nightmare: their neighbors, a family of four, had been murdered sometime Friday evening inside their home on Ellis Hollow Road and their house had been set on fire.

The freezing air of that Saturday—the temperature dropped to fifteen degrees below zero before dawn and rose to ten degrees during the day—only intensified the bone-chilling terror and disbelief. How could this vicious crime happen here in this safe haven from the real world? Who was the killer—or killers? And of all people, Tony and Dodie Harris, the nicest, kindest people you could ever meet, and their two popular children, Shelby and Marc. Were the Harrises intentionally sought out, and if so, why? Or was this a random killing, a tragic lottery that could just as easily have chosen them? A madman might still be out there, ready to strike again. It made no sense. People felt helpless.

Although burglaries were common in certain parts of the city, there were rarely serious crimes in Tompkins County. The well-entrenched illusion continued: Ithaca was a kind of country paradise where bad things just didn't happen. The small-town atmosphere and the cultural and intellectual tone set by Cornell University and Ithaca College gives the place an untouchable quality. The "ivory tower" appeals to many, because it seems detached and protected from the world in a cocoon fashioned by man and nature. Locals were proud of a recent study that named Ithaca the top small city in the East based on quality of life and the well-educated population of some thirty-five thousand people.

The town is located at the southern tip of the Finger Lakes region of New York State, where past geology sets the landscape apart, giving the area a grandiose beauty. Some twenty thousand years ago ice sheets moved down from Canada, leaving behind deep lakes and rocky gorges. A hilly terrain and the valleys below offer a pastoral contrast to the more rugged scenery. The eleven Finger Lakes (so-called because they look like slender, blue fingers on the map), are scattered over the western arm of the state below Lake Ontario between Livingston and Onondaga counties. They are intimately tied to the region's history. As far back as the Thirteenth Century the Iroquois peoples built their villages along the banks, fished in its waters, and hunted in the surrounding dense forests. Names of lakes and counties today, such as Owasco, Keuka, and Seneca are a reminder of the Iroquois tribes who were the first inhabitants of the land.

In 1779 during the American Revolutionary War General John Sullivan marched into central New York with over two thousand men to attack the Iroquois, who had sided with the Tories. His intention was to force the tribes to move westward and disrupt the Tory offense. Sullivan found most of the villages deserted (the Iroquois knew they were outnumbered), but by the end of the march he claimed his men had burned forty villages, 160,000 bushels of corn, well-established orchards, and quantities of vegetables. The Iroquois paid heavily for supporting the British.

The men in Sullivan's army saw great potential in these lands of forests and lakes that were "bluer than indigo" where acres of crops and fruit orchards flourished in Indian villages. Eventually tracts of land were awarded to war veterans by the Land Commission in Albany, the amount of land each was given was based on military rank. So began the white man's settlement of upstate New York.

Members of the Land Commission set about naming towns (twenty-six of them) for ancient military and classical heroes and empires, believing the rhetoric of the Revolution that compared American aspirations to ancient Greek democracy and Roman Republicanism. So we have, among others, Carthage, Fabius, Cicero, Romulus, Ovid, Virgil, Ulysses, and Ithaca.

Peleg Ellis, a war veteran, came in 1799 to settle on his tract of wilderness in what is now Ellis Hollow to the east of Ithaca. Most of the first settlers were of northern European stock. The next century brought Italians, Greeks, and Jews to populate the growing cities, to build the Erie Canal, and then the railroads. Immigrant groups in town formed enclaves for support. First on Ithaca's flats were the Irish, who then moved uphill to Irish Nob. There were 104 blacks living as freemen on the south side of town by 1830; they had the lowest paying jobs as domestics, janitors, or seasonal workers. A slave burial ground was discovered on Ellis Hollow Road on the J.D. Schutt Farm in 1928, settling the question about whether there had ever been slaveholders in Tompkins County.

The region's hopes of being a big commercial depot for northern and western markets in the 1800s were dashed twice; first when canals weren't built to connect Cayuga

Lake to the Erie Canal and second when major railroads by-
passed the town. In both cases the area's topography made
the projects too costly. With an abundance of water power,
mills of all sorts flourished, keeping Ithaca a small manufac-
turing center.

It was Ezra Cornell, a Quaker farmer and businessman,
who transformed Ithaca from the typical upstate village to a
university town. A man of extraordinary vision—he helped
to build part of the first telegraph lines in the country—he
wanted "to found an institution where any person can find
instruction in any study." His idea of offering everything
from the newest methods of farming to Latin and Greek, for
the poor as well as the rich, was a radical concept at the time.
Cornell took the European university model and made it into
something uniquely American: democratic with an appeal to
the diversity of individuals.

Cornell University opened in 1868 on some of Ezra Cornell's farm land atop East Hill overlooking Cayuga Lake.
Many of the 332 original freshmen climbed the legendary
Buffalo Street hill to the new campus that October day, finding one gray, austere building, Morrill Hall, barely completed for their classes and dormitory space.

Ithaca's steep hills and harsh winters have become syn-
onymous with the Cornell experience. The famous American writer, E. B. White, talked about putting on his sheepskin
coat the first of November to dig in for the long winter while
he was a Cornell student in the early twenties. He liked to
recall those cold mornings before six when he trudged up
the hill from the downtown offices the *Cornell Daily Sun*—
he was editor-in-chief—after putting the paper together for
another day, watching the lighthouses shimmer on the inlet
and feeling glad he had come to such a grand place.

The campus is well known for its spectacular scenery
with trails winding down rocky gorges and foot bridges over
waterfalls that drop hundreds of feet. Unfortunately the sheer

drops are also a temptation for those who can no longer cope with life. Students and townspeople have committed suicide down these precipitous slopes in spite of high guard rails that have gone up over campus bridges. It's a dismal part of local reality that isn't talked about.

The Wharton brothers, Theodore and Leopold, saw the filming possibilities of this dramatic scenery and turned Ithaca into the little film capital of the East between 1912 and 1920, churning out the popular melodramatic silent movies of the day with Irene Castle, Pearl White, and Lionel Barrymore. Heroines were thrown off cliffs, trolleys plunged down gorges, canoes were swept over roaring waterfalls, and bridges were blown up. Their operation folded when they ran out of money and Hollywood became the uncontested movie center of the world. By then Hollywood producers had started using more advanced filming techniques and the mild California climate made it easy to film year-round.

Because of the college-town atmosphere, it was probably inevitable that a town-gown division would eventually crop up. In the literal sense Cornell, high above Cayuga's waters, looked down on the town below, and as the university grew in stature and reputation around the world, the contrast and tension between locals and Cornellians increased. But the town knows that it prospers because of Cornell and Ithaca College, its other seat of learning on South Hill. The campuses define the town and are the drawing cards for people and business to settle there. Tourists often come from big metropolitan areas looking for a slower pace of life, clean air, and less crime. Migration picked up pace in the sixties and seventies and is still going on.

Many college students in the 1960s and 1970s reacted to the country's upheaval by dropping out of school and making Ithaca their permanent home. A walk on Ithaca's Commons is proof that the place remains a haven for alternative lifestyles. The small melting pot of well-informed Ithacans support all sorts of causes from saving the rain forests and whales to freeing Tibet and preserving Guatemala's Indian culture.

Small business firms, mostly home-grown, stay in Ithaca because it has a reputation for good public schools and a busy sports and cultural calendar. It's an attractive place for middle-management and other professional families to settle. It is also Cornell that sets the wage level for the area, which businesses must find appealing, since pay scales are relatively low, especially for clerical and blue-collar workers. Many residents commute to nearby Elmira, Owego, Binghamton, or Syracuse for higher wages. The few technical companies in Ithaca that hire skilled workers and professionals are small concerns with relatively few employees.

Although New York City is less than a five-hour drive down Route 17, when you're in Ithaca, the city seems light-years away. No passenger trains come to Ithaca, and flights are infrequent at the small county airport.

Part of the area's remoteness is planned, since no four-lane highways connect it to Syracuse and Binghamton, the two large cities nearby. A fight between developers and environmentalists has gone on for decades, especially over adding highways. So far, the purists have won. The steep and curvy two-lane roads that wind in and out of Ithaca add to the feeling of being sequestered. This is especially true during the winter when snow and ice are apt to keep roads hazardous. Local devotees will tell you, however, that it is the pristine white of snow-covered hills contrasting with the deep blue lake and sky of winter that brings out Ithaca's extraordinary beauty. But they may not mention the climate: long, harsh winters and many overcast days.

The city of Ithaca is surrounded by towns and villages; most are residential communities with pockets of commercial activity. The more affluent neighborhoods are situated in the northeast part of town, which includes Cayuga Heights, the area's gold coast.

These upscale communities contrast sharply with run-down trailer parks and shabby houses that sit on the edges of prosperity and dot the countryside. The majority of the small family farms on the outskirts of town are second-income endeavors: many look like transplants from Appalachia. There is no heavy industry in the region; most unskilled people work for one of the colleges or in the service industry.

Most of the city's less advantaged black citizens still live on the south side of town, where housing is often sub-standard. The more prosperous blacks are scattered throughout the area. Racial tension bubbles beneath the surface, erupting on occasion with incidents that usually involve young black men, the police, and drugs, in lively street disturbances in the Cleveland Street section.

Ellis Hollow, one of Ithaca's most desirable places to live today, is located on the east side of the city in the Town of Dryden. It was Ellis Village in the 1800s, supporting five mills (powered by the waters of Cascadilla Creek), a lumber business, its own school, post office, blacksmith shop, and general store. The stony soil made farming marginal but allowed for a productive quarry, which is still in use. Families broke their rural isolation by being good neighbors and forming a close-knit community where they often got together for socials and church.

People began to move into town to work at the turn of the century, and it wasn't until automobiles made commuting practical did Ellis Hollow transform itself into a residential area. In 1952 a few families renovated the old one-room schoolhouse into a community center to recapture the neighborliness of the past.

Ellis Hollow appeals to outdoor types who run and cycle in all kinds of weather. Ellis Hollow Road runs seven miles through the valley east-west, beginning at the East Hill Plaza Shopping Center and ending at State Highway 79. Among the gentle hills and dense woods Nineteenth-Century farmhouses contrast with elaborate, expensive homes built during the 1970s and 1980s. Although the area today is far different from 1799 when Peleg Ellis cleared the wilderness to build his log cabin, it has kept a measure of its independence and isolation. Tract developments are prohibited, allowing individual taste and spacious lots to remain the norm.

Most Ellis Hollow residents today are affluent and white. When Tony and Dodie Harris moved to the area in 1985 and decided to build their dream house on Ellis Hollow Road, they were looking for a country setting and a close-knit community. They wanted to be near people who cared about each other and especially about children. They liked the activities and facilities of the community center: swimming pool, tennis courts, an outdoor skating rink, ball fields, and programs for all ages. The Hollow seemed an ideal spot to raise their family.

Seven

McElligott and His Team

Senior Investigator David McElligott planned to take his two younger children Christmas shopping later that Saturday morning, December 23, to help them buy a present for their mother. It was the first day of his vacation. During the holidays he always tried to take time off to be with his family. Although divorced, McElligott adored his children and saw as much of them as possible on his days off from the narcotics unit in Binghamton. He was waiting for the kids to arrive when his boss called.

"You said you wanted to be assigned to Ithaca, David. Well, here's your chance," Carl Shaver told McElligott after giving him the bare facts of the quadruple homicide in Ellis Hollow. "I want you to head up to Ithaca right away and start coordinating the investigation." Shaver knew McElligott had worked on many cases in the Ithaca area, so he knew the place. Moreover, Shaver could count on McElligott.

McElligott hated telling his kids that their outing was off, and when he did, they were very disappointed. Once again McElligott felt guilty. He'd left them many times at the dinner table, and hadn't been at other family and school affairs, all because of his work. In fact, McElligott being on call like a doctor was a major reason his marriage had broken up.

David McElligott had been with the New York State Police for over twenty years, the last twelve as senior investigator in the Bureau of Criminal Investigation, Troop C, headquartered in Sidney. Troop C covered nine counties in the central part of the state.

"The only thing I ever wanted to be in my life was a detective, like my older brother, Jerry," he liked to tell his children.

He was proud of his Irish background. McElligott's father had come to America from the County of Limerick, as a young boy in the late 1800s. His father had worked hard to make something of himself. He'd tried professional baseball among many other pursuits, before starting a general contracting business in New Jersey. After the Depression, during which he'd lost all of his money, McElligott's father decided that railroads were here to stay and became a telegrapher for the New York, Ontario and Western Railroad in upstate New York. He moved his family to Sidney where he and his wife, thirty years his junior, raised seven children. David was second to the youngest.

McElligott's father was still working as a telegrapher in his early eighties. Having a secure job was so important to him, that he made sure that his sons learned a good trade. David started as a railroad telegrapher right out of high school following another brother, then spent four years in the Marine Corps. When he got out, David's brother, Jerry, already in the state police, suggested that David take the examination to be a trooper. David McElligott was accepted the day he got out of the service.

On Thanksgiving day four years later, he was promoted to investigator and sent downstate to Monticello, New York. It was an eye-opener for someone who had lived and worked in the rural part of the state. The Monticello station in Sullivan

County had eighteen investigators and sixty uniformed men. David had been used to the small-staffed stations upstate. At first he liked the excitement of being in a big operation. When he was sent to New York City on a homicide investigation, David began to think of himself as a city detective. But fate had another plan.

Less than a year later David's brother phoned him from Sidney and asked if David would like to replace an investigator who had passed away suddenly. McElligott hesitated, but called his brother back in a few minutes to accept the offer. He never regretted the decision.

He stood in a barn a week later, talking to a judge as he milked the cows, and looking down at his wing-tipped shoes in the manure. He murmured to himself, "I've come home. I belong here." He might have dressed like a city-slicker but he knew these people and could talk to them.

McElligott had the presence of a man who knew who he was and what he was about. Early in his career he'd taken advice from others he respected, especially his brother, who told him never to depend on a gun he carried for confidence. "You talk like you have it on." His talent at conversation—he could talk to anyone—made him one of the best interrogators in the BCI. He knew when to push and how to cajole a suspect into giving him information or a confession.

McElligott didn't let the military-style organization of the state police bother him. He wasn't like some of his colleagues who were clearly nervous in the company of higher-ranking officers. He had worked in an undercover operation for a year under the then Captain Tom Constantine who was now the superintendent. They were on friendly terms, but McElligott never forgot Constantine's rank, addressing him with military decorum.

Of course, there were times when he disagreed with his superiors. When this happened he might voice his frustration to a good friend, but to a boss it was always "yes, sir. I'll get right on it." The unfailing politeness fit his practical nature and made him popular with his superiors. He was a cop's cop.

McElligott was rooted in the team approach to solving crimes. Working in the narcotics unit for many years had taught him that. But as he progressed up the chain of command, he knew that someone had to be in charge and he accepted the role with ease. He liked to get things rolling as soon as he found out exactly what happened. Officers who took a slow approach to the job irritated him. He wanted action and he didn't mince words about what he wanted done. He'd tell investigators who hadn't worked with him before, "Patience is not one of my virtues."

McElligott's reputation became almost legendary in the BCI. He expected the best from the men on his team. He could blow his Irish temper with a flood of expletives if someone didn't follow his instructions or did something McElligott thought was stupid.

But investigators who got to know him on a personal level learned he had a big heart that went along with this demand for excellence. He understood human nature. He knew how to listen to a troubled or scared young officer and give him encouragement. He passed along tips to newcomers that his brother had given him when he became an investigator.

Having to witness the unsavory side of life on an almost daily basis hadn't embittered him or made him feel it was a rotten world. It was easy for him to understand how people who didn't have anything got themselves into trouble. The first time he saw several children sleeping on a bare and dirty mattress, his heart went out to them. He felt badly that any kids had to live in such shabby conditions. He often felt sorry for people he had to arrest.

The challenge of the work continued to invigorate him. Each new case meant a different puzzle to solve. And no matter how bleak the situation looked, he stayed upbeat. "We'll get 'um. It's just a matter of time," he'd say to his team.

However, there was stress on the job and sometimes it got to him. To relieve the tension he smoked over a pack of cigarettes a day. He had cut down some, but couldn't break the habit. Also, he sometimes showed a nervous trait of opening and shutting his eyes rapidly while in conversation.

He and his friend, Charlie Porter, gave up drinking altogether a few years back when both of them realized that alcohol had become a liability. He was middle aged and knew he had to change some habits to keep feeling good. Another one he'd given up was, after a bout with skin cancer, baking in the sun on the Jersey shore.

His work habits matched his neat, color-coordinated appearance. McElligott worked in an orderly fashion. Nothing was out of place in his office. No matter how busy he was, his desk was not cluttered. He could immediately find what he wanted because of a filing system he'd devised for himself.

There were visible contrasts to the man. He had a strong, intelligent face with the reddish complexion and rugged good looks of an outdoorsman—he looked easily capable of splitting logs, yet he dressed impeccably like a Wall Street banker.

He'd rather own a few well-made, expensive shirts than have a drawer full of cheap polyesters. The same with shoes and suits. He bought good ones and kept them in excellent condition. His shoes always had a military shine. What he wore looked well thought-out. One could imagine his closet and drawers organized by color and style.

He and his good friends in the force were all snappy dressers. When they went to a meeting in Albany, they'd try to out do each other wearing the nicest suit they owned.

McElligott's shoulders sagged a bit now on his slim five foot eleven inch frame and his thick, wavy hair was peppered with gray, but he approached his job as vigorously as he had those first years. There was still passion in his belly.

As David McElligott drove to Ithaca on Route 79 from Binghamton he spoke with Charlie Porter over the car transmitter.

"Where in the hell is this house on Ellis Hollow, Charlie?" McElligott asked. He'd never used Ellis Hollow Road as a shortcut to Route 79 as many people did.

"It's at the end near 79 just past Slaterville Springs. Turn right on Ellis Hollow and it's about a mile or so on the left."

McElligott pulled into the driveway alongside Porter's car. He'd heard there was a fire. He assumed he'd be looking at a burned-down building. Porter was waiting outside.

"Where's the scene, Charlie?"

"This is it," Porter replied, pointing to the left side of the house where firemen had vented out the upstairs windows and then McElligott saw the scorching and smoke.

Trooper Lishansky, standing next to Charlie Porter, hadn't been in the identification unit at Sidney for long. He had been on his way to a Windsor case when he was called.

McElligott looked at Lishansky for a long withering moment but made no comment. Then he said, "Where's Chandler?"

"Shaver said he'd be right over," Porter assured McElligott.

When the call had come through to the Oneonta station Saturday about a homicide in Ithaca, Karl Chandler was at his computer, entering information from lead sheets on a murder investigation in Windsor. He called Ithaca and was told to head for Ellis Hollow immediately.

Karl Chandler's specialty was homicide. He'd been a senior investigator with the state police for twelve years and in the force since 1960. Chandler could keep going longer than anyone else in the business. He slept little and with no family responsibilities, his work was his life. Around March when he got fed up with driving in snow and ice, he'd talk about the wonderful day when he'd get the hell out of this

God forsaken climate and retire to play golf in Florida. But his friends on the force knew better. Retirement would not come easy for Chandler.

He took the kidding that went on regularly among his fellow investigators with a shrug and a smile, except when it came to his dog, Reggie, his prize possession. He doted on Reggie like a mother hen. He bought a van so the Wheaton Terrier would have plenty of room. One day when his good friend, McElligott, asked him if he'd heard about a big dog being hit over on Interstate 88, it wasn't until he saw McElligott laughing that Chandler could breathe easier. Jesus, he thought, nothing was beyond a joke with these guys.

Someone asked Chandler how he handled fear before he was promoted to senior status—back when he faced dangerous situations in field assignments on a regular basis.

"I'm just always trying to figure out how in the hell am I going to get out of the thing. And I don't want to embarrass myself."

He once talked a fugitive out of shooting him after the guy told Chandler to get down on his hands and knees and beg for mercy.

"No way was I going to do that," Chandler said matter-of-factly.

Most of the danger was gone now as a suit and tie man, but the business of solving a homicide supplied enough excitement to keep Chandler keyed up. His pack of Camels stayed at arm's reach, a habit he couldn't break. He didn't mind admitting that one of the benefits of making senior investigator was sending others to autopsies. He never saw an autopsy he liked.

The job of solving homicides had joined the technology revolution and Chandler had been on board from the beginning. The computer fascinated him. It became clear to him that with a computer two investigators could do the work of ten. He was one of the first in the force to see the potential of computers in solving crimes and when the state didn't come through with the equipment, he bought his own. He tried to convince McElligott to give up the typewriter, but the old-timer kept postponing the transition. He said he'd do it when he had more time.

Coming on to computers fitted Chandler's practical nature. He put the crime puzzle together with a heavy dose of common sense. When headquarters sent him a specialist trained in behavioral science to set up a psychological profile of a murderer or rapist, Chandler was not enthusiastic. He knew enough about human nature after years of solving homicides and other crimes of violence to draw his own profile. He didn't believe in soothsayers.

Chandler arrived at the scene a short while later. He joined McElligott inside the house and Charlie Porter gave them a quick tour around the house. The investigators wanted to get an overall feel of what they had facing them.

McElligott noticed the overturned gas can in the living room. Quickly he went upstairs. He could recognize the figure on the floor as a female in the master bedroom, but standing in the other bedroom, he had to ask Porter: "Where are they?" He didn't see anything that looked like bodies. Porter pointed to some odd forms. McElligott walked closer and grimaced. Because the victims had been shrouded and bent down on their knees, they looked like charred lumps on the floor. McElligott leaned toward them and could see they'd been bound. He shook his head.

"Lishansky, gather every single piece of evidence you can find. I want every scrap of paper and strand of hair saved." McElligott had learned from watching others in the field and from his own experience to leave nothing to chance and he was a stickler for detail. It appeared there were no witnesses to the crime which made evidence gathering crucial.

He told Lishansky the way he wanted the photographs taken—a method he'd learned at a national homicide school. "Go to each corner of the room and take a picture of the body. That way the camera will pick up everything in the room."

"But that's not how we do it," Lishansky told McElligott.

"You don't understand, damn it. That's the way I want it done. As senior investigator I decide how it's done. I want those pictures like I told you," McElligott barked. "And make sure you get good pictures of every room in this house."

As a senior investigator in charge of a homicide investigation McElligott had to plan from the start how to prepare the case so the district attorney could present it in court, provided they caught the killer. Since there seemed to be no "smoking gun," keeping detailed records for the prosecution was very important.

They needed more manpower. A few days before the murders McElligott had met Sergeant David Nazer, the head of detectives at the Ithaca Police Department, and had mentioned to Nazer that he hoped to be assigned to Ithaca soon. They'd agreed to help each other out if the occasion arose.

McElligott had to cash in on Nazer's offer right away and asked him if he could spare a few guys. Nazer ended up by sending every man he could find on the Ithaca force that wasn't involved with a priority case.

The Tompkins County medical examiner, Dr. John Maines, was notified about the murders at 8:45 A.M. He came over immediately.

While McElligott waited for the medical examiner results, he called George Dentes to tell him about the Harris murders. Dentes had been elected Tompkins County District Attorney in November and would take over the position on January 1. What a way to start off, he thought. Worst multiple homicide that ever happened here. He'd seen nothing as bad as this in three and a half years as Assistant District Attorney in Manhattan. In 1985 he had moved his young family out of chaotic, crime-infested New York City to quieter pastures upstate—rural Ithaca where he and his wife were born and grew up (he had degrees in engineering and law from Cornell University). At least, it was a relief that the state police with a big organization and plenty of personnel were handling the case and that McElligott would lead the investigation. He had heard of McElligott's extraordinary ability.

One-half hour later Dr. Maines announced that each of the four dead Harrises was shot in the head. Since Maines was not a forensic specialist, he asked for assistance from the Onondaga County Medical Examiner's office in Syracuse. In a short while Dr. Humphrey Germaniuk, a forensic pathologist with Onondaga County, was on his way to Ithaca.

Lieutenant Bart Ingersoll of Cornell University's Public Safety Division was chief of the investigative arm of the campus police, but that Saturday morning he was standing in for the lieutenant in charge of the uniform patrol who had the day off. When the dispatcher walked across the hall to his office in Barton Hall and handed him the APB that had just come over the teletype about a missing GM van, the message contained little information except a description of the vehicle and that they were looking for it in connection with a homicide. He immediately radioed all patrol cars and told them to call blue light (secured phones where police could speak over closed circuits, located across campus under blue lights). Ingersoll instructed the patrolmen to look for the van in the sectors they covered. He then got in a car to do his own search.

Ingersoll started looking in places where stolen vehicles were often dumped. He'd been a campus investigator eighteen years, so he knew all the spots where hot cars had been found. After he checked those areas, he went out to Game Farm Road and looked behind Cornell's poultry barns; another location for stolen cars. He drove through the East Hill apartment complex, checked the area around Best Western Motel and behind East Hill Plaza, then swung around to the plaza parking lot, which was filled with cars and shopping carts by then. He drove slowly up and down each parking lane.

Across from the plaza was Ides Bowling Lanes and he remembered finding two stolen cars way in the back of the building on separate occasions. As he drove to the rear of Ides and around toward Marine Midland Bank, he spotted a van that looked like the one described in the bulletin. He got out of his car and glared at the license plate. It matched. Ingersoll radioed his base on campus what he had found. It was 10:38 A.M.

Ted Palmer and Charlie Porter went up to Ides to check out the van reported by Cornell safety. And an ID man was ordered to gather whatever evidence they could find in and around the vehicle.

A light coat of snow covered the van (it had been snowing off and on since 4:00 A.M.) They cordoned off a fifty foot area around the vehicle to prevent disturbance to the scene. Patrol cars and police stood at the various entrances to Ides Bowling Lanes and Marine Midland Bank to block cars and pedestrians from interfering with the site. Porter brushed the snow off the left rear corner of the van and peeked inside. He half-hoped he'd find a body in there—the boyfriend who shot himself after killing the family. He still yearned for a straightforward solution to the homicides. But he didn't see anything in the van.

They took pictures and the ID investigator fanned the snow back from the door of the driver's side with a 3 by 5 index card. He found three or four large footprints headed toward Ides Bowling Lanes and then disappear in a mishmash of tire tracks. The prints indicated the person could have been running. They took photographs of the footprints. Porter arranged to have the van towed to the police lab in Port Crane, near Binghamton, where technicians would go over it with a fine tooth comb for evidence.

Palmer went inside the bowling alley and talked with em-

ployees. They told him they saw a van like the Harrises'
parked in the same location at various times Friday night and
early Saturday morning; later they talked with a few Friday
night bowlers and they, too, remembered seeing a van like
the Harrises' parked outside.

While Palmer spoke with people inside the lanes, Porter
knocked on the doors of houses close to the Marine Midland
Bank and Ides to see if anyone noticed the van or persons
around it the previous night or early that morning. No one
knew anything about the van.

At times like this when he was working for McElligott,
Porter never forgot for a moment what a tyrant the man
could be when it came to investigating a homicide. He was
his best friend, but friendship had nothing to do with solving
crimes with McElligott. He demanded more than a hundred
percent and if you didn't ask all the right questions, he'd say
you screwed up, even if fifty people were around. He remembered when he was doing his first case as an investigator on a Binghamton homicide, involving a woman strangled
and left in the trunk of a car. He came back to the station
after interviewing the paperboy and McElligott said to him:
"How'd you do with the Perkins kid?" McElligott began firing questions like bullets from a machine gun: Did he tell
you this and what did he tell you about that? There were over
thirty investigators on the case and Porter noticed McElligott did the same with each one of them, never referring to
notes. He had all the facts in his head.

Investigators had to reconcile these van sightings at Ides
with fresh tire tracks that Trooper Beno saw at 7:20 A.M. Saturday on the Harris driveway and across the lawn. Did the
killer stay all night or come back before daybreak Saturday
to burn the evidence? And there was always the chance that
witnesses were mistaken about the vehicle they saw in the
parking lot. The Harrises' van was a common model and color
and at night in snowy conditions, vehicles can all look alike.

* * *

Tall, good looking David Harding, the upcoming star investigator with the ID section who had trained Lishansky in identification work, arrived at the crime scene and joined Lishansky inside the house. They had worked on many cases together that led to convictions and praise from their bosses. Harding called the shots and Lishansky followed.

They knew this one would take longer than the usual crime scenes they faced involving one or two rooms. They had a big house to deal with and to make things worse the fire left water damage and perhaps had destroyed evidence. Their work required technical skill and a calm, methodical approach to collecting evidence. But the immediate excitement of entering a murder scene pushed the adrenaline up a notch or two. Neither man had seen anything so horrendous before.

David Harding loved being in the hot spot of an investigation. When he entered the room, he'd work it like a politician, shaking hands with everybody and smiling broadly. He wanted his colleagues to like and admire him. Most of them did.

Harding and Lishansky soon realized that circumstances surrounding the multiple murders on Ellis Hollow Road were out of the ordinary: A well-respected, affluent family of four murdered in their own home three days before Christmas wasn't an everyday event. This was a major case. A piece of evidence they found at the scene and preserved might be the ammunition needed later to nail the killer. And if they fouled up and let something important slip by, it would not be pleasant facing McElligott.

Harding wanted to get the telephones working again and the furnace back in operation. He could see his breath when he walked inside the house. Icicles had formed on the kitchen faucet. It seemed to him there was no point in freezing while they did this long, painstaking job.

The two men took a quick walk through the house as they talked with officers who had been at the scene first. They wanted an overall impression before they examined the area in detail. They noticed a man's blue jacket hanging on the banister at the bottom of the staircase with a pair of men's gloves underneath it. There were envelopes scattered on the floor in the study and a small file cabinet was open. A closet in the study was filled with baseball cards. A briefcase stood on the floor against the island countertop in the kitchen. A Syracuse basketball still in its box lay on the same counter. A pan with a few noodles sticking to the bottom was on the stove next to a plate of Christmas cookies. Soup cans on a lazy-susan were toppled over. They kept searching. Two sacks of groceries were on the counter next to the sink. A set of keys were on a shelf beside the kitchen fireplace.

To the left of the foyer on the living room carpet lay a red and yellow gasoline can on its side with a nozzle five feet away. There was a strong smell of gasoline in the room.

On their next trip around, Lishansky took photographs and Harding inspected more thoroughly. It was a grisly scene upstairs where the smoldering fire charred the four bodies almost beyond recognition. The heat had made the clothing shrink around the bodies in a fishnet effect. In Marc's bedroom they found the body of Dodie Harris in a kneeling position leaning forward with coat-hanger wire and heavy shoelaces that secured her legs and wrists together and bound her to the bedframe around her neck. She had a bruise on her lower right leg.

Tony Harris's body was directly behind Dodie's, facing in the same direction. He was in a hog-tied position, wrists to ankles, bound by heavy shoelaces and coat-hanger wire. Heavy shoelaces also tied him to the bedframe on one twin bed. Coat-hangers wound around what they later decided were pillowcases placed over their heads. Other hangers tethered them to the bedposts. Tony had on his brown Docksiders; the only victim with shoes on. Broken glass was scattered on Tony's back. Harding noted a gold wedding band on his left hand and another large ring on his right hand.

Marc's body was bound to the foot of the other twin bed in his room. Wires were around his elbows and legs and his wrists were tied with a leather strap and his feet were tied together with shoelaces. He was covered with a pillowcase and secured at the neck with coat-hanger wire as his parents were. A straightback chair stood in the middle of the room. A gerbil lay dead in its cage. The fire was started on one twin bed and extended to the floor in the center of the room. Apparently diesel fuel was used for the upstairs fires. Its red container stood in the hall outside Marc's room.

Shelby was found naked face down on the floor of the master bedroom next to the charred mattress, her green prom dress over her. Her body was mostly decomposed as a result of the fire and at first glance they surmised the dress had been attached to her wrists. It looked like the fire had been ignited at the top of the mattress. Her left arm was folded behind her. A cord had been attached to her left wrist. A sock and another cloth gag were stuffed in her mouth. Her right leg was extended straight out on the floor. Blood had pooled on the carpet near her body and splotches of blood stains went down the bed's dust rufffle. The bedsheets were soaked in blood. She had been shot in the area of her right ear and eye.

Immediately the detectives thought of rape and searched for semen. They didn't find any.

The room was in chaos—open boxes, Christmas wrappings and bureau drawers strewn across the floor. All the windows were covered with either towels or sheets. Harding and Lishansky found yellow and brown stringed cord with loops on the end like makeshift handcuffs on top of the bed. Red bikini underwear lay at the foot of the bed along with an open jar of Vaseline.

While Harding was examining the floor around the burned bedsprings, a cat darted out from under the bed coughing and sputtering. Plastic was stuck on her face, her paws and whiskers were burned, and her coat was covered with gasoline. Harding tried to grab the cat, but she scooted out of the room.

The Harrises' dog, Annie, lay dead from smoke inhalation next to a blue upholstered chair that was near the door of the adjoining bathroom. Her eyes were open and a blue ribbon was tied around her neck. Eventually someone cornered the cat in the children's bathroom. None of them could guess how she survived the night. She'd licked her fur and ingested a dangerous amount of toxin before the police handed her over to a neighbor who immediately gave her a bath. She was the sole survivor of this massacre.

Tony Harris's leather wallet with his current Visa card was on top of the bureau in the master bedroom and a red Scripto cigarette lighter was on the dresser. After Shelby's body was moved, Lishansky found a ladies wrist watch on the floor next to the left side of the bed; the hands pointed to 6:33. He saw a panel of electronic buttons on the wall above the light switches. He found out that these buttons were connected to an elaborate security system that had been installed while the house was under construction. But the system hadn't been hooked up to a police or fire department.

In Shelby's room they noticed strips of panty hose dangling from the rungs on the back of a wood chair with some hose pieces entwined with human-looking hair strewn on the carpet. Cigarette ashes were on the floor around the chair. Bedcovers were pulled back and an empty piggy bank lay on top of the bed. All the shades had been pulled down. Tennis trophies were arranged in a cabinet. On top of the cabinet were a pair of scissors and a poster of Elvis Presley hung on the wall. A box in red Christmas wrapping was on top of the dresser with cutout letters in silver paper attached to the side of the package that read: TO JIM.

Clothes were heaped in a pile on the floor of the bathroom next to Shelby's room: A pair of jeans, a red sweater, socks and underwear. A Swatch wristwatch was on the floor. Cigarette ashes were in the toilet bowl.

They saw the contents of a purse or wallet, including coins and photographs, dumped on the hallway floor next to Marc's room. Cigarette ashes found on the 7th and 10th step of the staircase were taken in for analysis.

When they confirmed that the killer or killers put pillowcases over their victim's heads before they were shot, they suspected this was more than a robbery gone berserk. It looked like a planned execution by someone who wanted to inflict terror as much as the perpetrator wanted to steal. They could find no signs of a struggle after the victims were tied up. Marc was shot once in the head and twice in the face and Shelby had been shot three times in the head; Tony and Dodie were each shot twice in the head. The pillowcases reduced the area over which blood could splatter; since Shelby was not hooded when she was shot in the head, a substantial splattering of blood may have stained the killer's clothing. Harding took samples of bloodstains from the carpet and bed in the master bedroom.

Police searched the grounds and the garage for forensic evidence, hoping to find some trace of bullet casings or shell fragments. In the garage they found an air compressor with the cord neatly wrapped around it on the hood of the black Chrysler sedan. Nothing seemed to be disturbed at the Grey Goose, Dodie's store, when the police searched it. Investigators found a cash box inside the shop with $30 in it.

David Harding had seen enough crime scenes to suspect that the Harris family killer was experienced in crime; many surfaces were wiped clean on areas where normally prints would have been found in any house. He surmised that the intruder wore rubber gloves, at least some of the time.

He dusted practically everything in sight hoping to find fingerprints he could lift. Earlier Lishansky had pointed out what he thought were prints on the metal two and a half gallon gas can on the living room carpet. To check it out, Harding got down on the floor and at an angle directed the beam of his high-powered light to the surface. The light picked up some smudge marks near the bottom of the gas can and one at the top. He thought they must be fingerprints. Duct tape was stuck on the can which Harding could barely make out the word "unleaded" printed on it. The soggy rug reeked of gasoline.

Later Harding went back to the overturned gas can. He took the can upstairs to Shelby's room to see if they had latents. He needed an enclosed area where there was no movement to build a fuming chamber: Opening up a container of super-glue near the gas can and letting the fumes act as a fixative. But the process turned up negative. He couldn't lift any prints. It was frustrating. He called Lishansky over. He knew whoever handled that gas can had to be a suspect.

"I can't seem to get prints on this can, Rob. But we gotta be quiet about it, especially to McElligott. You can bet I'll get them so back me up with McElligott." He flashed Lishansky a quick knowing look.

"Yeah, okay. I want to nail the bastard who killed this family," Lishansky answered. "What kind of a son of a bitch could do this to kids?"

"We also want to help ourselves out," Harding reminded Lishansky.

As soon as he could get to it, Lishansky studied the envelopes strewn on the floor of the study. There was an empty envelope addressed to Warren Harris from Tompkins County Trust Bank. It was from their credit card department. He made sure the envelope got to McElligott right away.

Rob Lishansky liked the field work; going to the scene, trying to figure out the puzzle, talking with senior investigators and experts about all facets of the crime. What he could learn from autopsies intrigued him too. What he didn't enjoy was the slow, tedious process of looking at fingerprints under a microscope. It was the only boring part of his job. But he knew fingerprint evidence helped get convictions.

Often he strained his eyes to see if a finger's ridges matched another. When the sweat glands underneath the ridges do not release enough fluid as the print is made, it becomes harder to see the ridge detail for a positive match. Some prints may show curved or short ridges that stop abruptly, which makes it impossible to identify the print. Maybe they'd get lucky in this case or maybe they'd have to bend the rules a little.

They took cigarette ashes from the house to be examined by experts: two small heaps were found on the staircase, some around the straightback chair in Shelby's room and a cigarette butt under Tony Harris's briefcase in the kitchen.

Lishansky didn't know any thing about cigarettes, never having smoked. He got the name of an analysis expert from the crime laboratory in Port Crane, a town near Binghamton, who investigators had used on other cases. Lishansky learned that from a few ashes, they could tell the brand and type of cigarette. New technology could reveal the DNA of a smoker from saliva found on the cigarette tip, but the expert said the science wasn't at that stage yet. He could confirm from the ashes that the intruder smoked Benson and Hedges 200s.

The Harris house and van were full of animal hairs; for the most part they matched the long hairs of the Harrises' dog, but there were a few short hairs also. They took blood samples from both bedrooms and searched for any trace of blood that may have been transferred from the killer to surfaces in the house or van.

Lishansky measured the dimensions of every room in the house and the garage; it was information the police artist needed in order to draw a house diagram that showed the location of the bodies and other key elements of the crime scene. They needed this visual image in order to reconstruct the crime. McElligott wanted the diagram done right away, so that he and other senior investigators who were not at the scene daily could start brainstorming theories of what happened Friday night and Saturday morning, December 22 and 23. It helped to draw up the killer's profile after they had a reasonable idea of what took place at the crime scene. They had to know what sort of person or persons they were looking for.

It took Harding and Lishansky a while to establish the time when the killer or killers left the Harris home after burning the bodies. Lishansky talked with a fire and burglar alarm specialist at the scene. He informed Lishansky that the sophisticated $1,500 alarm system set up at the Harrises in 1986 was not wired to any fire or police station. The inside horn was on the wall in the hallway leading to Shelby's bedroom. It's outside horn was installed at the peak in the roof line of the garage. The sirens emitted a sound comparable in loudness or louder than a police car siren. Knowing that Dennis Regan's second call to police reported the alarm stopped at 7:16 A.M., they deducted the alarm must have started at 6:44 A.M.

A fire investigator, a specialist in tracing fires, ignited a fire in the Harrises' upstairs to see how long it took for the alarm to go off. In about a minute the smoke set off the alarm. The police assumed the killer was in a big hurry to get out of there after the penetrating shrill surprised him. It would have taken no more than a minute to run to the garage, back the van out and drive over the snow-covered front lawn. That would put him on Ellis Hollow Road by 6:45 A.M.

McElligott wanted to find out if the knots the killer used to tie up his victims would tell them something about who they were dealing with—were they tied by a left-handed person, were they specialty knots used in the military or some other line of work? After the ID men finished working on the crime scene, McElligott had investigators drive his car to the

FBI crime lab in Washington, D.C., loaded with the bedposts from Marc's room with the knots attached to them. Specialists could find nothing unusual about the knots. They were random and were tied in many different ways.

As the morning turned to afternoon, Captain Shaver arranged to use a nearby church on Ellis Hollow Road as a command post to run his investigation. It was close to the murder scene and as someone pointed out, it looked like the only public building around. They needed a headquarters quickly to coordinate the operation. Chandler and McElligott were the kind of partners who divided the work in a case without having to talk about it. They were well-acquainted with each other's style when they worked together in Troop C's major crimes unit, established in 1978.

Temporary headquarters were set up in the basement of the Ellis Hollow Community Church that stood on Ellis Hollow Road near the Ellis Hollow Creek Road intersection. The simple structure of white clapboard, built in 1896 on land that Peleg Ellis cleared and his daughter gave to Ellis Hollow a few years before her death, was still used as a community gathering place. The church had ample parking space and was half a mile from the crime scene. But it had only one phone line.

McElligott had John Beno and the other troopers who had been the first to arrive at the crime scene document all they had seen and done that morning.

McElligott quickly realized this was a particularly frightening and heinous crime to a well-liked family in what was thought to be a safe quiet neighborhood. He knew as soon as the media was notified the community would soon be in a state of panic. He was glad he didn't have to deal with the hysteria or the media. He could send those calls to his boss.

As the investigation continued that afternoon, it became clear to McElligott that the church basement didn't have the facilities they needed to run a command post. He knew they didn't have a simple case facing them. It might be a drawn-out investigation. Many things bothered him: the lack of a forced entry into the house, a missing van with one set of tire tracks buried in the snow and no footprints leading to the front or back doors. He assumed it was probably a robbery gone badly wrong. Porter had pointed out the gift shop to him. The brutality of the killings puzzled him. He hoped someone passing the house during the night or early morning might have seen something.

He assigned troopers to a roadblock in front of the Harrises, and sent others to make a door-to-door canvass within a five mile radius of the crime scene to find out if anyone had seen anything near or on the Harris property Friday or early Saturday morning.

A local resident who was stopped at the roadblock told the trooper she saw someone riding a bicycle late Friday afternoon headed toward the Harrises on Ellis Hollow Road, about two miles from East Hill Plaza. She couldn't identify the cyclist's sex, race or age, because the person's face was concealed by a hooded parka.

Ted Palmer, the police computer expert, arrived. Palmer, a senior investigator in Cortland, a town twenty-three miles northeast of Ithaca, routinely responded to nearby homicide cases, so as soon as he heard the homicide report from Ithaca sputtering over the station transmitter, he got in his car and headed for Ellis Hollow. As he approached Ellis Hollow Road, he received instructions over the radio to report to the white church located near the Ellis Hollow Creek Road intersection.

Chandler wanted Palmer stationed at the church to enter data into a computer as the leads came in. Palmer became hooked on computers after he participated in the first computerized homicide investigation in 1985. As he learned the mainframe software, he became fascinated with computer programs and what they could do in solving crimes. He spent two years (1987 and 1988) in Albany, designing database operations and traveling over the state, showing investigators how to use computers to solve crimes.

Palmer had his own Tandy laptop in the car; he knew that organizing lead data into the computer would be his main function after more investigators joined the case. He wasn't long at the church, however, when a call came through to check out a lead at Ides Bowling Lanes at the East Hill Shopping Plaza.

The primary lead McElligott wanted investigated was the robbery aspect of the crimes. When he saw the empty bank envelope from the credit card department found in the Harrises' study, it seemed obvious that the Harrises' credit cards were taken. Ted Palmer began to pursue the lead late Saturday afternoon. He was known for his thoroughness and the stamina to stay on a problem until he found a solution. He might look like a bespectacled professor with his calm, soft-spoken manner, but his appearance belied a suspicious, practical nature. He was highly regarded by his colleagues and superiors.

Palmer contacted the main office of Tompkins County Trust Company on Ithaca's Commons and spoke with Joseph Perry, one of the bank's vice-presidents, about their suspicion that the intruder in the Harris home may have stolen the Harrises' credit cards that were issued by his bank. It was something they had to pursue right away. They needed to find out if the cards had been used. Bank personnel went into high gear to try and track down the information Palmer asked for. They were anxious to cooperate with the police in solving the crime that had the community already becoming frightened for their own safety.

Meanwhile a news bulletin was released to the press that the four Harrises had been shot in the head with a small caliber handgun and their bodies doused with gasoline several hours after they were killed between 6 and 10 P.M. Friday night, December 22. It was not made public that the police were unable to determine the order of the killings because the bodies had stiffened from the combination of heat and cold air. The press release announced that intruders made no forced entry and robbery may have been a prime motive.

In the duplex they shared on Etna Road Shirley Kinge hadn't been up long when her son Tony came over, his Doberman at his heels, and found his mother and grandmother drinking coffee in the kitchen. Shirley's Doberman lay at her feet. Her dog was as laid back as Tony's was aggressive. That's probably why the Dobermans got along. It was a few minutes before three o'clock in the afternoon.

"I want to go out and get some things. Drive your car, Ma, an I'll buy gas," Tony said to Shirley as he rubbed his cigarette out on the floor with the bottom of his sneaker.

"I hate shopping and you know it and besides I'm tired." Shirley got up from the table and left the room after taking out the leftover slices of pepperoni pizza from the carton for the dogs. They were tall enough to grab the food from the table.

"Shit, what's Christmas suppose to be? You're suppose to get things, not that we ever did that." Tony followed Shirley upstairs to her bedroom.

"All right," she sighed. "Give me time to dress and brush my teeth, will you? I don't have any money to buy anything," Shirley said loudly enough so her mother could hear her.

Forty-five minutes later they were in the Subaru. Tony told his mother to drive to Marine Midland Bank on Triphammer Road.

Joanna heard about the Harris murders on the radio Saturday afternoon and saw television coverage later that day. She remembered the credit cards Tony put down on the kitchen table in the morning. She was too scared to confront him and she knew if she asked him questions about the credit cards, he'd say it wasn't any of her business.

* * *

By 3 P.M. the police had moved from the small church to the police barracks and began to run the operation from there. The station had just put in a new Merlin phone system with ten lines and they had plenty of room for extra desks and computers.

Later that day the bodies were removed to Syracuse for the autopsies to be conducted by Dr. Germaniuk and other forensic pathologists on the medical examining staff.

The autopsy team got sick and tired of calls from McElligott. He'd call every hour and tell them he wanted a report—right then—and he wanted them to continually call him with an ongoing assessment of what they'd found.

Eight
Christmas in Ithaca

Captain Robert Farrand, Commander of Troop C, briefed the media Sunday night with the barest details of the investigation. No official cause of death was announced, nor was any possible suspect named. They could find no evidence of forced entry.

It soon became evident that David McElligott had been right about the effect of the media and the anxiety that would be aroused. The wire services picked up the story and by the next day it appeared on the front page of papers as far away as North Carolina and the Midwest, as well as in *The New York Times*.

The public was asked to call the police if they had any information about the case. Meanwhile people in Ellis Hollow were getting hysterical. Rumors flew. Residents badgered the police and were angry about their close-mouthed policy. The townspeople were terrified. They were afraid the killer might strike again.

The Tompkins County Sheriff's Department was barraged with inquiries about police permits for carrying guns. Gun shops had record sales after Christmas. Charles Muzzy, an Ithaca gun store owner for thirty years, said he had never seen people in this town react the way they did to the Harris family murders.

One locksmith told a reporter she couldn't keep locks on the shelf. They were bought up immediately. Rumors persisted that Tony Harris had been in a witness protection program for an indicted former Syracuse mayor; others suggested that a jilted boyfriend of Shelby's was getting even. Anything seemed easier to take than the idea of a random killing. That was the worst nightmare that people could imagine. It made everyone vulnerable.

McElligott was impressed that despite their anxiety the people of the community wanted to help the police. One of the main reasons McElligott wanted to retire to Ithaca was because he liked the people he had met in the area.

During the Christmas weekend a trooper found a basket of cookies and other holiday foods left outside the front door of the barracks with a card that read, "God Bless You." A physician stopped by and offered her services at no charge in the event medical care was needed. Others left special foods and small gifts.

McElligott made sure his team got off for part of the holiday to be with their families. He left Ithaca late Christmas Eve and spent most of Christmas day with his children. They opened gifts at his house in the morning and had a big brunch before he packed up more clothes and returned to Ithaca. McElligott had managed to stay close to his four grown kids from his first marriage and the two younger ones. They didn't come out and say they were proud of their father—in fact, they had complained over the years about the demands of his job—but McElligott knew he was a hero in their eyes.

Perry worked over the holiday weekend with the bank's credit card management company and clearinghouse in Omaha, Nebraska. First he established that Visa Gold cards were issued to the Harrises, then he traced any activity on the cards. He discovered that 1990 Visa Gold cards, issued to Warren and Dolores Harris, had been sent to them during the third week in December. It all made sense. The intruder found the envelope unopened in the Harrises' study and took the unsigned Visa cards as part of his loot. The Harrises' 1989 Visa cards were left in the house.

As Ted Palmer learned the intricacies of following a credit card trail, it soon became apparent that his Tandy laptop computer didn't have sufficient memory for the job. Chandler remembered seeing an IBM personal computer in the Harrises' study on one of his trips through the house. He mentioned the PC to McElligott, and soon it was arranged with Don Lake, Dodie Harris's brother, to loan them the computer until the state came through with one for their use. State police headquarters in Albany kept promising individual stations across the state they'd have personal computers soon, but so far no one had seen any.

The bank and clearing house personnel worked closely with police to speed up the paper trail process.

Nine

A Lost Bicyclist

On Tuesday, December 26, the media reported that police were looking for a bicyclist seen headed east on Ellis Hollow Road around sunset on the day of the murders. Captain Carl Shaver told reporters that police were interested in talking with the cyclist, because they were trying to find out how the intruder got to the scene, and they hoped the biker had seen something relating to the murder of the Harris family.

McElligott returned to work early Tuesday morning to find the command post's bank of phones ringing constantly. Callers from all over the United States had stories about seeing cyclists and cars in or near the Harrises' on December 22 and 23. The police didn't automatically tape calls coming into the post but when they heard something good, a switch on the phone would start the tape rolling. On McElligott's orders, police listened to everyone who called—from the people who made sense, to crackpots who told outlandish tales.

McElligott took a call from a woman named Beatrice Doll in Connecticut who said she had a precise memory of what she had seen on the afternoon of December 22. He took down notes as she clipped off her story with Yankee precision.

"On Friday, when I was en route to visiting my family on Genung Road for the holidays, I saw a man riding a bicycle on Ellis Hollow Road headed in the direction of that gift shop. He looked like he was having a hard time with the snow and blowing wind. He had a parka around his head."

"About what time did you pass by this cyclist? Can you remember?"

"It had to be between 4:20 and 4:35 P.M. And I saw him after I'd gone by the intersection of Ellis Hollow Road and the Hollow Creek Road. I thought it was strange to be out that late in such terrible weather. He was a black man."

McElligott didn't put a great deal of stock in the woman's comments. It was snowing and getting dark when she saw the cyclist. He thanked her for calling and put his notes on a pile of lead sheets on his desk.

Some of Ellis Hollow residents thought it was preposterous that police were looking for a bicyclist.

"Having lived in Ellis Hollow for twenty-five years, I know this is a favorite bike route," said Janet Sitchen. "I see bicyclists on Ellis Hollow Road almost every day. There are certain unusual customs around Ithaca."

Another Hollow resident claimed that many people commuted to work by bicycle. "There are a lot of rugged types out here."

Later that busy day, Dr. Germaniuk, the forensic pathologist, informed an impatient McElligott that the bullet wounds indicated the victims were shot while someone stood over them at close range.

As the day progressed, a bank official called to say they had found out that two purchases were made December 23 on the Harris cards. The bank gave Palmer some details about the items purchased in Auburn, a town forty miles north of Ithaca. A pair of red Reebok women's sneakers, size 7, were bought on the Warren Harris Visa card at the Footlocker store at Auburn's Fingerlakes Mall and a pair of white Reebok women's sneakers, size 9, were bought on the Dolores Harris card from the Marjax store at the same mall.

On Tuesday, during the afternoon, McElligott called David Harding at the crime scene to check on how things were going. He liked to get a frequent update.

"How's it going, Dave? Anything new?" McElligott asked.

"Yeah, I got something. I was about to call you. I found three prints on the overturned gas can left on the living room floor." Harding explained the prints were on the long side of the red and yellow can.

"Good going, big time. What else you got?" McElligott asked.

Harding told McElligott there were a lot of prints they had to check out as soon as they had the Harrises' finger-prints. He said he was having a hard time lifting the gas can prints.

"But I'll get 'em. It may take a while, but I'll get 'em off," Harding assured McElligott. "We're covering every inch of that house."

"Good," McElligott answered, his mind elsewhere. He didn't put a lot of stock in fingerprints. They were usually hard to match, but he was first to admit to knowing very little about prints. He left them to the specialists. Just like firearms. He was a terrible shot.

David McElligott announced there would be a briefing session every morning down in the basement of the odd-shaped single-story building, referred to as "the pit." He borrowed chairs from the Varna fire department and set them up in semicircle rows facing a table where he, Karl Chandler, and the Captain were seated. Except McElligott never sat on them, he stood at the blackboard or walked back and forth in front of his audience.

From the outside, the Varna barracks looked like an ordinary private residence: white aluminum siding with black shutters framing the windows and evergreen shrubs on both sides of the entrance. A split-rail fence encircled the drive-way. Perhaps this look was a throwback to the days when troopers lived in their barracks. The interior had long, dimly lit corridors that seemed to go in all directions with some parts added as the organization grew. It was jokingly referred to as the structure built by committee.

One of the front offices was converted into the investigation's nerve center, from which the principals ran the operation. Karl Chandler and Ted Palmer set up their computer equipment; David Nazer of Ithaca's police department sat at a desk across from McElligott. Nazer and McElligott fielded the incoming calls and made out lead sheets for the investigators. Chandler worked to keep the records up to date on the computer as well as running leads himself. The setup allowed for easy and ready access to each other. They threw out ideas, discussed them, and made their decisions. McElligott felt this was the best mix for solving crimes. He and Chandler made sure their most trustworthy officers were sent to Ithaca from stations across the state. McElligott had no use for the "I can do it myself" type of investigator. If a loner was found on board, he was soon dismissed. Everyone had to be dedicated to the team philosophy.

McElligott liked to walk down the corridors, in and out of offices, coffee mug in hand, listening to others as they hashed over leads, inserting an opinion or fact here and there. His sense of humor was the oil that kept his engine running. Although the job was serious, he liked to have the working climate relaxed enough for investigators to kid each other and joke around. It helped to relieve the tension.

There was no micro-managing on his part. When his men or women received an assignment, they were on their own with the knowledge they'd be grilled later by their boss. He was in the habit of telling investigators who didn't know him, "I'm the best and worst of guys, but I'm right on the money." Most of them already knew the kind of man he was. He was often referred to as "Monsignor."

McElligott warned his team, "When I'm waiting for you to get back from an assignment and I find out you've stopped off for dinner and drinks, just make sure your stuff is all packed up at the motel, because I'm going to throw it out on the goddamn curb and send you back to your station. Don't make us wait for you. You come back, give us your report, and I'll take you out to dinner."

Lead sheets were the building blocks to the investigation for McElligott. He believed one promising lead on top of another would eventually bring them to the solution. McElligott read every lead sheet turned in at the end of the day before Chandler entered them into the computer. Chandler pulled those facts from lead sheets that he thought should be followed. He possessed an instinctive logic for picking out the treasures from the trash. In case he was mistaken, Chandler could rely on Ted Palmer, whose job it was to see that every word of a lead sheet went into their database.

This was the first major homicide case in which McElligott had relied so heavily on computers. He had to admit they made it easy to keep track of what had been done so far and by whom. Everyday, a printout showed him a name index of everybody they'd talked to and a matching lead number. McElligott used these printouts at morning briefings to bring everybody up to date.

The next day's lead sheets were based on what they had found out the previous day. McElligott believed in this cumulative process. The leads became a part of him; at briefings he connected information from a day or so before to an investigator's current findings. He often asked questions to dig deeper, inquire further, and to get at the logic of the thing. McElligott insisted everything be written down, but he rarely referred to notes. He lived the case and once he had the facts they never left him. Easy recall of names, dates, and places was an important asset in running a big investigation.

As much as he wanted to see the case solved, McElligott

believed the process couldn't be hurried. But he gave another impression to the team. McElligott had to make them feel their work was urgent. He had to motivate them. Each person on the team got the chance to suggest his own ideas after the investigator told the group what they'd done the previous day. McElligott told them often that "a lot of heads are better than one" and that they were going to solve the case soon. Although the Captain or Major would be present at these meetings and McElligott told the team they were the bosses, McElligott did most of the talking. He outlined the major facts of the case—what they knew so far—on the blackboard.

Experience had taught McElligott that the pieces of the puzzle would come together if everyone was patient and worked hard. Three-ring binders of all lead sheet reports were kept across from Nazer's desk for investigators to go through at any time.

After the Harrises' bodies had been removed to Syracuse for the autopsies, McElligott had made every investigator in the case walk through the Harris home and view the scene of the crimes. He believed in opening every possible avenue. Something might cross an investigator's mind later that connected a piece of information to what he observed while viewing the crime scene.

When McElligott learned from Harding and Lishansky that most of the surfaces inside the house had been wiped clean of fingerprints and that they couldn't find a murder weapon or any bullet shells or fragments left behind, he suspected they were dealing with an experienced criminal. They searched their files but came up negative after checking out all parolees and well-known "bad guys" in town. It didn't look good.

Ten

Running Hot and Cold

It was never good news when there were no suspects after the first forty-eight hours. You could see cars bumper to bumper in the parking lot in back of the Varna state police barracks and along the sides of the half-circle driveway. More than forty investigators were now working on the Harris case. They were mostly taken from BCI staffs across the state, plus detectives from the Tompkins County Sheriff's Department and the Ithaca Police Department. Forty uniformed men and women supported the effort with roving patrols in the community and a twenty-four hour guard on the Harris property.

McElligott and Chandler remained at the command post later than anybody, often until 11 or 12 o'clock at night. Usually they ordered food in, sometimes they'd go out late, calling their favorite restaurant at East Hill Plaza, to ask them to save two steaks for them. The owner became a friend and kept his place open after regular hours to serve them and sometimes their bosses—the Major or Captain. Both men kept going on cigarettes and coffee.

The two senior investigators roomed together, talking

until two in the morning about the case and making up a list of things to do the next day. All of the out-of-town investigators stayed at Howard Johnson's on Route 13. The management gave them a good discount on the rooms. They almost filled the motel.

Everyone gathered for breakfast in the restaurant next door between 7 and 8 A.M. where most of the conversation centered around the case.

Later, a Bank personnel informed Palmer that the Harris cards were used for expensive purchases at a shopping mall in Camillus, a suburb of Syracuse. Items included a pair of $500 diamond earrings, a $400 VCR and a $300 television.

Palmer fed the leads to McElligott, who assigned investigators to question the store clerks about these purchases. If things went favorably, they would come back with a description of the buyers and signed receipts. The police noted that whoever made these shopping trips didn't choose the more popular malls in Syracuse up Interstate 81, but more than likely they drove the two-lane Route 34 to the out-of-the-way Fingerlakes Mall in Auburn and then on Route 5 to the lesser known Camillus Mall west of Syracuse.

McElligott hoped the Visa cards would be used again; so he had Palmer ask the bank to keep the Harris account open for a while longer. He knew it was a long shot. Since the advent of computers, most people who steal credit cards know they don't have much time to run up expenses, so it's the first twenty-four hours they go on a spending spree.

McElligott talked to his team about this lead. He liked to keep the optimism flowing with everybody, but McElligott realized that the credit card trail might go sour. Stolen credit cards are big business. They're sold everywhere; even in broad daylight on Ithaca's Commons. The intruder could have easily gotten rid of the Harris cards for cash. But it was their only real lead so far.

Barbara Ostrander, a teller at Marine Midland Bank on Triphammer Road, discovered a Tompkins County Trust bank access card inside the ATM during her routine check on the morning of December 26. The name looked familiar. She checked the newspaper to make sure and handed the card over to the assistant manager, who called the police immediately.

Soon both banks started getting information about other uses of the Warren Harris bank access card. After checking their ATM logs, it was clear that while police and firefighters were discovering the Harris bodies on Ellis Hollow Road, someone was five miles away trying to withdraw money on a bank access card stolen from Tony Harris.

At 7:38 A.M. on December 23 someone had made three attempts to withdraw money on Warren Harris's bank access card at the Triphammer branch of Tompkins County Trust. But the computer was down in the main office. At 7:50 A.M. two attempts were made to withdraw money at the bank's Pyramid Mall branch. They also failed due to computer malfunction. At 3:44 P.M. on December 23, $200 was withdrawn on Warren Harris's card at Marine Midland's ATM outside the bank's Triphammer branch. *Who had done it?*

Charlie Porter and his partner, Tim Boehlert, followed the lead. Bank personnel pointed out to them that whoever used the access card had to know the cardholder's P.I.N. number (personal identification number). The ATM seized the card after completion of the $200 transaction, probably because the card was left in the machine too long. The user hadn't withdrawn the card when he punched in the P.I.N. number a second time for another withdrawal. The access card must be inserted for each transaction.

The banks supplied investigators with names of customers who transacted business at their Triphammer branches around the same time that the machine ate up the Warren Harris card. They hoped someone who used those machines on Saturday, December 23, would remember something. Many phone calls later, they got lucky.

John Burton reported that he and his son, Scott, were in

their car waiting to use the Marine Midland ATM at the bank's North Triphammer Road branch on Saturday, December 23, around 3:45 P.M. They remembered the car in front of them. Police asked the Burtons to come in and give a description and statement of what they had seen.

"Our station wagon was behind this dirty, light-colored car, a black man got out of the passenger side and went to the machine. After a few minutes, he waved to the driver of his car to move ahead. Then he motioned to me to pull up to him. The man said he'd lost his card in the machine and would I use mine to see if it would spit his out? I used the machine, got $100 cash but his card didn't come out. I turned to him and said, 'Well, it looks like you're stuck.' He just shrugged his shoulders and answered, 'Too bad.' I thought it was strange that he seemed so undisturbed about losing his card," Burton told Investigator Porter.

Bank personnel explained to investigators that often access cards get trapped inside the machine, because the user leaves them in too long. Some customers encounter difficulty when they first try automatic machines. Police surmise their suspect might not be accustomed to ATMs or he was in a big hurry.

The Burtons gave the forensic artist as many details as they could remember about the two people: He was a lanky, black man with a five o'clock shadow who was smoking a cigarette. Scott Burton said he had loose curls cut short in the front and his hair went to his shoulders behind his head. The driver was a black woman who had "poofed-up" hair. She was probably older than the man, but they didn't see her well enough to describe what she looked like.

By Thursday, December 28, Ted Palmer had traced six purchases that were made on the Harris credit cards December 23. A forensic artist accompanied investigators to Auburn and Syracuse to make composite drawings from the store clerks' descriptions of the customers they waited on who used the Harris Visa cards. Fortunately some of the clerks remembered those purchases even though they were made on a busy night before Christmas when the malls were crowded with last-minute shoppers. Other clerks were either doubtful or said they couldn't remember anything about the transactions. Investigators had hoped that some store or bank had surveillance cameras operating at the time, but none did, which made the clerks' memories of that night even more crucial.

He was disappointed but it came as no surprise to McElligott that the credit card trail now had turned cold. There'd been no more purchases on the Harrises' Visa card after December 23. McElligott and his team waited long enough to see if the stolen cards would be used again. Then he and Chandler decided on Friday, December 29, to release the composite drawings to the media. Maybe someone would recognize a drawing and come forward.

McElligott thought there was probably more than one killer in that house. And a female accomplice hadn't occurred to him. The Harrises had no connections to blacks and blacks were rarely seen in Ellis Hollow. McElligott felt they had to find the two people pictured in the drawings to know who the intruders were. If the police could find out who sold the couple the cards, they might make headway. But the whole thing was puzzling. To steal credit cards and sell them, the robbers could only get $20 to $40 dollars at the most and maybe there had been $100 they took from the house and the $200 from Tony Harris's bank access card. *Did it make sense to brutally murder four people for that?*

The police artist drew eight composites (four of them from descriptions by store clerks and two from bank witnesses); there were five drawings of a black male suspect, one with curls, one wearing a hood, and all showing a five o'clock shadow; three drawings of a black female suspect, one with glasses and all wearing some type of cap.

The whole case, McElligott thought, had too many missing pieces to construct a logical outline no less a complete case. No matter how impatient he and the others were they would have to wait and hope that further investigation would bring out more of the facts.

Funeral services for the Harrises were held that cold blustery Saturday at Holy Cross Church in DeWitt, the same church in which Tony and Dodie were married in 1971. More than four hundred people filled the pews and the extra chairs set up for the ceremony. At the wake held the day before, 700 people passed by the four caskets.

The funeral was an emotional gathering, an outpouring of sympathy for the Harris and Lake families. In reflecting on the unknown murderer, Reverend James Gehl told the assembly, "Jesus loves even that sinner."

As Al Hundskamer sat in church and listened to the eulogies, he thought back to when he first got to know Tony Harris. Tony was on his team at age thirteen when Al coached Babe Ruth baseball. He remembered how he stood out from the other boys, not in talent, because he had average ability, but in his outgoing personality and self-confidence. Tony was the first kid at practice and the last to leave; he wanted the team to win, his individual achievement didn't seem to matter as much. When they were playing for the team championship in Booneville, New York, the team's catcher jammed his thumb and had to be taken out of the game to the emergency room. Hundskamer moved Tony from first base to behind the plate, a position that he'd never played before. It was a pressure atmosphere in a tight game for the division title and his teammates were pumped up to win. Tony took charge as though he'd been groomed for the job. Hundskamer never forgot the poise of the young boy.

When the mourners left the church to bury the Harrises on a hillside in St. Mary's Cemetery next to Holy Cross Church, the day had grown even colder. The Harris family was laid to rest under pink granite stone engraved with their names, birth dates and the date of their death—December 23, 1989. The grave site overlooked the city and its surrounding hills.

Later a memorial service was held for the Harrises at the Immaculate Conception Church in Ithaca. More than six hundred attended; many family friends and religious leaders spoke about their remembrances of the Harrises and tried to console the gathering.

Reverend Charles Marks said, "We are angry that humans could treat others like this. We become indignant when we realize that the very qualities that made the Harris family real and lovable, also made them vulnerable. Their openness, friendliness, their trust made them vulnerable."

The media had the eight composites by noon of the day the Harrises were buried. They were shown on local and regional television news programs that evening. The release was too late for the Saturday edition of the *Ithaca Journal*. With no Sunday paper, the story was to be front page news in Monday's January 1st edition.

By the time the drawings were released to the media, Captain Shaver had arranged for an 800 number at the Varna command post. In the release they asked the public to call the 800 number with any information pertinent to the case. Chandler always dreaded this part of an investigation. He wished there was some way to weed out the nuts who loved to call the police from those who had real information.

Ted Palmer had devised a look-alike tip sheet with a format easy to enter into the computer. He hoped the form might help speed up the process when the calls started coming in.

Some in Ithaca's black community were outraged that in the composites all the suspects had the stereotypical look of Afro-Americans with big lips and protruding jaw line. One woman accused the police of racism: "Now the police will stop every black man and woman to question them about the murders."

Indeed she was right. Blacks reported that they were being indiscriminately stopped and queried by cops, especially young men seen in parts of town where whites usually hung out. Black mothers urged their sons to stay close to home. Some voiced the suspicion that if the Harrises had been black, the community would not have been so driven to solve the case. A white Ellis Hollow resident asked her neighbors not to be intolerant toward all blacks just because the suspects might be Afro-Americans. She reminded them they wouldn't put all whites in a bad light if the murder suspects happened to be white.

Her words, amid the anxious atmosphere, did little good. Racism had reared its frightened ugly head and further polarized the community.

Eleven

Coping

As more rumors in the town grew, fear multiplied. It became obvious to Marc Walker, president of the Ellis Hollow Community Center, that his neighbors and friends desperately needed some answers. The police were so tight lipped about the murders that residents were fueling their own hysteria by exchanging unreliable information. Walker convinced Captain Farrand that a meeting with the police was essential to calm people down. On Sunday afternoon, December 31, about three hundred and fifty area residents packed the Caroline Elementary School cafeteria where state police, community leaders, school officials and counselors addressed questions concerning the brutal murders.

"Nothing in our investigation of this particular case leads us to believe this will happen again in this neighborhood," Captain Farrand assured the crowd. "If I thought there was even a slight, remote chance that some crazed killer was running around the neighborhood and might strike again, I would be remiss in my duty if I did not warn you about that."

He asked the audience to understand that the police could not release information that might compromise their investigation. Here lay a bone of contention between residents and the police. Ellis Hollow people felt they deserved more "inside" information because they lived in the neighborhood where the crimes had been committed and they were still very frightened. A tug of war was developing between the people and the police.

Ithaca is full of assertive individuals who by nature, or profession, or both, are accustomed to speaking out and getting results. "People feel they're experts on everything here," one old-timer told a reporter. Now they wanted more than advice and reassurance. They wanted new information about the Harris murders. But the police stayed firm and released no new facts. "I think this has really built up fear," said one man. "We don't know whether there are psychopaths running around, or whether robbery was the motive or if it was something else."

Captain Farrand and Trooper Michael O'Connell fielded a barrage of questions about crime prevention, home security, how to establish a Neighborhood Watch organization and how to respond if approached by someone with a gun.

"If someone approaches you with a gun, do whatever they tell you," O'Connell told the audience. "Try to avert any kind of a conflict." With what had happened to the Harrises it seemed even what would have been good advice took on an eerie cast. When asked about how people arming themselves could be a potential for accidents, O'Connell said, "The last thing we should be thinking about is arming ourselves." Despite this, one man in the crowd told a reporter, "I now sleep with a knife beside my bed." Even though the police insisted the crime was an isolated tragedy, the anxiety of the townspeople could not be easily dissipated.

A day after the composites were released, the command post received a hundred calls. With the 800 number, police heard from individuals as far away as California. Many local calls still involved descriptions of cars seen in or near the Harris home from December 22 through December 23. By

now, investigators had ruled out the two bicyclists seen on
Ellis Hollow Road Friday afternoon, December 22; one was
an eighty-year-old gentleman who cycled every day and the
other was an Ellis Hollow resident.

McElligott picked up an incoming call from a man who
insisted the killer was an Iranian terrorist. McElligott tried to
cut him off politely, but the caller persisted. Finally in desperation, McElligott told the man he'd switch him over to
Senior Investigator Karl Chandler, their expert on international terrorism and hostage situations. McElligott grinned
over at Chandler as he picked up the phone.

Many callers said they knew absolutely that they'd seen
vehicles parked at the Harris home on the Friday or Saturday
around the time of the crime. A station wagon, a green van,
a red car, a silver and blue older model sedan—the list of vehicles supposedly seen went on and on. About fifty car sightings were reported. It was virtually impossible to rely on the
sightings because there were so many and if all of the cars
had been at the scene they would have been parked on top of
each other. But vehicle sightings, just like the bicycle sightings, raised more speculations on how the killer or killers
had gotten to the Harrises.

From the avalanche of calls, one woman particularly impressed McElligott. Alice Pickert told him she had passed by
the Harris house on the way to pick up her daughter from the
airport around ten o'clock and had seen lights flickering in
an upstairs room. When she came by about an hour later, all
the lights were out. Mrs. Pickert said everything was quiet at
the house. She didn't see any cars parked in the driveway or
near the property on either trip. McElligott took note that her
description of the weather was accurate. He and Chandler
were coming to the conclusion that there were no vehicles
parked at the Harrises' after late-afternoon on the day of the
murders.

More information reinforced the theory that the intruder
arrived by bicycle: Alice Pickert's testimony put the cyclist a

few yards before the Ellis Hollow Creek Road intersection at 4:35 P.M. and later a statement from Alicia Alexander and her son, Ian, corroborated the Connecticut woman's story. The Alexanders reported seeing a bicyclist on Ellis Creek Road at Thomas Road (a short distance from Ellis Hollow Creek Road) headed toward the Harrises' around 4:30 P.M. The cyclist was having trouble with the snow; they noticed his tire tracks on the snow-covered shoulders, starting at the Genung Road turnoff. He wore a parka with a fur lined hood. Alicia Alexander said the cyclist was a young, good-looking, black male.

There were no bicycle sightings after the one at 4:35 P.M. reported by Alice Pickert. Ted Palmer made drawings showing all the vehicles reported at the house. They eventually ruled out every vehicle parked in the Harrises' driveway or near the house after 2:00 P.M. on December 22.

The cyclist theory began to look even more plausible. The medical examiners were not absolutely sure, but they concluded after the autopsies, that the killings probably took place between 6:00 and 10:00 P.M. It was likely that the intruder had arrived at the Harrises' close to 5:00 P.M. Those two pieces of the puzzle—time of arrival and the last bicycle sighting—fit together.

Two composites of a black male were added to the eight drawings first released to the media: One showed a figure with a hood and the other had a short haircut, both described by clerks at the 16-Plus Store in Camillus. Every call coming into the command post (two more lines had been added to the regular service) about composite look-alikes was taken down by staff members assigned to the desk. Investigators sifted through the stack of telephone calls for leads that looked promising.

One of the many leads on McElligott's desk was from an informant who had called about having hired a woman to clean his house. The woman looked like the female composite drawing. The caller's heavy accent made him hard to understand. He said the woman was "Shirley King" and that she lived with a younger guy, either her husband or boyfriend, who looked like the male composite.

The communication specialist tried the name on the police network and the state drivers' license database. All that came up was a "King" from Locke, New York. It was one of hundreds of leads that had come in. Nobody could make anything of it, so the tip-sheet sat on McElligott's desk along with dozens of other look-alike leads.

Lieutenant John Grant was sent over from BCI headquarters in Albany to offer assistance in the case. He was trained at the FBI's Behavioral Science School in Virginia. Major Farrand—he had been promoted from captain during the first week of the investigation—wanted to touch every base and he knew Grant was good at offering ideas about the type of suspect with whom they were dealing. After a detailed study of the crime scene, a criminal's profile can be pinpointed to the person's personality and what kind of car he drives. Grant said at a morning briefing that the brutality and circumstances of the Harris crimes suggested the behavior of a psychopath and he didn't think drugs were involved. Chandler wasn't impressed. Neither was McElligott.

Another call came in which seemed more valid. On December 23, Professor Dean Sutphin and his family left their home on Ellis Hollow Road to spend the holidays in Virginia. When they returned, the media was full of the Harris murder investigation. Sutphin read in the *Ithaca Journal* that the police were requesting that the public call them if they'd seen anything on Ellis Hollow Road that Friday afternoon or Saturday morning.

Sutphin knew he had to call them right away. He didn't like the idea of getting involved, but he knew it was his duty as a good citizen. He spoke with Karl Chandler, who asked Sutphin to come in and make a statement.

Sutphin distinctly remembered looking at the digital clock in his car as he and his wife pulled out of their driveway, and headed for Virginia. It was 6:48 A.M. Sutphin told the officers that he drove down the driveway and stopped to put a Christmas package in the mailbox. Before turning left onto Ellis Hollow Road, Sutphin noticed a van heading west—the direction he was going. He waited for the vehicle to pass his driveway, but the van slowed almost to a stop, then slowly turned right on Game Farm Road, about one hundred yards from the Sutphin car. Sutphin noticed the van moving at a snail's pace. A black male was driving the van and the passenger, considerably older, looked like a black female. The man was wearing a light-colored stocking cap.

Sutphin recalled driving slowly because of the slippery roads, and before reaching the intersection at Judd Falls Road, there appeared to be a van behind him. It turned right, into the East Hill Shopping Plaza or into the apartment complex. Chandler took the statement, walked with Sutphin behind the barracks where the van was parked and asked him if the vehicle he had seen in the early hours of December 23 looked like this van. Although Sutphin could not be positive, the GM van parked behind the police barracks looked like the one he had seen December 23. Chandler thanked the professor for coming in and told Sutphin they might have to contact him later.

Four students in Cornell University's School of Veterinary Medicine got in touch with the campus police after they returned from the holiday break to inform them about an incident in the vet research tower on Friday, December 22. Two men were roaming around the building between noon and 2:00 P.M., the students said. They described their encounter with two black men that afternoon. The men looked suspicious as they wandered in the halls and into offices where no one was around. One of the students asked if they could help the men, who said no, they were just looking around. Since there were holiday parties going on in the building, offices were left unattended. Later it was discovered that personal checks were ripped out of checkbooks as well as credit cards and some cash were taken from five people. The vet students thought it was likely that there was a connection between the thefts at the research tower and the Harrises' stolen credit cards. The vet school is on the eastern edge of the campus, only six miles from the Harris residence.

During their interview with campus police, the students identified men from the composite drawings. Despite the students' convictions, the investigative team didn't believe the thefts at the vet school on December 22 were related to the Harris case, but rumors spread like wild fire on the campus that a killer had been at the school. Students and staff were getting more tense and frightened. Cornell's safety division received calls from top Cornell administrators putting on the pressure to see that the vet school incidents were properly investigated. Captain Shaver explained that the police were swamped with tips and it was their job to put investigators onto leads that held the most promise.

However, the heat from Cornell forced McElligott to take men off other leads to probe the school thefts. McElligott didn't like it, but he accepted that kind of meddling as part of the job. Hearing about it, Karl Chandler said he was glad he didn't have to handle those public relations issues. He hated politics getting in the way of doing the job, and thought a criminal investigation should be left to the professionals.

Tom Kelly headed up the investigation of the vet school thefts. He had joined the state police after being discharged from the Marine Corps twelve years before. Kelly had wanted to become a state trooper since he was a kid. He and his family had taken summer vacations to the Finger Lakes from their home on Long Island. There, he had seen some troopers and realized that this was the kind of cop he wanted to be—away from cities in open spaces. To Kelly, central New York State was beautiful country. It was also a better environment than the New York City area to raise a family. Kelly loved police work. He had the personality and skill of a natural investigator. Kelly could talk with anyone, pulling out information with ease. However, so many checks were routinely stolen at Cornell University that for Kelly to trace the vet school thefts was like trying to find the proverbial needle in a haystack. The process required many days of legwork by many men, following tips that often led nowhere.

McElligott had a strong feeling there were no logical links between the two cases. The time frame wasn't right. The guys roaming around the vet tower were sighted as late as six o'clock. They would have had to race one hundred miles an hour to be way out on Ellis Hollow Road at the time when the crime was committed.

Investigators finally zeroed in on the vet thief, Charles Haynes, at a friend's apartment in Syracuse. He was hiding inside a laundry basket. Kelly arrested Haynes as one of the men who stole checks at the vet school on December 22, on a forgery charge. The arrest of Haynes led to the break-up of a forgery ring that had been going on for years in central New York. Haynes had been convicted in 1967 of first degree manslaughter after killing a man in a barroom fight in Syracuse and had served five years in prison.

The vet school witnesses had told police the thieves looked like they were in their twenties. McElligott interviewed one of Haynes' associates. As they sat across from each other in an empty office at the barracks, McElligott noticed his pockets were bulging.

"What's in your pockets?"

The suspect emptied them on the table.

"What the hell is that?" McElligott asked, pointing to one object.

"False teeth, man," he said.

"For Christ's sake, how old are you?"

He turned out to be fifty something.

Meanwhile, Doug Vredenburgh had been going up to Syracuse every day to check out the forgery lead and agreed with McElligott that these guys were not their killers. They were wasting manpower, yet some men assigned to the detail still believed they had the right suspects. They grumbled to Vredenburgh after hours about the "suits" not taking them seriously.

At the next briefing when the forgery guys were brought up, a fatigued and dispirited Vredenburgh said in a loud voice that he was tired of going up to Syracuse on a dead-end lead.

"The next person who says they're good suspects is gonna have to deal with me."

McElligott had heard that some investigators had gone to the Captain to tell him they had the right guys, but McElligott wouldn't listen. McElligott explained to the Captain that these suspects' alibis checked out. The police knew where the two men were the night of the murders.

The press, which was critical of the police for holding back information about possible suspects, picked up the story. They acted as though Haynes was being looked at as the possible perpetrator in the Harris murders. Police were telling the media very little, so Haynes became a suspect by default.

The townspeople were growing more frightened day by day as news spread that lead after lead was going nowhere. Robert Dean, president of Deanco, the company for which Tony Harris had worked, announced that the firm was offering a five thousand dollar reward for information leading to the arrest of the murderer or murderers. When asked by the press if he knew of any reason why Tony Harris would be targeted for murder, he replied that he knew him to be a man of integrity. Tony had been a well-respected and popular Deanco employee for many years and had a lovely family. He could think of no reason why anyone would harm any of the Harrises.

Richard Steele, a Syracuse reporter, got McElligott on the phone. Although McElligott had earlier thought he could divert these calls to his boss, Shaver wasn't around to talk to the media. Steele said, "I've heard from reliable sources that Shelby Harris had been raped, sodomized and tortured with cigarettes. We're going to print it unless you can give us hard information about what's going on."

Trying to keep his temper in check and important information about the crime out of the media's reach, McElligott replied, "All you heard was conjecture, it just isn't so." McElligott took a deep breath, "but go ahead and print it. Be my guest." He didn't have much patience with reporters.

More than a hundred people sought help from the Tompkins County Mental Health Department during these first weeks after the murders, said psychotherapist Tom Schneider, also a neighbor and friend of the Harrises. Harry De-Libero, a counselor with the state's Division of Veteran Affairs, told the audience at a citizens' meeting they were experiencing posttraumatic stress disorder, a response to catastrophic or traumatic incidents or events. He urged them to talk about the tragedy with friends, family or counselors and to make sure their children were listened to. Counseling services at local schools would be available after winter vacation. Caroline Elementary School principal Connie Tobias was roundly applauded when she announced a new after-school program to keep latchkey children at school until 6:00 P.M.

Farrand said he was confident the crime would be solved. "Murder is the most solvable of all crimes. That's a fact."

Donald Culligan, who sat on the Tompkins County Board of Representatives from the City of Ithaca, proposed donating one thousand dollars to the reward fund from the board's reserves. "This is to give the feeling of the County Board representing all of the people," Culligan said.

A second reward fund was established at a public meeting for information leading to the arrest and conviction of the murderers. By the end of the session, over ten thousand dollars was pledged. Captain Farrand made it clear that reward money was important in solving crimes; the higher the bounty, the more likely it was that someone would give them key information. Soon the two reward funds were up to twenty-six thousand dollars.

Fifty parents gathered at the Ithaca High School cafeteria on January 3. Stewart Grinnell, director of the county's mental health clinic, told the group that he had turned away a stranger who appeared at his door last week and asked to use his phone. Grinnell had never done that before and he wanted the audience to know that his reaction was normal under the circumstances.

Galer Zimmer, a DeWitt Middle School counselor, admitted to a similar crowd gathered at DeWitt: "I'm feeling real sad and real angry. But I don't want to let those emotions go yet. Because if I let those go, it would be like letting Marc go."

When Marieke Widmann thought about the tragedy, she remembered a remark Shelby had made to her in the autumn. Since this was Marieke's first year on the varsity girls tennis team at Ithaca High, she didn't know many of the girls. Shelby broke the ice for her and started up a conversation on their first out-of-town trip. Marieke told Shelby, "I'm getting nervous; there have been so many robberies in our neighborhood lately that my family has decided to put in an alarm system."

Shelby replied, "I don't think anything would happen to me, because I feel my neighborhood is extremely safe."

David Harding had developed close ties with Don Lake, Dodie Harris's brother, and his family after having to ask them so many questions about the Harrises. He had escorted Don through the house after the bodies were removed. Harding was ardently sympathetic to their loss. He kept in regular contact with the Lakes and became personally involved. Harding assured Don, "We'll find whoever did these terrible crimes. Count on me to do everything in my power to nail the killer."

Don Lake felt that with people like David McElligott and David Harding investigating, it was just a matter of time before the case would be solved. He had complete confidence in the authorities.

Lake became the family spokesperson and the one who dealt with problems and details left behind in Ithaca. He and his family, along with the Harrises' friends and neighbors in Ellis Hollow, decided to rebuild the Harrises' house when the weather warmed.

On January 5, Carl Shaver announced to the media that the bicyclist so many people reported seeing near the crime scene didn't appear to be connected with the case. This stand appeased Ellis Hollow residents while investigators went ahead and pursued the lead. Police knew how to work the press to their advantage. If the cyclist turned out to be their killer, Shaver wanted to make him relax his guard. Maybe he'd show his face around town and someone would recognize the man.

Twelve

The Young Tipster

George Dentes telephoned David McElligott during the fourth week of the investigation about a call he'd received from Paul Albanze.

"I'm not sure I have his last name right. I asked him to spell it out but he had a real heavy accent. He said he'd called you about a black woman he'd hired a few years ago to clean his house. She looks like one of the composites and the guy she lives with looks like another composite drawing," Dentes said.

"Why did he call you?" McElligott asked.

"He said he wanted to make sure you were following through with his tip," Dentes replied.

"Just a minute George."

McElligott rummaged through the stack of papers on his desk and found the Albanze call.

"Yeah, George. The notes I took are in front of me. I got Barnes to run the woman Albanze said cleaned for him, a Shirley King, through the computer and all he could get was a King in Locke, New York. Did he mention anything about this woman living in Cayuga County? I've got in my notes he said she lived somewhere in Etna."

"No. No mention of Cayuga County. He told me the woman and her husband or boyfriend worked down at Ides Bowling Lanes," Dentes said. McElligott could tell from the sound of Dentes voice that he felt the tip was a serious one.

"I'll send a team over to Ides and check it out."

"The man sounded real sure—that much I could get through the accent," Dentes added decisively.

"Okay, George." McElligott reassured him. "We'll try to run with it again and see what we come up with. I remember the guy's call because it was so hard to understand him."

McElligott sent two investigators to the bowling alley to inquire about a black man and his wife with the name of "King" who may have cleaned for them in the past. The person in the office told the police that two blacks had cleaned for them a while back—an older woman, a man named Michael Turner, and a blond girl called Bonnie.

Barnes ran the new name through the computer but didn't find anything under Michael Turner.

McElligott spoke with Paul Albanze again and asked him about the Locke address. *Did the person he knew as Shirley King ever live in Locke?* He didn't know, he told them.

The tip sheet stayed on McElligott's desk.

McElligott always told the group of investigators at the close of morning briefings that maybe this was the day they'd get the break they needed. Spirits were down, some were frustrated at the way the case was going. He pulled aside the two guys he knew were most disgruntled.

"Come on in at the end of the day and beat on Karl and me. We'll listen. I don't promise we'll do it any different, but you can blast us good if you want. We'll buy you guys a drink and listen to you gripe."

He knew investigators in the field sometimes felt they were "busting their butts" out there, trying to solve the crime while the senior officers sat in comfortable offices ordering them what to do. McElligott had to keep morale up any way he could. It was important to keep the investigators believing in their own abilities, but even he was getting jumpy. He felt they would solve the Harris case, but just to be sure, McElligott sent out for more help.

Surveillance and drug raids were Arthur Daniel's fortes. He learned from some of the most experienced cops in the business: Narcotics investigators with the New York City Drug Enforcement Task Force combined with the Federal Drug Enforcement Agency (DEA). Daniels started state police undercover work in New York with professionals who made so many entries on drug busts that they became almost routine—a way of life. From New York, he was assigned to the Narcotics Enforcement Unit in Binghamton where he worked with David McElligott.

Daniels headed for Ithaca on January 20 after finishing his duties on another murder case. He handled routine investigative work on the Harris homicides, first going through the Grey Goose records to see if they led anywhere.

On January 24, ten thousand posters announcing the Harris case reward went to nine central New York counties. The bold red lettering read: *REWARD/WHO KILLED THE HARRIS FAMILY?* The reward funds reached twenty-six thousand dollars by that time. A local company did the printing at no charge. The company's vice-president, Tom Parziale, was a close friend of the Harrises.

By this time some area residents didn't think the crimes would ever be solved.

"No one in Ithaca is intelligent enough to solve them," one disgruntled man told a reporter.

Another added, "The Ithaca area is a place where killing can be done with impunity. If I were murdered, I'd rather it happened anywhere else than Ithaca."

Many assumed the killers were on drugs. How else could you explain the risk involved?

On Thursday, January 25, a young, piquant looking, dark-haired woman appeared at the front desk of the command post. She said she had something to tell the police "about those drawings in the paper to do with the Harris murders." Her eyes were fixed on an invisible spot on the wall.

Connie Littleton had just gotten off the night shift. It was eight thirty in the morning. Karl Chandler came out and directed her through the corridors to an interviewing room.

"I felt like I had to come up here and tell the police what's been on my mind for a while," Littleton's voice shook as she spoke to Chandler.

"Go right ahead and tell me whatever you'd like, Miss," Chandler reassured her.

"My name is Connie Littleton," she paused, took a deep breath and went on quickly, "and one of my jobs is at a bed and breakfast and that's why I'm here. I had to tell you that the woman in the newspaper looks like a person that works at The Peregrine House where I work and another picture looks like Tony [Michael Kinge]. But my boss said it didn't look like Shirley and I got the feeling she didn't want me to get involved," Littleton said in one breath.

"Who is this Shirley?" Chandler asked quietly.

"Shirley King works like I do, part-time."

Littleton explained that the place was owned by Bernice Crawford and her daughter, Anne Maples.

"They don't know I've come up here, but I had to. I hope I don't lose my job over this," Littleton said biting her lip. "That picture looks a lot like Shirley King."

Littleton's words made Chandler remember a lead with the name King and her husband or boyfriend that went nowhere. He'd heard McElligott spout off about not being able to do anything with the tip about which the informant had seemed so positive.

"Was Tony her boyfriend?" Chandler asked.

"Oh, no. That's not her boyfriend. He's her adopted son. The picture looks like Tony, all right."

Chandler's thick eyebrows raised.

"Do you know how old Shirley King is?" Chandler asked.

Littleton shook her head. "I think she's fifty something, but I don't know exactly."

"Where does she and her son live?" Chandler asked.

"Over on Etna Road in a two-family house. Tony lives on one side with his girlfriend—she's white—and baby, and Shirley lives with her mother on the other side."

Chandler tried to keep his manner calm. He didn't want to jump on this timid lady and frighten her. "What do you know about Tony?"

"Well, I think he's been arrested. That's why he uses a different name—Michael Turner—I think."

"Do you know where he works?"

"He does jobs around town like paint and cleaning jobs."

"Do you know if he worked at Ides Bowling at any time?"

"Yeah, I think he and Shirley cleaned there," she said.

"Can you give us a phone number for Shirley King?"

"Her phone is under her mother's name, Sallie Reese. She's real close to her mom, I know that," Littleton nodded her head.

As the young woman read over the statement Chandler typed up for her to sign, she told him that Shirley spelled her last name with an "e" at the end.

Chandler thanked the young woman for coming in. "Your information was very helpful."

Now they had two unrelated informants identifying the same person. That fact alone made the Kinge tip stand out from all the other hundreds of calls they'd received so far.

"Christ, these people are in close range, just over on Etna Road. It's a stone's throw from here," (only two miles from the Varna station) Chandler said to McElligott as they discussed the young informant's statement.

"Now maybe we can get somewhere," McElligott replied. But again their communications specialist couldn't get anything on the computer. They had no birth dates to go with the names.

A few hours later, his frustration growing, McElligott sent Tom Kelly to The Peregrine House to check out Littleton's statement. Anne Maples, the owner's daughter, was at the desk. It was obvious that Maples didn't want to talk about the possibility that one of her employees could be the person in one of the composite drawings. But Kelly was there with his badge and she had no choice.

Reluctantly, she gave them Shirley Kinge's social security number. Maples said that Shirley had worked for them the last two years as a part-timer, once every two to three weeks.

"Was Shirley working on December 22 or 23?" Kelly asked.

After checking her records, she said, "No." When the semester ended at Cornell, business was slack, she explained.

Maples said Shirley drove a white Subaru coupe and she suspected it might be in her mother's name, Sallie Reese.

"I wouldn't be surprised if everything is in her mother's name," Maples continued.

Maples described Shirley as a very unsociable person. The last she saw Tony was about a year ago when he was hired to paint a few rooms at The Peregrine House.

"I felt very uncomfortable around Tony Turner after he made several advances toward me," Maples told Kelly.

They asked her to describe Tony.

"He's a very dark black man with large lips. And he's got some broken teeth in the front."

Kelly's heart jumped a beat but he said nothing.

As the conversation wound down, Maples said her mother would be in later.

"I'll be back to see her," Kelly replied.

When Kelly returned a few hours later he sensed right away that Bernice Crawford didn't like the idea of talking with police any more than her daughter did, but sometimes his courteous manner worked wonders.

Kelly spoke to her for a few minutes about how much he

appreciated her cooperation. When Crawford seemed less hostile, he asked her about Shirley Kinge.

Shirley was a good and dependable worker. She seemed well educated too, Crawford said. She didn't know Kinge's birth date, but she knew where Kinge lived on Etna Road. Crawford gave him Kinge's address. She knew that Shirley rented her apartment from Mary Tilley who had a real estate office downtown. Crawford suggested they talk with Tilley, because she probably knew Shirley well.

Crawford added, "I hardly know Tony Turner. He did odd jobs around town and occasionally painted for me."

"Could you please give me some samples of Shirley Kinge's handwriting?" Kelly asked. After rummaging through a file drawer for several minutes, Crawford pulled out a few receipts that Shirley had written out and gave them to Kelly. He thanked her again and left.

As soon as McElligott heard the report, he sent a team back to Ides Bowling Lanes, this time to talk with the manager, Scott Hamilton. They asked Hamilton if he had had a Tony Turner or a Shirley Kinge working for him at one time. Hamilton told the police that after Shirley Kinge answered an ad he ran in the newspaper for cleaning help, he had hired her on the spot. She had presented herself so well and seemed to be a very well educated woman. She worked for Hamilton about six months and then left town. Her son took over for her and cleaned the premises until 1987. Hamilton told the officers Tony was a quiet and polite young man. Hamilton knew Tony had been in trouble with the law and was trying to make a clean start. He had offered to help Tony go back to school.

"They were the kind of employees I would give a good reference to," Hamilton told the investigators.

But Hamilton didn't know anything about Shirley Kinge living in Locke. As far as he could remember, she lived somewhere in Etna.

The day after Littleton's tip, a call came in from Pat Holden, a Dryden woman, who told the investigator that she had worked in a cleaning service with a woman who very strongly resembled the person pictured in the newspaper drawings. Holden also said she thought the woman's son had been arrested at one time. She was asked to come in and give a statement. She did.

In the difficult Harris situation, as in his other cases, McElligott followed the rule of investigation. Three separate, unrelated calls that identified the same people meant they were now on the right track. Two calls were a good sign but three made it a dead-ringer. The Dryden woman was the third and McElligott kept his fingers crossed waiting for further confirmation.

The next day, McElligott assigned two investigators to talk with Mary Tilley, Shirley Kinge and Tony Turner's landlady. Tilley told them she'd known Shirley Kinge since she started cleaning Tilley's office back in 1983. Shirley's son, Tony Turner, and Tony's live-in girlfriend, Joanna White, also cleaned for her on occasion. Tony began renting the Etna Road apartment in 1984 and Shirley became a tenant in 1987. They lived in 520A and 520B Etna Road.

Tilley shook her head, saying they were always behind in their rent, but since they helped her out with cleaning jobs, she didn't evict them. The investigators informed Tilley they were looking at a number of suspects on the Harris case and would appreciate it if she kept quiet about their inquiry.

Information from Kelly's interviews still hadn't produced anything on the computer. Names or aliases without corresponding birth dates had led to a dead end. They could not find any vehicle or driver's license issued to the suspect. McElligott was at an impasse but he pressed on.

Thirteen

Stakeout

Not only McElligott, but everyone in the department was getting antsy. McElligott, like the others, just pressed on. He found Tom Kelly. "Go on over to Etna Road, Tom, and see if you can talk to our suspect," McElligott said. "It can't hurt."

It was after dark on Friday when Tom grabbed Charlie Porter, who happened to still be working in one of the offices at the command post, and they set off for Etna Road.

Kelly talked to Porter on the way over about how he'd approach the suspect's house with the excuse he was making a neighborhood check to see if anyone had noticed unfamiliar cars or vehicles along the road on the night of December 22, when the Harris family was murdered.

A short while later, the police car pulled into the driveway in front of 520B Etna Road. The two officers got out, went up to the door, and knocked. No one came to the door, but a man with a baby in his arms pulled the curtain to the side on a window to the right of the door, and stood back. They could vaguely make him out, and couldn't see his face. There was enough background light to see the man's long hair reached to his shoulders in corn rows with something attached to the ends. That matched store clerks' testimony. Kelly saw that the man had on a wool-like scull cap. One clerk had testified that the customer who used Warren Harris' Visa card wore a small wool hat.

Kelly called to him.

"Sir, I'm Tom Kelly and this is Charlie Porter. We're investigators with the state police looking into the Harris homicides." He pulled out his ID and kept it in front of him. "We're checking the neighborhood since this road is close to the airport to see if anyone saw unfamiliar vehicles or people along here on December 22, the night of the Harris murders."

The man was silent.

"Sir, we need your name and birth date, please," Kelly said loudly.

The man answered he was Michael Anthony Turner. "I was born August 28, 1956."

"Where were you the night of the murders, December 22?" Kelly asked.

The man's voice showed no expression. "Baby-sitting, and I didn't notice anything. But maybe my wife saw something. She works from eleven at night till seven thirty in the morning at a nursing home downtown," he said.

Kelly wanted to keep the conversation going as long as he could, but he saw the suspect move further back from the window. Kelly yelled, "Please have your wife call the state police barracks in Varna. Here's my card, sir."

Kelly knocked loudly, trying to hand him the card, but he wouldn't open the door. Kelly and Porter watched as he disappeared from their view.

Kelly knocked next door at 520A. There was no response. He knocked again. An attractive, older, black woman stuck her head out of an upstairs window. Both investigators craned their necks trying to see her features more clearly, "We're investigating the Harris murders and wonder if you saw anything on the road the night of December 22," Kelly asked.

"No, I didn't see anything. I don't pay attention to what goes on outside my apartment. I stay inside for weeks at a time," she said, irritation plain in her voice.

When Kelly asked for her name and date of birth, she cut him off.

"You don't need to have that information. It's none of your business." She slammed the window shut.

Kelly and Porter drove back to the command post immediately to see if the new information matched other facts. "We finally have a date of birth," Porter told McElligott. "Maybe we can get somewhere now."

McElligott told Barnes to try the criminal history database again with the new information. Barnes entered the name Michael Anthony Turner with the birth date Turner had given Kelly.

"We've got something," Barnes called out. "Look at this." The fictitious name with a fictitious birth date brought up the real Michael Anthony Kinge. Their suspect made a costly mistake when he gave Kelly an alias and birth date he'd used for a previous arrest.

The computer then brought up all the aliases for Michael Anthony Kinge and his criminal record. They found out where he was born, his record of robberies, prison time, what firearms he'd used, and that one arrest involved a silencer.

"Judas priest," cried McElligott, holding the printout Barnes had handed him on the suspect.

"This is one hell of a dangerous guy we're looking at."

His criminal record included Cayuga County, where Kinge was arrested in 1978 on loan fraud, a month after he obtained a false personal identification card in the name of Anthony Stone.

* * *

After his encounter with Tom Kelly, Tony Turner phoned Jo at the nursing home and spoke to her in the threatening voice that she hated. "Call Kelly at the police barracks in Varna and tell him I was home all night December 22, taking care of the baby. Make sure you tell him you didn't notice anything out of the ordinary on Etna Road when you left for work or when you came home at eight the next day or you'll have hell to pay and more if you don't do what I want," he said.

The Varna barracks received a call from Joanna White at about nine o'clock Friday, January 26. She asked to speak with Mr. Kelly.

"This is Joanna White. I'm calling from work. My husband said you stopped by our house and you wanted me to call."

Kelly was taken aback, but he kept his voice calm. "Yes, Joanna. We're investigating the Harris homicide and since Etna Road is near the airport, we're having to check out all possibilities. We wondered if you saw anything unusual on your road the night of December 22?"

The woman seemed ill at ease. "No. I didn't see anyone or anything out of the ordinary when I went to work about ten thirty that night."

"What about when you drove home the next morning?" Kelly asked.

"No," she said in a monotone, "I didn't see anything."

She spoke in such a low voice Kelly had to press his ear to the phone. "Did you leave and come home at your usual times that night and the next morning?"

"Yeah."

"Did you come straight home from work?"

"I drove straight to work and came right home when I got off at seven thirty on Saturday."

"Can you tell me if your husband was at home the night of December 22?" He heard her sigh.

"Yes, he was home all night taking care of our son while I was at work," Joanne said.

"We appreciate your calling us, Joanne."

Considering that part of the information they'd just retrieved on Tony Turner/Michael Kinge included how much he hated cops, investigators were a little surprised his girlfriend had called them. Furnishing police with an alibi for the night of December 22 so soon after investigators came to his house suggested the suspect had panicked. *Or had he been tipped off to the fact that the cops were looking for him?*

Kelly reported the call to McElligott. "Finally some breaks," McElligott said and then he added, "Of course, I knew they'd be coming."

McElligott arranged with Mary Tilley on Saturday to rent a vacant apartment in another duplex she owned that stood several hundred yards south of the Kinge house. "We'll set up an observation post in that building," he announced. Then McElligott assigned Arthur Daniels to head the Etna Road surveillance. He could rely on Daniels to run a flawless undercover operation; the suspects won't have a clue they're being watched.

The team started surveillance on both Kinges and on Joanna White about midnight on Friday, January 26. Cars were posted at both ends of Etna Road from the Hanshaw Road turnoff to beyond the suspects' duplex. There were seven people on each of the two twenty-four hour shifts. Daniels set the hour for changing personnel at times when he thought the least amount of activity would be going on; 8:00 A.M. after most people had left for work in the morning and by eight in the evening when families were usually inside their homes watching television. Daniels and his partner started at 10:00 A.M. and worked till one or two in the morning. They were a roving patrol and filled in as back-up detail if needed. Daniels decided who would follow which car and he made sure that fresh cars with different people were in place, so the suspects wouldn't become suspicious. Seldom did one undercover car follow a suspect from home to a destination. Officers and vehicles were switched at frequent intervals.

Two investigators manned the observation post in an upstairs room of Mary Tilley's duplex, around the bend of the road from the Kinges' house. From there, they could see the driveway of the Kinges' residence, but because of trees in the way they didn't have a clear view of the front doors. During daylight hours the investigators could determine which suspect left the premises. With the night scope they could see figures, but they weren't able to identify who the people were, because of the great distance.

Using a CB radio and code names that were frequently changed for each vehicle and suspect, it was the job of those stationed at the post to advise the team of any movement from the house. Everyone on the surveillance used a handle and those names also changed from day to day as did the changed CB channels used. A detail would pick up the vehicle for a period of time and then drop off and another undercover car would take over. This continued until the suspects reached their destinations.

When Trooper Linda Brady came to work on the late shift January 26, McElligott told Brady they needed her for surveillance duty on a suspect. She'd be contacted soon with her assignment. She was glad for the chance to get involved with the Harris case again. The senseless murders of the Harrises had preyed on her mind and made her anxious to do something.

On the day of the murders, Brady had been called in for security detail. She had sat in a patrol car from 3:00 A.M. to 3:00 P.M. on Ellis Hollow Road in front of the Harrises' house every day for a month. She made sure no curiosity seekers disturbed the premises and watched to see if the killer returned. It was an unlikely prospect, but they wanted to prepare for anything.

The memory of seeing the grisly crime scene on the morning she was briefed lingered in Linda Brady's mind. When she sat alone in the patrol car in the middle of the night, she'd look up at the window in the bedroom where Shelby had been murdered and wondered what went on in there that awful night. Brady swore she could see shadows moving behind the window panes. A trooper on the shift right before hers said that one night as he sat alone in his car guarding the property, one of the garage doors opened on its own.

Now Brady was given the 8:00 A.M. to 8:00 P.M. shift on the Etna Road surveillance. She was to be partnered, at first, with other investigators.

While Brady and the others watched the house, other aspects of the case moved forward. The fire arms specialist had told McElligott the bullets that killed the Harrises were tainted with particular markings that threw off his judgment at first as to what kind of gun had been used. No shells were found at the scene, which made the specialist think of a .22 automatic pistol, the only gun that has a bag adapter. A .22 bullet twists and turns before it's expelled, leaving it with grooves and layers. A silencer produces similar revolver-type markings on the bullet. After feeding the computer all the ballistic data they had on the case, the readout was inconclusive. But the examiner thought the weapon in question had to have been either a revolver, a sawed-off rifle or a gun with a silencer.

Karl Chandler felt they were on the right track. After he saw the look-alike handwriting samples on the canceled checks from The Peregrine House written by Shirley Kinge and the signatures on the Harrises' Visa card receipts, he almost felt relieved. Chandler felt sure the same person signed both pieces of evidence, but, of course, they would get a handwriting specialist to verify the match.

An investigator was sent to pick up the Cayuga County 1978 color mug shot of Michael Kinge and a copy of his fingerprints on Saturday, January 27. State police in Cayuga County had told them over the phone that it was a clear, good picture of Kinge.

Although the frontal view of Kinge showed his features clearly, the Afro hairstyle was dated and might make it harder for people to identify him now. They needed a current photograph of the suspect.

Harding reported to McElligott late on the 27th that Michael Kinge's fingerprints from Cayuga County didn't match any crime scene prints.

Knowing they were looking at a man who had threatened a couple at knifepoint in New York City, and who had skipped town on a robbery charge, McElligott ordered a twenty-four hour surveillance on the Etna Road duplex. They wanted to intervene in case Kinge tried to leave the area or commit another crime. And believing they were closing in on their best suspect, they urgently needed a current photograph of him. They'd have to try a long-range shot as he came out of the duplex.

The command post received another call about their prime suspects on January 27. As soon as the investigator on the line heard the type of information the caller was giving, he asked the man to come in and make a full statement.

The informant, James Bryant, was a former employer of Sallie Reese who said that after he saw composite drawings in the newspaper (he'd been out of town on a long vacation), Bryant had realized the female pictured resembled Sallie's daughter, Shirley Kinge. He explained that Sallie had been a live-in nanny and housekeeper in his home for several years in the mid-eighties. "The black male resembled her grandson, Tony," Bryant said. Police learned from him that the grandson drove the women around in a tan pickup truck and they lived on Etna Road. He knew that Shirley had a lot of financial problems, because Sallie often talked about them. Sallie said Shirley spent more money than she had on clothes and expensive jewelry.

"We're cooking," McElligott announced. "I'm going over Kinge's record. Maybe there's more."

McElligott learned from Michael Kinge's Cayuga County record that Kinge had burglarized with Ron Callie. They coded Callie as coconspirator to find out if he'd been arrested with Kinge. It turned up that Callie had a record himself. Tom Kelly and his partner went over to Callie's house late Saturday, January 27.

Ron Callie was at home when Kelly and his partner knocked on his door in Danby (a rural hamlet just outside Ithaca). Callie told them he was about to go to work. He explained he had odd working hours because of a cleaning business he ran with his wife.

Kelly told Callie they were investigating the Harris murders. He asked Callie if he knew Tony Turner.

Callie hesitated at first, but he'd been in trouble with the law recently and he knew he had to cooperate.

"Yeah, I know Tony but I ain't seen him in a long time," Callie said.

It slowly emerged during Callie's conversation that Tony was even more dangerous than they'd thought. He had guns and he liked to modify weapons to suit his purpose. Callie had seen a drill press in Turner's apartment that he thought Tony used to make knives. Callie, as an afterthought, described a homemade silencer that Tony showed him one time. The two officers flashed each other a knowing look.

After hearing Ron Callie's testimony about the suspect using a press at home to alter weapons, Chandler wanted to find out what could be made with a drill press. Chandler didn't have the faintest idea and had to get more information about the machinery. Harry Paceman and Chuck Morris were put on the detail, and they were instructed to track down the place where their suspect had bought the equipment.

Paceman and Morris made numerous phone calls and then headed for Sears and Roebuck at the Pyramid Mall. There they spoke with the manager of the hardware department, explaining as little as possible about why they needed the information. Paceman asked the manager if he would show them sales records of drill presses sold within the last six to eight months. Since drill presses are expensive items, and not many are sold, the investigators were able to search through the records.

They discovered that John McNamara, a hardware clerk, had sold a thirteen-inch drill press and set of drill bits to a Sallie Reese on October 15, 1989. On October 21 a four-inch vise was charged to the same account. Morris asked him, "Sir, can you recall the sales transaction?"

McNamara told the investigators he remembered selling a Craftsman floor model drill press to a black male and it was paid for by an older black woman, who the clerk took to be the man's mother. McNamara showed them the model he sold to the man, saying it was the top of the line. The price was four hundred dollars. Paceman asked, "Is a drill press for hard materials as well as wood?"

McNamara said, "With metal drill bits the machine could go through steel." The two investigators discussed the press's capability of altering weapons and McNamara agreed that it would be possible to cut off a gun barrel. The policemen described throwing stars (long, sharp knives). McNamara said he guessed a person could make knives with the press if he knew what he was doing. "It would take a lot of skill to do that," he added.

As soon as the two men returned and Chandler received their report, he entered the drill press information into the database under suspect Michael Kinge/Tony Turner. There was proof now that Michael Kinge had purchased equipment at Sears on Sallie Reese's account. That press was more than likely used to modify or manufacture firearms or silencers.

Kelly asked Callie to describe Turner's looks.

"He's about five-eleven, medium dark skin, I'd say. Sometimes he wears his hair mashed down under a stocking and sometimes in them corn roll type things."

Kelly asked him to name Tony's friends, people who knew Turner fairly well.

"Well, Tony's a loner-type guy. You know what I mean? He don't hang around with people much," Callie answered.

Kelly pushed harder. "Callie, you must know somebody Turner has associated with." He paused and looked Callie in the eye. His voice hardened. "This is a serious crime we're investigating. You can't hold out on us, Ron."

Callie told them Tony knew John and Henry Riser. He'd worked for them in their construction business.

Callie said he'd known John Riser for years. Kelly leaned toward him, "How did Tony get to know John?" he asked.

Callie replied, "It was through buying pot. John sold it to a lot of guys he knew."

As the conversation went on, Callie gave them more details about Tony Turner's history. He said he was sure Tony had used false names like Anthony Stone and Michael Turner.

"Thanks for your help," Kelly said. "We'd like you to keep our inquiry confidential. We'll call you in to make a statement," the other investigator added.

After Kelly and his partner questioned Callie, the investigators followed a lead from their conversation with Mary Tilley. Shirley Kinge had worked for a man named Douglas Sutton who was also in the real estate business with a special interest in land development. Sutton was very willing to talk about Shirley Kinge.

"I hired her first to clean my house in the late 1970s and later she did the bookkeeping for my business. Occasionally she baby-sat with my adopted son who's black. But I haven't seen her in a long time, probably it was '83 or '84," he told investigators.

"Her son, Michael, came to pick her up occasionally. They lived in an old farmhouse up in Genoa at the time."

The two officers smiled at each other. They'd finally made the Locke connection (Genoa is a small rural area near Locke in Cayuga County north of Tompkins County).

Investigators had learned that when Shirley Kinge worked for Sutton, his business office was located in his home at 1665 Ellis Hollow Road, a few houses west of Thomas Road. At that time he owned a 157-acre tract along Ellis Hollow Road. They mentioned it to Sutton.

"I'm sure Shirley was familiar with the property," Sutton said. Other studies had produced the fact that Tony and Dodie Harris bought their lot from Sutton in 1985. Police asked to see samples of Shirley's handwriting he might have. Sutton said he knew they were somewhere in boxes in his cellar. It was so long ago however, he needed time to find Shirley Kinge's records, but since he didn't throw out any business paperwork, they were definitely there.

The officers reported to McElligott. When he heard Sutton had lived in Ellis Hollow, McElligott knew they had to protect him. "It could be that the killer or killers had meant to hit him and not the Harrises. They may have killed the wrong family," he observed.

With Art Daniels, McElligott drew a line between Etna Road and the Sutton house. "Daniels, you and your surveillance team take the suspect if he attempts to go beyond that point," McElligott said decisively. Then McElligott called Sutton, suggesting that he might want to send his family out of town for the time-being.

Kelly followed through on Callie's leads and found Henry Riser at home in Lansing on Saturday night. He asked Riser for information about Tony Turner. "We're looking for him to talk about the Harris murder case," he explained. Kelly emphasized how tentative the whole thing was; they had several leads to check out and to please keep their conversation confidential. Riser told the investigators that Turner had worked for him as a subcontractor, so Riser didn't have Tony's papers. It was several months before, and Henry hadn't seen Turner since. His brother, John, who worked for Henry too, probably knew Tony better than he did. *Where could they find his brother?* Kelly asked Henry Riser to give them John's address.

John was on his way out the door of his apartment when Tom Kelly and his partner arrived. John was on his guard when talking to them; he'd been in a few scrapes with local authorities, mostly having to do with growing and selling marijuana. "I'd like to ask you a few questions about a possible suspect in the Harris homicides," Kelly said.

According to John, he knew Tony Turner, but not too well. John told Kelly he'd worked with Turner on construction jobs. "Turner was a cool, laid-back type of guy who didn't like to work too hard. Henry and I couldn't always count on him. But when he showed up he did a pretty good job."

Kelly asked him to describe Turner's looks.

"He wears his hair in those corn rows with some kind of beads in them, you know the way you see a lot of black guys," John said.

Kelly nodded, asked John if he knew Tony Turner to be in any trouble with the law and if he owned weapons of any sort. "No," John said. "I don't think so."

Kelly wondered if he was telling the truth.

Kelly asked John to keep this conversation to himself.

"We have a lot of leads to follow. This is just one of dozens and we don't want to get anybody alarmed."

"Oh sure. I understand," John said as the detectives left.

Fourteen
A Straightjacket

David Harding didn't talk anymore to McElligott or Chandler about the fingerprints he had supposedly found on the gas can in the living room. He waited to see how the case unfolded. He told the boss, "Lishansky and I are still analyzing the evidence we gathered from the crime scene and we're working with the Harrises' fingerprints to compare them with ones found in the house."

McElligott barely acknowledged Harding's explanation; he was too busy concentrating on the prime suspect, Michael Kinge. Although Kinge had never been picked up on a murder charge, his criminal record showed a potentially violent man who hated cops and loved weapons.

McElligott was beginning to believe they were onto the right people but he wanted closure. What the police needed right away were good photographs of Michael Kinge to compare with the drawings police artists had composed and to show Kinge's picture to potential witnesses. The 1978 Cayuga County mug shot of Kinge was not recent enough—showing the suspect with Afro-styled hair.

McElligott was getting more impatient by the hour. Kinge

hadn't budged from his house since surveillance started. "We have to think of a way to get him out," McElligott said with disgust. He brainstormed with Chandler and they came up with an idea. Mary Tilley had said Tony had sometimes cleaned her properties to help pay his rent. McElligott and Chandler explained to Tilley the need to get Michael Kinge out of the house. Would she ask him to clean an apartment? She agreed and said she would let them know when it was set up.

Tilley phoned Shirley Kinge soon after speaking with McElligott. She asked Shirley to give Tony a message to call her back about a cleaning job; this was the only way to communicate with him since he had no phone of his own.

A short while later Shirley knocked on the back door of Tony's apartment. It stayed locked now day and night. Tony was in the kitchen, emptying dog food into a plastic dish on the floor. The Doberman kept his eyes on Tony.

"Tilley wants you to clean an apartment. I told her you'd call her back," Shirley said.

Tony shrugged. "Hell, I hardly owe the bitch anything. I worked for her the other day."

"Well, I'm giving you the message. Do what you want. I've been called in to work a few hours. Jimmy's with mother. Where's Jo?" Shirley asked as she opened the door to leave.

"She's on a double shift today."

Shirley left. Tony began mumbling to himself. He was in no mood to work for Tilley but he still owed her rent.

His last paying job had been in December when he'd painted some rooms in the Red Cross building downtown. He didn't mind painting as much as cleaning jobs. He decided to coax his mother into helping him clean the apartment. When Shirley had wanted them to run their own cleaning business, Tony was not enthusiastic. But he and Jo went along with Shirley in the venture, starting at Ides Bowling Lanes. He ran the floor machines and they did the lighter work. Gradually Tony slacked off, doing a sloppier and sloppier job, knowing that the women would cover for him.

Tony heard a bang on his wall. That had to be his grandmother, Sallie Reese. That was her way of communicating with him and Jo.

"Let her wait," Tony murmured. Seconds later the banging got louder.

"What in the hell does she want?" Tony said and sauntered next door. Sallie said he had a phone call.

"The guy insisted I get you."

It was John Riser.

"I thought I better tell you. The cops came by to see me. They were asking questions about you. They said they're investigating the Harris murders," John said.

Silence on the line.

"What the fuck did they ask you?" Tony said in a low voice.

"Nothing much, routine questions like how long I've known you. Did you own a gun and all that crap. I told 'em I never seen you with a gun," his words trailed off.

"Shit, they don't know nothin'. Those stupid cops. I got nothin' to worry about." Tony's hand trembled as he put down the phone.

He quickly walked back to his apartment. "I'll have to stay inside for a while," Tony decided. But he reassured himself. *How could the police prove anything on him?* He didn't leave evidence behind. He'd wiped the place clean. He was smarter than they were. He'd gotten away before, he'd do it again. He had an alias; so they wouldn't be able to find anything on him.

Tony went next door to get Jimmy. The baby might be good protection against the cops. And he had the Doberman. He'd trained the dog to leap over the five-foot board that separated the animal from the rest of the front room and to attack at his command. The dog could rip somebody apart in seconds. His image of the Doberman's invincibility fit his obsessive need for power. The dog was his prize possession.

Tony took the sawed-off shotgun from the bedroom closet and carried it with him wherever he went in the house. He put one of the long knives he'd made in one side of a leather shoulder holster and strapped it on. In the corner of the same closet stood the rifle Tony had modified into a silenced semi-automatic pistol. It was the Charter Arms rifle Jo bought for him in 1987 at an Ithaca gun shop. When he'd started to modify the gun, he'd cut the barrel off too short. It wasn't long enough to create gas back pressure to operate the bolt; so he had to buy another barrel. He cut the new barrel to make it a little longer this time, drilled holes and filled the space between the barrel and the sleeve with chore boy. This was his silencer.

Despite these protective measures, Tony's nerves became more frayed as the days wore on. He had a constant headache and his whole body felt stiff and chilled. After John had warned him that the cops were looking for him in connection with the Harris homicides, Tony went into a defensive mode like a soldier holed up in a bunker, knowing that the enemy was out there and time was running out. Tony kept his sawed-off shotgun with him wherever he went in the apartment and wore the shoulder holster with a long knife in each side and a bandoleer of .20 gauge shotgun shells around his waist all the time. When he tried to sleep a few hours after Jo returned from work about eight o'clock in the morning, he put the weapons and ammunition on the floor beside his bed within arm's reach. He hardly spoke to Jo and he didn't want the baby near him.

The curtains on the downstairs window were drawn all day (except the kitchen window where he pulled back the bottom half to watch the road and the front of the house). He'd covered the rest of the windows with sheets and blankets. The only light he had on at night was in the back room he used as his workshop. Tony ate very little, pizza was the only food that appealed to him, and he drank instant coffee. He kept the kerosene heaters going full blast and still he wasn't warm enough. Sometimes Tony grabbed a blanket and threw it around him as he sat at the kitchen window facing the road. He kept his dog near him, believing the Doberman was extra protection.

Tony had his police scanner going all the time. It stayed on the kitchen table where he could listen as he sat beside the window and waited. He was obsessed with where and what the cops were doing every minute. They were the enemy. He had to be prepared.

When his heart started pounding, he'd collect himself by taking out his gun and examining its chamber. Sometimes he would clean or polish the barrel with a chamois. Or he'd sit in a chair backed up to the kitchen wall and shoot buckshot or arrows from his crossbow at a target on the back door. He aimed for the circle he'd painted red a long time ago that was supposed to be at the center of the door, but was really several inches too far up. He hit inside the circle or on its rim every time.

This exercise calmed him down for a while. There were other targets he had set up downstairs and in good weather he liked to practice shooting with a rifle in the back yard. His neighbor across the road, from whom he often borrowed gasoline (the pickup had a leak in the gas tank) asked him once if he was a hunter or did he just like to target practice. Tony told her he didn't like to kill animals, he just enjoyed shooting as a sport.

Being on constant guard sapped his sex drive. The hardcore pornography magazines he had all over the house had usually been a turn-on or at least a distraction from boredom and worry but now they didn't help. He got Jo to bring him the more expensive variety: explicit scenes of bondage and other erotic examples of violent sex. But he was too wrapped up in fear for his own survival to be excited by pictures.

As time passed the rooms downstairs had the locked-in

smell of dog odor, cigarette smoke, and kerosene fumes with a trace of marijuana sweetness in the air. Tony kept the temperature between seventy-five and eighty degrees night and day. He had a cigarette lit whenever he wasn't smoking pot. As soon as his supply of marijuana dwindled down, he called John for another bag. John was prompt with his deliveries. He stopped by after dark one day, sold Tony a bag, and said he had to get going. John didn't want to hang around. He could see that Tony didn't want to talk either; he was in one of his unsociable moods. Maybe Tony wasn't a killer, but John couldn't be sure.

The tension Shirley, Sallie and Joanna usually felt with Tony had become a never-ending straightjacket around their lives since the investigators had knocked on their doors January 26. They didn't talk about it, trying to deny all the signs of imminent danger lurking around them. Joanna had been a part of Tony's web of deception and indulgence before, but now it was different. Her child was at risk too.

Joanna kept the baby over at Shirley and Sallie's apartment most of the time. Nervously she'd run in and out, asking them if they wanted anything from the store. If she was picking up pizza, she would ask if they wanted one.

Her stomach was in knots all the time. The only way to cope was to keep moving. Thank God she could do errands. Driving relaxed her nerves. It was a short respite from the constant worry. Tony yelled at her, "It'll be over if you tell the cops anything. If you say one goddamn word about it, I swear I'll put a bullet in your head."

She wanted to leave, to take the baby and get away from Tony and his madness. But fear paralyzed her, and she didn't have a place to go. All she could do was try and get through the day. It crossed her mind that she probably had this coming to her. She'd been stubborn and a real fool to get involved with someone like Tony.

When she first started seeing Tony she never thought it would last long. But she fell for him hard. Back then he could be a real charmer; he could talk her into anything and the sex was the best she'd ever known. He made her feel like she belonged to somebody. To her, that was love.

When their son was born, she had tried to be hopeful about their future. But it was then things began to get out of control—Tony wasn't working much, and the bills kept piling up. She felt more of his rage as he swore at her continuously and demanded that she do exactly what he wanted. They'd never had an easy time of it, but they were in a crisis now. She didn't know him anymore. He might do anything.

Fifteen
The Peregrine House

A cursory view of Shirley Kinge's handwriting on The Peregrine House receipts and in Sutton's checkbooks showed a striking resemblance to the signature of "Dolores Harris" on the December 23 Visa card transactions. When Karl Chandler looked at the handwriting comparisons, it seemed obvious to him, but they still needed the opinion of a handwriting expert. He called Chris Landis, a Secret Service agent in Syracuse. Chris was a friend of Chandler's and Chandler asked him, "Could you come down and take a look at some suspects' handwriting in the Harris case?"

In addition to the samples of Shirley Kinge's handwriting, they also had Michael Kinge's signature on Cayuga County arrest forms, and on a few check stubs provided by Ides Bowling Lanes. Landis studied the samples. They looked like a positive match to him, but Landis recommended that they get the expert from headquarters to look at them.

On January 29, Aaron Carter, a Secret Service handwriting expert, flew up from Washington, D.C., to make comparisons between the suspects' handwriting samples and the credit card receipt signatures bearing the names of Dolores and Warren Harris.

Carter concluded, "I can give no opinion regarding the Michael Kinge handwriting samples." He said, "In all probability the Shirley Kinge handwriting samples and credit card slips were signed by the same individual. But to give a positive match, I'd need controlled signatures."

Still trying to put together a photo lineup for their two witnesses, McElligott sent a surveillance team on Monday, January 30, to The Peregrine House. He wanted long-range photographs of Shirley Kinge as she got in and out of her car. The investigators had arranged for Shirley Kinge to be called in to work that day.

The team searched for the right spot; it was hard to get into a good position to take pictures on the narrow one-way Cook Street that ran alongside the bed and breakfast. They needed one where the parking lot could also be watched. They were too far away and there wasn't room to double-park for long. As they considered their options, they saw Shirley's white Subaru pull into the lot. Luckily, no cars were coming, so the investigators quickly snapped pictures as Shirley got out of her car and walked to the back door.

When he saw the photographs, McElligott grumbled, "They aren't good enough for our purposes. We need clear shots of Shirley Kinge's face in order to put her picture along with other women for a lineup sheet."

McElligott's intention was to have store clerks identify the person who made purchases on the Harrises' Visa card on December 23.

Since the surveillance photographs of Shirley Kinge going in and out of The Peregrine House were taken from too far away to get a good image of her features, McElligott and Chandler realized they had to try again.

"Let's get her boss to call her in again. Maybe the guys

can find a way to get a closer shot," McElligott suggested after a late afternoon briefing session on January 29.

David Harding stood in the group around McElligott and Chandler as they were discussing their options.

"Maybe we should go undercover to the motel and really get a good look at her," Chandler said.

"I can do it," Harding said decisively.

"Stop taking on all these jobs, Dave," McElligott laughed as he scrutinized Harding. "You volunteer for everything. You're like the guy on a TV commercial picking up phones, saying to each caller, 'I can do that, I can do that' and when he puts the phone down, he says, 'How am I going to do that?' "

But McElligott realized their experienced undercover guys were on surveillance and if they took them off the detail, it was possible Shirley Kinge might recognize them since they had been following her around town. The rest of the investigators were interviewers, not undercover cops. Harding was involved in a sting operation and had worked other undercover assignments. Even though McElligott didn't wholly trust him, it looked like he was the only person available.

It was worth a try to see what Harding could find out. To McElligott, Shirley Kinge was still a secondary issue although he felt that through Shirley they might learn more about her son, who was their prime suspect.

They had to get a look at her close-up. She'd been described to them, with wide discrepancy, as a woman in her late thirties to someone in her fifties with various hairstyles and facial features. And controlled handwriting specimens were a must to compare with the signatures and other writing found on the Harris credit card receipts.

That night, after weighing the possible consequences, McElligott assigned Harding to the job. Harding went over to The Peregrine House. He had phoned to make sure Bernice Crawford, the owner, would be there. Harding explained his intentions and asked for Crawford's cooperation in calling Shirley Kinge in to work the next day for an early evening shift. Crawford said she'd have to make up some reason why she needed Kinge again. They weren't very busy right now, especially during the week. Harding flashed her his captivating smile and left.

Driving back to the station, Harding's mood darkened. Harding didn't like the way McElligott ran an investigation, but he kept this discontent to himself. The boss's style was autocratic, especially at times like these. This didn't allow Harding to use his initiative; to lend his personal stamp to solving a crime. Harding liked to take the ball and run with it. He had to get along with McElligott, but Harding tried to sidestep McElligott whenever he could and report to Chandler, who he didn't find so intimidating.

Harding had never liked taking orders from anyone. He hadn't thought about the military rigidity of command in the state police when he signed up. Harding had banked on being so good, so smart, and smooth-talking that his reputation would bring admiration and lessen the chances of being questioned by any boss. To achieve this purpose, he made sure the higher-ups in the organization knew he was available to anyone who needed him and that he was willing to work long hours. His strategy paid off. Harding had been promoted quickly and had generated the feeling in Albany and at Troop C headquarters that he was an outstanding officer—a rising star in the organization.

One of the main reasons Harding became a specialist in evidence gathering was that it insulated him from taking orders from people like McElligott. He was the authority on fingerprints and other pieces of evidence that were needed for convictions. People looked to him for answers. McElligott's often repeated statement, "There are no heroes in this business," didn't mean anything to Harding. He couldn't relate to that philosophy. He didn't believe it.

Mary Tilley came up to the barracks on Monday, January

30, to let the investigators know that Tony had just called her to say he hurt his back and wouldn't be able to work for a while. By then, under court order, the police had Sallie Reese's phone connected to a DNR (dial number recorder), a mechanism installed at a telephone sub-station. The device alerted police to what numbers were called out. For incoming calls, they could tell how long the call lasted but not its source. Tilley's story checked out. There was an outgoing call from the Etna Road telephone to Tilley's number that morning.

At least, they knew the suspect was inside. But what they really needed was a picture of him. Still, more evidence was piling up. Douglas Sutton informed investigators that he'd found old payroll checks and checkbook stubs that had samples of Shirley Kinge's handwriting. An officer was sent to Sutton's house to pick them up.

Investigator Doug Vredenburgh and Trooper Charlene Hippenstiel were assigned to watch The Peregrine House at the time when Shirley Kinge was expected to arrive. They would inform Harding of her arrival and try snapping more long-range photographs of her. The two officers saw the suspect drive up in the white Subaru and park in a space behind the building at about 4:00 P.M. This time, Vredenburgh found a parking space at the side of the building on Cook Street, close to the building's parking area, and took pictures of the suspect as she entered the rear door. They radioed Harding that Shirley Kinge was inside. A few minutes later, the officers observed a white female exit the inn and walk over to a blue car in the same parking area. The woman got inside the car and drove off.

The Peregrine House, advertised as a Victorian Inn, stands two blocks from the Cornell University campus on the corner of College Avenue and Cook Street. The three-story, red brick house that faces College Avenue was built in 1874 for the John Snaith family. It was the first residence in that section of what was then called Huistis Street during Cornell's early years. Now, a black iron fence surrounds the property to further distinguish it from the transient, almost seedy character of the rest of the neighborhood where ordinary frame houses, divided into student rooms and apartments, are bunched together. The bed and breakfast is one block from Collegetown's commercial district. Just beyond is the main entrance to the University. When Cornell is in session, the avenue and its narrow, steep side streets are jammed with cars and students night and day. After hours, it was relatively quiet.

About 4:30 P.M. on January 30, Harding went up to the front door of The Peregrine House. Harding's clean-cut looks reminded one of a fifties heart-throb—slim, medium height, classic features, clean shaven. His light brown hair, cut in the current style, was short in front and came to the nape of his neck in back. Only an eyetooth slightly out of line marred his picture-perfect smile. Looking good was important to Harding. He liked to dress as he did today in fashionable three-piece suits and silk ties.

Although Harding was a smooth talker, he didn't come off as slick. His boyish charm, including the broad smile that looked effortless, made him seem vulnerable as well as appealing. Being well aware of his attributes made it easier for Harding to pull them out of his reservoir for whatever the occasion demanded. He was like an actor putting on the right costume and make-up.

Carrying one piece of luggage, Harding gingerly rang the doorbell. Smiling at the petite, middle-aged, black woman who opened the door, he asked, "Are you Anne Maples?" Maples was one of the owners to whom Harding had spoken.

"No, Anne isn't here now. But I work here. Can I help you?" The woman had an appealing, throaty voice.

"Hi, I'm David Savage from Albany. I called earlier for a reservation."

"Yes, Anne told me she had somebody coming in," the woman said as she slowly opened the door.

Upon taking a closer look, Harding noticed she wore large fashionable glasses with tortoise shell frames and her black hair, though neatly styled, had flecks of gray throughout it. She looked fit and thin in dark green corduroy slacks with a white sweatshirt and black sneakers.

"You need to register over here," she told him while walking over to a table in the entryway. He assumed the woman was Shirley Kinge, but decided to ask her name later.

Harding followed the woman, put his bag down and said, "I'm sorry but I've broken my index finger. It's put my writing hand out of commission. Would you mind signing in for me?" Harding was wearing his left hand in a splint.

"Sure, what happened, were you in a fight?" she asked with a slight smile.

"No, I broke it in a basketball game; it was sorta stupid when you think about it. I just play to keep in shape and now I can't even write," he gave a wry grin.

While he dictated, she wrote his name, his address, and his phone number in Albany in the reservation book.

"It's forty-nine dollars and ninety-five cents plus tax for the single. Is it going to be a credit card?"

"No, I've got the cash," Harding told her as he pulled out his wallet. Showing a touch of awkwardness, he handed her three twenty-dollar bills. When the woman returned, Harding noticed she had changed her glasses and wrote out his receipt. She said she had to go to the office to get change.

"This is new to me," Harding gestured with his right hand. He wanted to keep the conversation going. "I've never stayed in a bed and breakfast, but there's a first time for everything. I've got business with Cornell tomorrow, so I wanted to be close to campus."

They chatted about the driving conditions, how much of a

walk it was to campus, and how hard it was to find a parking space. Harding was good at small talk.

Shirley explained the house rules as she escorted him upstairs to room 203—a single room at the front of the building.

"If you'd like something to drink when you come down, just ask. I'll be glad to get you tea, coffee, whatever," Shirley told him.

"Thanks very much. Is it okay if I hangout a while? I've got to kill a little time."

"Sure. No problem," she nodded.

"I think I'll change into comfortable clothes first. I'll see you downstairs," Harding said, smiling and looking into her ebony eyes. He was also good at charming the ladies.

After she left, he flipped on the television in the room. It took about twenty minutes for him to change into slacks and a sweater. During that time he collected his thoughts about his next move and got his camera loaded. Then he strolled back downstairs and found Shirley in the office standing over an ironing board.

Shirley was spraying starch across a tablecloth before she pressed it. She took deep draws on a cigarette in between ironing and spraying the starch. Harding watched intently for a few minutes as she kept the cigarette in her mouth while pushing the iron up and down. After a few strokes of the iron, she laid the cigarette in an ashtray behind her and used both hands to pick up the part of the tablecloth she'd just ironed and drop it over the far side of the ironing board.

A television was on and tuned to CNN news. It was the same news he'd been watching in his room. Harding started right in, "Isn't that something what's happening in Europe? I just saw the news about these communist countries turning to democracy. It's amazing. Freedom is catching on everywhere."

Shirley shook her head. Her voice rose, "Yeah, so-called freedom. We're suppose to be a free country but I've never been free. I was sunning on the richest beach in the world and you brought me over here to pick cotton. And then when I wanted to learn to read and write, you beat me for it. When it was over, we were all supposed to get forty dollars and a mule. That was two hundred years ago and it should be worth three million dollars and a small Mercedes now." The words flowed out of Shirley as though she'd given the same speech before.

Harding nodded. He noticed that it didn't take much to get this woman going. He kept his eyes on her as he made mental notes of what she said.

Harding remembered what Bernice Crawford told him about Shirley's fastidiousness. She'd move the candy dish back to its spot on a side table if someone moved it. Glasses or mugs were taken out of the sitting parlor as soon as they were set down.

"Could I have a glass of orange juice when you finish ironing?" Harding asked.

"Sure, I'll get it now, 'cause it'll take till I leave to get done with this huge pile Bernice left me." Shirley pointed to a full laundry basket next to the ironing board.

She went to the kitchen and came back with a carton of juice and two glasses.

Harding noticed that Shirley smoked constantly. She offered Harding a cigarette from the pack of Benson and Hedges Light that lay on a desk in the office. "Thanks, but I don't smoke," he said. As she poured the juice into both glasses with her right hand, she let the cigarette dangle from her left.

Harding sipped the juice and left the empty glass on a small table. It wasn't long before Shirley picked up his glass and the one she had used and with the cigarette still lit in her mouth, she took the glasses back to the kitchen. He was glad when she came right back. That meant she hadn't washed them.

For ten or fifteen minutes he stayed silent, watching the news broadcast while Shirley kept ironing. Finally, he said,

"Say, I apologize for not properly introducing myself. You know I'm David Savage since we got that over with when I registered, but I didn't get your name," Harding said in his friendly tone.

"I'm Shirley Kinge," she said softly.

The news switched to a recent arrest made by a narcotics unit. Kinge began ardently speaking above the television's hum. "Nothing's equal in this country. If I rob a store and kill a black man, that doesn't matter. If I kill a white person, it's a new set of rules."

Shirley pointed to the white newscaster:

"If I kill him or her that's where it's at. If I get caught with a gun in New York that's an automatic fifteen years. If a black has a silencer on a gun, he'll get double time. That's even before you get to the robbery or murder."

Harding listened intently, not taking his eyes off her. It wasn't necessary for him to respond. Obviously she liked doing monologues.

She went on, "You can't talk like that around here or men with badges will be at your door. I just want to be left alone." Shirley continued, "Drugs aren't a black problem you know, like they're always saying. It's a white problem and it's all about money. White people have all the control. I can't find employment because they say I'm overqualified. Hell, I have to pay for shelter and food like everybody else. And I'm still a 'Three thirty-fiver.'"

"What's that?" Harding asked.

"Someone who makes minimum wage. I make more than that, but I'm still under-employed," she said with disgust.

When the news covered the freeing of Nelson Mandela in South Africa, she talked about how ridiculous it was to keep him in jail. "It's because the powers that be just want to exert their control."

Shirley kept ironing as she talked. The can of spray starch lay at one end of the ironing board; she picked it up to use on the table napkins she was pressing. Harding remembered to move the candy dish to another table after taking a piece of lemon hard-candy from it.

He took his 35-millimeter out of its case as he talked, "I really like different styles of architecture. Photography is a hobby with me," he explained. "It's a good way to remember the places I've been." Harding paused, glanced at her to see if she was listening, then continued, "Would it be all right if I took pictures of the interior of the house, especially the ornate woodwork. I really like old houses." Shirley said she didn't see any reason why he couldn't take pictures.

Harding made sure he looked awkward using the camera with his right hand as though it felt strange to him. In fact, he was right-handed. As he began to snap pictures, he asked Shirley to stand in front of the stairway. "I like to have people in my photographs because they make them more interesting," he told her.

"No, I don't like to have my picture taken," she said firmly.

He tried to tease her into posing for the camera, but she was emphatic.

After snapping a few pictures of the staircase and sitting room, he lowered his 35-millimeter to put in his pocket. When he had the camera at waist level, he let the shutter go off. Shirley was standing two feet away and could hear the click.

"Well, I just took a picture of the ceiling. Guess I'm completely incompetent with my right hand," Harding said, laughingly explaining that the camera had gone off accidentally.

After the incident, Harding told her that the Cornell friend he was meeting for dinner wouldn't be free until after eight o'clock. He knew that was the hour she got off work. "I'll just go up and put this away," he said. Harding went up to his room, took the camera out of his pocket and put it in the suitcase. He grimaced. Disgusted about not getting a good shot of Shirley Kinge, he grabbed his briefcase and a few minutes later, left the room to go back downstairs.

Once there, Shirley asked him if he'd like anything to eat. "No," he said. "I'll wait to have dinner later on. But don't let me interfere with your eating though," he told her. Shirley said she'd get something for herself and went back to the kitchen.

Harding was taking out a pile of envelopes from his brief-case when Shirley, with a sandwich in her hand, entered the office. He explained that he was late mailing invitations to his high school classmates for a reunion in June. He told her about the high school he had attended in a small town near Harrisburg, Pennsylvania. Harding said he was responsible for the first half of the class list and another member of the class had the rest. Then he asked, "Would you mind address-ing the envelopes for me since I have to get them out right away?"

"No problem," Shirley said. She'd help him out. She pulled a chair over to the desk and Harding gave her the list of classmates with their addresses. Some of the twenty-five were to Harrisburg and two were to individuals with the last name of Dolorean. Shirley and Harding remained in the of-fice since there seemed to be no other guests in the house.

When Shirley began addressing the envelopes, Harding commented on how nice her handwriting was; then he ex-cused himself and went up to his room. He jotted down the bulk of what Shirley had said so far, detailing her comments about crime and race. He had a good memory, but he had a lot on his mind and was afraid he'd forget what she'd said.

When he returned to the office, Shirley was still writing. "I've got three more to do," she said.

Harding began talking about why he was in town. "I have appointments with some people at Cornell who need help in writing state and federal grants." Picking up her head, Shirley stopped writing for a moment and asked him what he did.

He explained. "Yeah, it's an interesting job actually, and

it's always nice to help people get money for their projects." Harding took the addressed envelopes from Shirley and put them in his briefcase. "I'll have to mail them tomorrow at the post office since I don't have any stamps. You really got me out of a jam," he told her.

Shirley asked more questions about the grant process. She told him about an idea she'd had for a long time and wondered if it would work.

"I've got two hundred acres in Watertown that I want to retire to someday and I've thought about starting a hospice. Do you think there are any grants for something like that?"

Looking into Shirley's eyes, Harding wondered if she was putting him on. That sounded kind of far out, but he played along with her to see where it led. He asked her a few questions about the exact location of the property and how long she'd had the place.

"I might be able to help you," Harding shook his head affirmatively. "I don't know how busy my schedule will be in the next day or two, but if I have the time, I'd be glad to help you in pursuing a grant." He rattled off some information about what types of projects the state and Feds were apt to fund, remembering his years as a school administrator in Waverly, New York, where he had applied for grant money.

"Maybe we can get in touch in the future and arrange a time to meet." Shirley got a piece of paper from the office and on the top of the sheet she wrote down Harding's address and phone number in Albany as he dictated them to her; she tore off the bottom half of the paper and wrote down her name, address and phone number and handed it to Harding. Then she invited him to her home to discuss the grants.

As she smiled at him he wondered if she had other things in mind too. Harding automatically thought that way in the presence of women; they'd been falling for him for years. "I probably won't have time this trip to come out, but I'll be back in town soon," he assured her.

He thanked her for addressing the envelopes and keeping him company. "I enjoyed talking with you," Harding said softly. "We'll keep in touch. It was nice meeting you," Harding shook her hand.

"Yeah. Maybe I'll see you again," she said, smiling again and taking her jacket from the coat tree in the entryway, she put it on, and walked to the kitchen. Turning around, she looked at him standing in the office, waved her hand, and said in a slightly raised pleasant voice, "Good bye." It wasn't the same angry voice he'd heard from her earlier when she spoke about white racism in the world.

Harding heard the back door shut. He waited until the sound of a car motor started up and he could hear it leave the driveway. Glancing at his watch, Harding noted that it was a few minutes after 8:00 P.M.

He went up to his room, waited a few minutes, and then brought his suitcase downstairs. Wearing gloves, he collected items to take back to the barracks: The two juice glasses, a mayonnaise jar Shirley had used to make a cheese sandwich for herself, the can of spray starch, and a cigarette butt that Shirley had left in an ashtray. She hadn't bothered to move the candy dish back in its place. He went out the front door at 8:25 P.M.

McElligott and Chandler were at their desks when Harding strode in. He recounted how he'd spent the hours at The Peregrine House with Shirley Kinge. He read them her words about black versus white crime. The words that interested the two men most were the ones about a silencer.

"Wow, that's a different thing to say," McElligott commented. "She sounds like one hell of an angry woman. Sorta reverse racism."

Harding nodded, "I got twenty-five samples of her handwriting, plus the receipt."

"Those should tell us something. But I doubt you got a good picture of her taken from your hip," Chandler said. He went on. "You filled in a few gaps, Dave. Maybe we'll be able to match the handwriting, but we need more information."

Harding smiled, "She invited me to her house. I can go over there, get a good look at what's going on, and we can get surveillance to take a picture when I lure her outside or maybe her son might be there and I can see him up close." Harding felt he was on a hot trail. He was itching to keep going—his way.

"Absolutely not," McElligott blurted out. "Are you crazy? We're looking at a very dangerous man. If the suspect's on to us, you could get shot. Going to her house is out of the question. We've got to lure her some other way."

Harding was beginning to get on McElligott's nerves. McElligott couldn't stand Harding's grandstand plays. He could feel tension building up between them but he didn't really care unless it got in the way of the investigation.

McElligott already annoyed Harding but the younger investigator knew that when McElligott's mind was made up, it was final. Arguing with him wouldn't help, but he hated following the orders McElligott barked out.

They waited for the photographs. Chandler was right. The "accidental" picture of Shirley Kinge Harding snapped wasn't good enough for a lineup photo sheet. They had to find another way to see her again, so better photographs could be taken. Harding frowned, "I'll check out the glasses and mayonnaise jar I took for fingerprints."

Despite McElligott's misgivings, a scheme was devised during the night at the Varna post. Harding would call Shirley Kinge the next day and arrange a meeting to help her with the grant process. They selected a spot close enough to the campus, the Friendly's Restaurant in the Cayuga Mall off North Triphammer Road, so Harding's reason for meeting there fit in with his busy schedule at Cornell. They needed a place where the surveillance crew, without being noticed, could easily take pictures as the suspect entered and exited the building.

Wednesday, a few minutes before 3:30 P.M., Harding pulled into Friendly's busy parking lot. Taking a look around, he saw the surveillance van to the east of the restaurant where Investigator Doug Vredenburgh and Lieutenant Craig Harvey were positioned to take photographs. Trooper Charlene Hippenstiel was assigned to arrive at the restaurant a bit later than Harding and Kinge. She came in a separate vehicle.

Shirley Kinge pulled her white Subaru into Friendly's parking lot. Harding stood by his car waiting for Shirley to walk over to him. The police planned it this way so photographs could be taken at close range. Vredenburgh shot frame after frame as Shirley walked over to Harding's car. He took even more shots as they walked toward the restaurant.

Hippenstiel came into Friendly's a few minutes after Harding and Kinge were seated. She got a table several booths down the aisle from them.

Harding started talking about the bad road conditions that he wasn't used to. It had been snowing off and on all day. "But at least, I don't have to deal with the traffic here like I do in Albany." Shirley said she traveled back roads all the time, no matter how bad the weather was. She avoided the main roads, because she hated traffic.

They ordered coffee. Harding asked for ice water and Shirley said she'd like some too. They were seated in one of the larger booths. It was the middle of the afternoon and few customers were in the restaurant. As Harding intently studied Shirley, he noticed that she still wasn't wearing earrings in her pierced ears and this time she had on white Reebok sneakers.

Harding leaned towards her, "I've forgotten to bring the application form with me, but I can take down the vital information from you and start the process." He apologized because again he had to ask her to write for him because of his broken finger. There were no awkward pauses in the conversation. Shirley's gift of gab matched Harding's.

As soon as the waitress brought them their coffee and the ice water, Harding handed Shirley a yellow pad and asked her to write down the information as he gave her the questions that appeared on grant application forms from another yellow pad in front of him. "I know these items by heart after working so long with the grant process." He explained that the first ones were biographical in nature.

Lighting up a cigarette, Shirley looked at him. Instead of just writing down the answers to his questions, she wanted to tell him about herself, as if the meeting was social as well as business.

Where and when was she born? Her parents' names and addresses? Her Social Security number? Was she married? Her husband or ex-husband's name? How many children she had? The names of her children and where they lived?

She gave her birthdate and place of birth. "My mother is Sallie Irving Turner Reese and she lives with me at the same address on Etna Road. I have a daughter, Gabrielle, who lives in Columbia, South Carolina. I have a son, named Robert, who lives in Flagstaff, Arizona." Harding asked her if she had any more children. "No," she replied. She wasn't sure of the children's birthdates. She only had minor contact with her daughter and never heard from her son.

Shirley didn't seem to mind his questions so Harding asked her more as he glanced down at the yellow pad on the table.

What about past employment? Shirley said she worked for Port Authority in New York City from 1959 to 1974. She had been at The Peregrine House for about three years, worked at the Ithaca Child Care Center last year for a few months, and before that she was employed by Douglas Sutton, who was a real estate developer. During the years unaccounted for, she had taken cleaning jobs for various individuals. Shirley wrote the names and addresses of three local people to use as personal references.

Harding asked her how long she'd lived in upstate New York.

"Well, I got fed up with all the crime in New York City. My apartment was robbed so many times, so I decided to quit Port Authority, I really hated that job, and moved to where I could find peace and quiet."

"How long ago was that?"

"In 1974, I bought this property I told you about in Watertown. Rather, a friend and I bought it together for thirty-five thousand dollars. I saw it advertised in a New York paper—all this land with an old farmhouse on it. My friend didn't want to come up then, she had a good job in Florida, so I came up and lived in the farmhouse."

Apparently, Shirley, a lone black woman, had been conspicuous in Jefferson County, a rural, and predominately white, upstate county. But she didn't mind. She kept to herself except for the job she had with a federally sponsored nutrition program for the elderly.

"What made you move here?" Harding was off his application questions, but the more he learned about this woman the better. He was thankful that she liked to talk.

"That's a long story, but the gist of it is, the house caught on fire one freezing night in February in 1976 and sent me running out in the cold. The house burned down, but I had the sense to grab my furs." She laughed. "Then I moved here. You ask a lot of questions, just like a cop," Shirley said with a smile, as though she was talking with a friend. He gave a small laugh in response but didn't reply. She'd already told him about being turned down by H.U.D. for financing a home. Obviously she felt that this nice guy who wrote grants might be easy; he looked like the kind who might help her one way or another. She had good reasons for wanting to make a good impression on him.

Harding laughed again, this time heartily, "Yeah, well, you know the government. They want to know everything, especially when it has to do with giving out money."

He asked the next question in routine fashion.

"Have you ever been in trouble with the law?"

There was a pause while Shirley took a long drag on her cigarette. She began telling him about an incident in Charleston, South Carolina, in 1976 or 1977. "I was unjustly accused of a larceny while on a baby-sitting job," Shirley said matter-of-factly. The two ten-year-old children of the household had a sleep-over party one night and after she left at eleven o'clock to go home, the police came to the door and took her to the Charleston police department on a larceny charge of about $570. She was fingerprinted and photo- graphed. She had to appear in court three times for the charge. When she was scheduled to appear a fourth time, Shirley got nervous and left the state.

"Why did you get nervous?" Harding asked.

"They found a black guy shot with his hands tied behind his back. He was shot seventeen times. The cops were white and they called it a suicide. Do you get my drift?" She took a sip from the almost empty water glass in front of her.

"Don't worry, grant applications don't require information that far back," Harding said. Leaning towards her, he asked Shirley if there had been any recent problems.

Poker-faced Shirley leaned over, put her hand on top of Harding's and said, "You mean, have I killed anybody lately?"

Her skin was very dry and her touch made Harding feel uneasy. He slowly moved his hand away from hers and repeated the question. After taking a drag on her cigarette, she continued. "No, I'm not that way. If you had a .357 Magnum in my face, I might make you eat it. But, if I could get away from it, I would." She told Harding there were things that happened down there in the South that would shock him,

Michael Kinge, a.k.a. Tony Turner, had already made his criminal debut when photographed here in a 1978 police mug shot—eleven years before the Harris family would be tortured and then brutally murdered.

A 1990 police mug shot of Joanna White, Michael Kinge's girlfriend.

Shirley Kinge, Michael's mother, listens attentively during her trial as an accessory to murder. *(Photo by Bill Warren, The Ithaca Journal)*

The Harris House in Ithaca is cordoned off after local and state police respond to what a neighbor first reported as being a fire alarm sounding. *Inset:* Shelby, Tony, Marc, and Dodie Harris pose for a family picture in 1989—the same year a murderous, chain-smoking criminal would botch his robbery of their crafts business and idyllic home just two days before Christmas, then decide that he didn't want anybody who could implicate him left alive. *(Photo of the Harris House by David Grene,* The Citizen*)*

District Attorney George Dentes displays a fingerprint chart to the courtroom during New York State Police Officer David Harding's evidence-tampering trial. *(Photo by Robin Wishna, The Ithaca Journal)*

Defense attorney William P. Sullivan, Jr. holds the gas can from which David Harding lifted finger prints—the same gas can used to set the Harris family's bodies and home on fire. *(Photo by Robin Wishna, The Ithaca Journal)*

New York State Police Senior Investigator David McElligott *(above)* was suspicious of how the young and overly ambitious officer David Harding *(right)* always seemed to uncover crucial evidence from crime scenes after other veteran detectives had left empty handed. *(Photo of David McElligott by Jay Reiter,* The Ithaca Journal; *photo of David Harding by Gayle Shomer,* The Ithaca Journal)

"You're white and insulated from the real world." She paused and went on. "There are things locally that I could tell you that would shock you too," she shook her head.

Harding began to imagine the layers that made up this woman; layers of experiences real and unreal that must constitute her life. As he made more small talk, an icy feeling began to grow in the pit of his stomach. He wanted to get out of there as fast as possible, to grab the data now that they needed. But Harding knew he couldn't be too abrupt. A few minutes later he looked at his watch and grimaced, "Someone is waiting to see me on campus, so I'll have to go. I'll be in touch with you about the application." He left the money for the check on the table and stood up.

Shirley asked him in a joking manner, "I haven't cost you too much on your expense account, have I?"

"Oh, no, not at all." Harding smiled, wondering if she'd been flirting with him all along. It had been a delicate balance for him between being friendly with her so she'd talk with ease, and not getting embroiled in a compromising situation. He was a good actor, maneuvering his way in and out like a professional con man.

Outside, Shirley stopped near Harding while he put his coat on in front of the unmarked police van that was parked next to her Subaru. "I'm going over to pick up a few things at the Grand Union next door," Shirley said.

"I'll process the application and then get in touch with you, Shirley," Harding waved as he walked over to his car.

Lingering, she smiled at him and said, "Okay. See you later."

Inside the restaurant, Hippenstiel waited a few minutes after Harding and Shirley left. Then she explained to the restaurant manager that she was a police officer investigating a crime, "I need to take the lady's water glass, coffee mug and silverware to the station." The manager gave Hippenstiel a paper bag in which the trooper put the articles. Walking to the door, she checked outside to be sure Shirley and Harding were gone before quickly delivering the items to Lieutenant Craig Harvey in the surveillance van.

Sixteen
Getting the Evidence

On February 3, events occurred which were to influence the investigation in the immediate sense and to have drastic long-range implications.

Harding had ridiculed Rob Lishansky for not solving any crimes with fingerprints during Rob's first year in the ID unit. "You want to move up, you'd better make your bosses notice you," Harding advised.

When it became clear the investigation was closing in on the Kinges, Harding knew what he had to do. He had to prove Shirley Kinge had been inside the Harris house. David Harding had kept the gas cans found at the crime scene. His theory was helped by Professor Stuphin who said he had seen a black male and an older black woman in a van on Ellis Hollow Road near his house on the morning of December 23 around 6:45 A.M. Harding knew they wouldn't have an opportunity to trick Michael Kinge and get his current fingerprints. He was an experienced criminal and hadn't left his house since January 26 when McElligott had ordered a twenty-four hour surveillance detail on the property. They had nothing to compare to the prints from his 1976 Cayuga County arrest record.

Harding wanted to immediately pursue the New York City Port Authority lead where Shirley Kinge had been employed. McElligott called Albany to say they needed a NYC contact to ferret out Kinge's personnel records at Port Authority. A lieutenant came through with the request in less than an hour.

David Harding expressed special interest in seeing Shirley Kinge's fingerprints and McElligott wanted any information that would shed light on one of their suspects. Kinge's prints, taken when she was hired in 1959, were in her folder.

McElligott called Keith Barclay, who was one of his investigators. Barclay was temporarily assigned to New York City but couldn't wait to leave. McElligott told Barclay he could come home after he picked up the suspect's employment folder at Port Authority. The material was at the Ithaca barracks within hours. They learned more about Shirley Kinge but Harding examined the prints and discovered they were too smudged to make any reliable comparisons.

Harding was determined to get Kinge's fingerprints. He had two more possibilities to try right away. He remembered that part of the information Shirley gave him at Friendly's Restaurant for the so-called grant application included an encounter with the law she had in Charleston, South Carolina. He called Charleston's police department and asked if they had a record on a Shirley Kinge, a larceny charge in 1976 or 1977. Harding explained why he was interested in her and informed them about the circumstances of her arrest in Charleston. He was hoping they had her fingerprints. Several hours later a Charleston detective called back to say they could find no record of any such arrest.

When George Dentes was informed of the Charleston dead-end, he was disappointed but not surprised. "Arrest records for minor charges are sometimes thrown out after so many years," he said.

Harding, however, seemed furious. He wasn't about to give up. Shirley Kinge's Port Authority records showed previous employment with the United States Treasury Department beginning in September 1957. A call to Washington, D.C., determined that the FBI held all prints from federal agencies and the armed services. Captain Shaver asked an FBI fingerprint expert to look at Shirley Kinge's Treasury Department prints to see if they were worth flying up to Ithaca. He called Shaver back to say the prints looked okay. He'd make a glossy and send them up by airline priority mail. Investigators also learned that Shirley Kinge was fired from her job as information clerk at New York City's Port Authority Bus Terminal in 1974 for absenteeism; the reviewing officer cited excessive sick leave and tardiness.

Although they faced minor setbacks every day, the investigation moved ahead. McElligott felt they were closing in on the Harrises' killer or killers. He wanted someone to walk the Shirley Kinge fingerprint card from the FBI to the National Airport in Washington, deliver them via an agent on a flight to Ithaca, and he'd have an investigator pick up the prints.

But Albany had other ideas. As was the custom in highly visible cases, Captain Shaver was on the line with Albany whenever they faced a major decision. Superintendent Tom Constantine, head of the New York State Police, wanted to be kept informed and in some instances called the shots.

Albany decided to send the Treasury Department prints by regular air mail express, which due to bad weather, landed them in Detroit. This resulted in a ten-hour delay.

McElligott exploded at Karl Chandler when he heard about the prints landing in Detroit, "Damn them, what did I tell you? I knew there'd be some kind of goddamn screw-up if they did it their way. They shoulda put them on the plane when I told them."

His old friend silently listened to McElligott sound off. Chandler knew the pain of this kind of frustration. He also knew there wasn't a thing they could do about it. It was in the heat of an investigation when they were getting close to solving the puzzle that McElligott's nerve endings seemed to tighten and he had to watch his self-control. He lit another cigarette, walked to the coffee room, refilled his mug, and tried to think about something else. "What's done is done," McElligott mumbled. He wasn't the kind of person to dwell on negatives or hold grudges. He had blown off steam; now he let it go.

It was not as though McElligott looked on these finger-prints as the major weapon in getting their suspects, but he knew that if the prints matched, it could add to the police's increasing arsenal against the Kinges. McElligott wanted anything that told them more about their suspects. He didn't like or trust Harding, but was thankful Harding and Lishan-sky, the ID men, seemed to be on top of their job and doing all they could to help out.

Captain Shaver gave Harding the Treasury Department folder as soon as it came in. It held a glossy reproduction of Shirley Kinge's fingerprints. Now, Harding had Shirley's government documented fingerprints and the lifts he had taken of her left middle and left ring fingers from the mayonnaise jar she used at The Peregrine House. Although Harding tried all morning, he couldn't lift anything from the Friendly's water glass. Harding remembered how parched Shirley's skin felt when she touched his hand at the restaurant and assumed he couldn't lift the prints because of her dry skin.

During a lull in the afternoon, McElligott and Chandler were alone in the operation room; McElligott had been typ-ing up lead sheets when Harding suddenly stormed in and excitedly announced, "Boss man, I gotta match. I matched two prints on the living room gas can with Shirley Kinge's government prints."

"Hold it, right there, Dave." McElligott rolled a new sheet

of paper into his typewriter. He looked up and scrutinized Harding's hyperactive manner. "Okay. Hard prints. Tell me what you got," McElligott said.

Harding told him again.

McElligott was stunned. "Wow, Dave. You said you were having trouble getting them off the can."

Harding's face was expressionless as he spoke. "Oh, no. I got these two prints on the short side of the can. The others, on the long side, I couldn't lift." Harding held up an imaginary gas can, pointing to the short side from which he said he had lifted the two prints.

McElligott scratched his head. He couldn't remember Harding ever mentioning two prints on the short side of the can. "Dave, I don't remember any other prints," he said, watching the younger man closely.

"I mentioned we had others," Harding smoothly replied. "We can go in and arrest the mother too with this kind of evidence," he continued.

McElligott was puzzled. The discrepancy between what he thought Harding first told them about the three prints and now these two prints bothered him. Weighing Harding's words and his own skeptical feelings, McElligott decided he had to rely on Harding since he was the fingerprint specialist. Later, though McElligott tried to forget his dubious thoughts, the conversation remained in his mind.

When Lishansky found out that Harding announced his print match on Lishansky's day off, he was furious. Now Harding would get all the credit.

The prints continued to bother McElligott so he finally called a second fingerprint expert and Harding's supervisor in the ID unit in Sidney. Lieutenant Craig Harvey, who was involved with cases in other areas of Troop C during this time, came over. He looked over Harding's print match-up and verified the findings.

The fingerprint evidence added another notch to the police case against the Kinges, but they had already set the wheels in motion. The process of obtaining search warrants for the Etna Road duplex had begun even before Harding's dramatic announcement.

The breakthrough news swept through the command post like wildfire. One investigator who had worked on several cases with Harding exclaimed, "He's incredibly lucky or awfully damn good or maybe both." Albany also heard the news. Officials congratulated Harding for his excellent work.

Meanwhile, the other investigators found that the surveillance photographs taken of Shirley Kinge as she approached Friendly's Restaurant on January 31 and while she shopped on other days were good enough close-ups to use for identification purposes. McElligott could see a clear resemblance between the photograph of her and the artist's drawing. As he studied the pictures, he understood why she had passed for a younger woman.

Investigators took random photographs of five other black females, who appeared to be in the same age category and who had physical builds similar to that of Shirley Kinge's, as the women went in and out of stores in the Syracuse area. Police created photo lineup pages in which they showed the same subjects in different settings with a page of Shirley Kinge photographs interspersed. It was an unorthodox method, but they had to try it.

The same procedure was applied to the 1978 photograph of Michael Kinge using other mug shots of black males. A police artist altered the old photograph of Michael Kinge from the Afro hair-style he wore then, to his current shoulder-length, Jheri Curl look.

Later that afternoon, at Syracuse's Public Safety Building, the police showed the lineups to the store clerks in Camillus and Auburn who handled the Harris credit card transactions on December 23. The police asked each clerk if he or she recognized any of the individuals as the customers who had used the Harrises' credit card.

All but one clerk tentatively picked out Shirley Kinge and

only two clerks who waited on the Warren Harris credit card user could tentatively pick out Michael Kinge. Sarah Clark, the jewelry store clerk who had waited on the woman buying diamond earrings using Dolores Harris's Visa gold card, gave a positive identification. Clark said, "There's no doubt in my mind," as she pointed to the photographs of Shirley Kinge. Clark also told an investigator that in a conversation she'd had with the suspect on December 23, the suspect had told her, "I'm probably going to regret this." And then the woman had said she'd take the diamond earrings.

The same photograph lineup sheets were shown to Professor Dean Stuphin on February 3. He tentatively picked out Michael Kinge as the person he had seen in the van on Ellis Hollow Road on December 23, but he said he'd have to see him in person to be sure. He also expressed doubts about the statement he made to investigators on January 8. He said that after thinking about it for a long time he might be mistaken about the day he saw the van with these two individuals in it. "It could have been another time I saw him."

Stuphin changing his story came as a blow to the investigation; he was an important link to their theory that the suspects had left the Harris home after the fire alarm went off about 6:45 A.M., December 23.

There was, however, nothing McElligott could do except take Stuphin at his word. He had to accept the professor's reservations, but McElligott dreaded telling George Dentes.

Scott Burton picked Michael Kinge out of the lineup photographs. He didn't have a doubt that was the man in front of him and his father at Marine Midland Bank's ATM on North Triphammer Road, Saturday afternoon, December 23. His father, John Burton, was not as positive. He thought it was possible that this male on the lineup sheet was the man who asked him to dislodge his bank access card, but John wasn't sure.

McElligott informed Dentes about Stuphin's retraction and that Michael Kinge's criminal record included a bench warrant from New York City. Like the pragmatic attorney he was, Dentes put the disappointment out of his mind, and got on the phone with the D.A.'s office in Manhattan. He found out Kinge had been arrested in New York on possession of a loaded firearm in September of 1982. Kinge had failed to appear in court on the charge, so a bench warrant had been issued. Authorities hadn't searched for him, but if he was picked up on something else, this 1982 offense would show up. Kinge's record revealed that he was apprehended in Lansing on a burglary charge in 1985 under the name of Anthony Turner. He gave his address as Etna Road. The connection had not been made with the person wanted in New York City. When Dentes got down to preparing for the arrest of Michael Kinge, he asked New York City to dismiss the 1982 bench warrant case against Kinge in order for Ithaca authorities to interrogate him. (The "other case pending rule" in New York State was in effect, which meant a defendant with a pending case could not be questioned on a new case because that would violate his right to counsel.)

The Etna Road stakeout team stayed busy. Undercover police had followed Joanna White to grocery stores, to gas stations where she filled a kerosene container, to a video store on the other side of town, and to pick up pizza at East Hill Plaza, which she did almost daily. She usually left the house alone by 10:30 or 11:00 A.M. in the Ford pickup. Trooper Brady and Ithaca Detective Doug Martin followed her to a supermarket. While inside, they pretended to be buying food for dinner as they stayed close to Joanna, following her up and down the aisles. When they saw her get in the checkout line, they dumped their basket and left the store to be able to get into their car and continue to trail her. They tried to see if Joanna wore any of the items purchased on the Harris Visa card, but had no luck. In their opinions, she didn't.

*   *   *

Now as the suspects looked hotter, the police wanted more cars available. Linda Brady, who in the beginning was partnered with other investigators in the surveillance detail, was assigned a car of her own since she was from the area and knew the local roads. Most of the other investigators on the detail were from out-of-town. Four to six undercover vehicles were positioned so that the suspects could be trailed in whatever direction they went. One team was stationed in a sheriff deputy's driveway just beyond the intersection of Etna and Hanshaw Road, while another car sat in a trailer park driveway on Hanshaw Road. Brady was assigned to keep her car in the parking lot of the Guthrie Clinic across Route 13 and another team parked outside a long-term storage facility.

Several area residents who observed the unmarked cars lingering for a long time in parking lots called the police. They thought the people looked suspicious. Many of the undercover cops from the narcotics unit grew beards and long hair to blend into the drug culture. They looked the part. McElligott decided to move them from public locations. It was too risky to give out any information about what they were doing there.

McElligott and Chandler were aware that their prime suspect might try to leave by hiding in the trunk of a car or by some other surreptitious manner. One evening the undercover police observed a car pulling into the suspects' driveway. Two people came out of the house and got into the car. Trooper Brady picked up the vehicle as it traveled secondary roads in the Etna and Freeville Townships. Not knowing if their main suspect was in the car poised to pull off another crime, a uniformed trooper was called in as a ruse to intercept them. Finally the car pulled into a private driveway, but no one emerged from the automobile. The trooper went up to the parked car and explained that a suspicious vehicle had been reported in the area and he had to check it out because of the Harris murders. The trooper radioed back that Sallie Reese and Shirley Kinge were with a Realtor looking at houses to either buy or rent.

Brady was told to do a drive-by on the suspect's house as it was getting dark. She passed the duplex, not seeing anything, and kept going on the road past the few houses until reaching an old logging trail cut through the woods. As she backed into the path, she saw headlights shining from a car parked across the road. It turned out to be a sheriff's deputy, who thought that Brady looked suspicious. He came over to her car and asked what she was doing there. Brady told him she was a state trooper doing undercover work and showed him her badge. He said he had heard that the state police were on some kind of surveillance having to do with drugs. Brady let it go at that.

Surveillance continued. The weary detectives noted that Shirley Kinge sometimes took Tony's child with her when she did errands. Sallie Reese left the apartment infrequently. They waited for Michael Kinge to make a move. After dark, as police drove by in undercover cars, a figure was seen several times at the front downstairs window on his side of the duplex. The police surmised it was Kinge.

McElligott brought Ron Callie into the Varna station on Sunday, February 4, for a late briefing before they executed the search warrant. McElligott wanted to talk with Callie again. He was their best informer. While Callie sat in an interviewing room near Captain Shaver's office, he overheard Shaver's loud voice on the phone talking about going into the suspect's house. Callie panicked. He had been told that the evidence pointed to his former friend as the Harrises' killer; he was scared that Kinge might try and kill him for being a snitch. McElligott decided it was safer to put Callie up in a motel in Owego, a town 35 miles south of Ithaca, until the search warrant was over. He didn't want to take a chance that Callie would tip off their suspect.

Tom Kelly flew down to New York City Monday morning, February 5, to ask Ron Altman, a credit card customer from New York City who had been at K-Mart in the Camillus Mall in Syracuse on December 23, to identify Michael Kinge from their photograph lineup sheet. Investigators and bank personnel working on the credit card trail had turned up his name and address. It looked as though Mr. Altman had made a credit card purchase after a Panasonic television set was bought on the Warren Harris Visa card.

Kelly called Altman, an attorney in Manhattan, and told him about their need for identifying a prime suspect in the Harris homicide case and asked for his cooperation. Altman told Kelly he was in Syracuse visiting his daughter over the holiday weekend and he did remember standing behind a black male at K-Mart. Altman recalled that the man wore a blue sweatshirt with a hood and a dark brown coat.

Kelly went to the lawyer's office in New York and showed him the photo lineup sheets. Altman picked out Kinge and said he was positive Kinge was the man he had seen at K-Mart. Kelly took down his statement, thanked Altman for his help, and said he would be hearing from the Tompkins County District Attorney's office soon.

By Monday afternoon, February 5, they had enough evidence to take the Kinges in for questioning. Positive identification had been made of the two suspects from store clerks, from a witness at the bank machine where the Harris access card was used, and from a shopper at Camillus Mall. They knew Kinge made weapons and a silencer, and that he fashioned himself as a criminal. They knew his criminal record. And they had evidence of Shirley Kinge's fingerprints on the gas can found at the murder scene.

Knowing that Michael Kinge was well-armed, and having been informed by New York City police and by Ron Callie that Kinge was prepared to shoot the cops rather than be taken, McElligott knew they had no choice but to make a forced entry and prepare for the worst.

McElligott was satisfied they had the right man. He told

Daniels to prepare for a forced entry on the duplex. As they watched the evidence building on Kinge and learned about his habits, Daniels felt it was a distinct possibility they would have to go in and take their suspects. He had already been thinking abut how they could do it. A conflict had erupted between Ithaca and Albany over who would make the entry. Albany officials wanted the statewide SWAT team to do the job. The Mobile Response Team was created to perform highly dangerous missions across the state. McElligott felt the MRTs were armed to the teeth and might blow up the evidence. They were designed to break up huge standoffs such as the takeovers of buildings and McElligott wanted to take their suspects into custody, not blow up the house or the evidence.

He liked the fact that Daniels' team included several former New York City drug enforcement veterans who together had participated in over two hundred entries. The team also had been working together on the Harris case and knew each other so well from narcotics work that they knew how every officer would react in tense and unexpected situations. Their confidence came from trusting the people they worked with. "I need all the pluses I can muster," McElligott said. "Our suspect is dangerous and we have to deal with a possible hostage situation with the Kinge baby."

The layout of Tilley's duplex in which police set up their observation post was the mirror image of the Kinge house. Daniels had the team go over every detail in the house. They knew how many steps to the front door, where the light switches were, where there were likely hiding places, how many steps to the stairs from the entrance, and the location of bedrooms. The team brainstormed, trying to think of every possible situation they could run into and made their plans accordingly.

One vital piece of information was finding out where the baby slept. They were determined to protect the child from any gunfire. The team was thoroughly briefed on the suspect's criminal record, his violent nature, and what guns he probably had in the house. They were aware that he'd told police officers in New York City he wished he'd shot it out with them and taken the cops with him.

Daniels presented his plan to McElligott, then McElligott had to get it by Captain Carl Shaver, and finally have it approved by Albany. At the end of the day on February 5, Daniels still didn't know who would be making the entry. McElligott assumed his men would do the job, so he and Shaver made sure they had the equipment they needed: military flack vests and bulletproof helmets borrowed from the National Guard, appropriate weapons, and a helicopter stood by in case of injuries. McElligott was a fanatic about protecting his men. He would spare no cost or inconvenience to see they were equipped with the best that was available, especially in a volatile situation such as the one they were about to face with Tony Turner.

Seventeen

Firefight

On Tuesday, February 6, McElligott informed Daniels that Albany had given him the go-ahead. "I want your men assembled here by 5:30 A.M. tomorrow, Ozzie. Come on in as soon as you can. I want to go over a few things with you. Looks like this is it, my boy."

McElligott didn't play favorites on his team, but if he did have one, it would surely be Daniels. Daniels was a big, strong man who wore his hair long, and grew a beard and a mustache as an undercover cop. He could look very intimidating when it was needed, but those close to him knew that Daniels was caring and sensitive. He also knew entries like nobody else, could always be relied upon, and planned a raid like it was an army invasion; no detail too small for his attention. McElligott felt Daniels was a person to be trusted with dangerous assignments and people's lives.

Senior Investigator Bob Courtright and Tom Kelly rang the doorbell at the front entrance of Ithacare Nursing Home. Joanna White came to the door along with her coworker, Trudy Curtis. Courtright showed them his police badge. "We're state police officers and this is Tom Kelly. We want you to go with us to the barracks where we can talk. And we have a search warrant for your pickup truck," Courtright said.

"But I can't leave with only one other staff member on duty," Joanna told the officers as she looked over at Curtis.

"I've already talked with your supervisor," Courtright fired back.

Without another word, Joanna went downstairs to get her coat and pocketbook. Upon returning, Joanna handed over the keys to her truck. She didn't ask Courtright or Kelly why she was being taken in. She didn't ask them anything. Head down, she meekly left with the two investigators.

They drove to the command post in an undercover vehicle. Another officer took Joanna's truck to be searched. During the trip, Kelly read Joanna her Miranda rights. She still was silent. The only time she spoke was to ask if she could smoke a cigarette.

On arriving, the investigators escorted Joanna into the station and headed for the zone sergeant's office to conduct the interview. Courtright sat in a chair next to Joanna and Kelly was across the table from them.

Then the two police officers began to interrogate her. "We wanta know the layout of your apartment. We're going in there for Tony and Shirley Kinge in connection with the Harris murders. We have a search warrant for the premises. We don't want to see anybody get hurt," Courtright said.

As they spoke Joanna began looking more and more tense. And when they asked in which apartment the baby was sleeping, she became very upset, pleading with them not to go in and harm her baby. Over and over she repeated her entreaties.

Watching her, Courtright was sympathetic. He operated under the principle that even with the worst of criminals, you can't strip a suspect of his or her dignity. You have to treat them with a certain amount of respect. He never taped interviews or took notes in the beginning of a session, feeling that both techniques made suspects more uncomfortable. Usually, he didn't yell during an interview, but feeling the pressure of time, he was becoming frustrated with Joanna, who was not answering any questions. They needed facts about their prime suspect right away to protect the entry team and the baby.

Nevertheless, Courtright assured Joanna several times that her son, Jimmy, would not be harmed. The officers said they would see to it that the child got out safely. The young woman appeared to relax a little. She asked when she could see Jimmy. "We aren't sure," Courtright said, "but the social services department will take good care of the baby temporarily."

Joanna, constantly smoking, began to tell them about the duplex. She said that she wasn't sure where the baby would be sleeping. "He could be with Tony or with Shirley and Sallie. Tony usually sat by the kitchen window, looking out. He kept both doors locked," Joanna said. "He'd be waiting for the cops." She drew a map that showed the bedroom where Tony slept. Now, however, he stayed up all night and would only go to bed when she came home. Joanna then offered details about the rest of the rooms, including a closet where Tony kept a weapon. The officers asked what type of weapon he usually carried with him. "A gun," Joanna said softly.

They inquired about the storm door at the front of the house. "Was it locked?" Courtright asked.

"Yes, Tony keeps it locked," Joanna told them.

As they continued to question her, Joanna became more defensive of Tony. Her voice trembling, Joanna denied that Tony had been involved in any criminal activities. Joanna said he was home baby-sitting the night of the Harris murders and insisted she didn't know anything about the murders except what she saw on television. Courtright had a strong feeling that Joanna was lying and that she knew more about Tony's actions than she said, but he could not get her to admit it. Kelly took over questioning Joanna and she went on denying that she knew anything.

Courtright raised his voice: "You aren't telling us the

truth, Joanna. We are not stopping until you come forward with what really happened."

The two men's eyes met. They agreed without words that the conversation was going nowhere. Kelly offered to get Joanna something to eat, but she said she wasn't hungry. Courtright started to ask her what she knew about the Harris murders. He watched her closely, noticing that the cigarette in her right hand began to shake.

After Kelly and Courtright had finished talking to Joanna, they met to discuss their next step. Courtright then went down to the "pit" where the entry teams were gathered and told the team leaders what they had learned from Joanna. He handed them the sketch she'd drawn of the apartment. It helped to know where Tony might be sleeping, but not knowing on which side of the duplex the baby would be, reminded them they could still get into a hostage situation.

The team members were already worried about Tony's state of mind. It was not only what Joanna had told them that made them apprehensive, but what she didn't say as well. The whole idea was to take the suspect alive. McElligott wanted the chance to talk with him. There were so many unanswered questions: *Was his motive robbery? What happened inside the Harris home that December night? How long did he stay there? When did he come back to burn the bodies?*

It was a difficult situation, one they didn't want to blow. They'd been working long hours to solve the Harris murders, and the case had become a part of them. Karl Chandler thought the community deserved to know the full story behind the crimes that had destroyed its sense of security.

Once again the investigators discussed the entry plan. McElligott and Chandler would be in separate, undercover cars parked on Etna Road at the Hanshaw Road intersections. Chandler would stay behind McElligott, who would be with

Major Farrand. They'd go in after the police radioed from inside the house that the scene was secure. The investigators made sure the school buses were rerouted and patrol cars blocked off that end of Etna Road. They didn't want vehicles passing in case there was a firefight at the doorway. A helicopter was standing by at the county airport for any emergency that might arise. The helicopters could fly the wounded to a hospital or be used in the unlikely event of a car chase.

There were two entry teams going in separate vans, seven men to a team, including the driver. That meant there would be a team for each side of the duplex. Daniels was in charge of taking Michael Kinge and Don Vredenburgh headed the other team, whose job it was to find Shirley Kinge and to move Sallie Reese out of the house. Both were prepared to get the baby out.

Daniels wanted the team to have plenty of time to get ready, so by 4:45 A.M. they had gathered for a final time at the station. The team went over every detail of the plan plus the new input from Joanna White, and changed a few of their original plans. After making sure they had all their equipment in the vans, they left to put the plan in motion.

It was 6:20 A.M. and still dark on the crisp, cold morning, when their cars and vans pulled out of the Varna barracks parking lot and headed for Route 13. The team members needed some outside light when they went into the house in case the lightbulbs had been pulled. Also it would save time not to bother with light switches. When they learned from Joanna White that Michael stayed up all night waiting for them and sometimes only went to bed after she got home, they had decided to change from their usual forced-entry tactics of going in between 4:00 and 5:00 A.M. and instead hit Tony Turner after daylight. A street-wise guy who was heavily into marijuana knew that raids were made during the night. They might get lucky and find him sleeping. It was their best chance of taking him without a fight.

At the scene, sitting in the vehicles waiting for daylight,

the team was visibly nervous. After nearly thirty minutes, David
Beers, the driver with Don Vredenburgh's team, opened his
door. It was no longer dark, but he realized they couldn't see
any light through the vans' tinted windows.

Beers pulled out onto the highway and the other van followed. That was the part of the job Daniels looked forward.
It was exhilarating work from here on out. And it was a relief
to finally get the criminal after hours of tedious planning and
rehearsals. Beers tried not to think about the danger, but he
was as worried as the other team members were about the
gun with a silencer. They wouldn't be able to hear Tony if he
started shooting and that kind of situation made everyone
nervous. Despite this, the teams training and experience helped
to keep them focused on the task at hand. Nevertheless, hearts
began to beat faster and hands got sweaty as they waited inside the vans. Doug Vredenburgh hummed an oldies tune,
Gelinger talked louder than usual and Lohan squeezed his
hands together.

Even though they were anxious, all of the members of the
SWAT teams identified with the Harris murders. Each thought
of his own children and was horrified at the brutality of the
killing of an entire family. The Harrises were good people
who'd done no harm to anyone.

The vans pulled into the gravel front yard of the duplex,
only about thirty feet from the road. The officers sitting on
the passenger side got out first. They ran to the front of the
house to protect their people from possible incoming fire.
The first person out of the rear of each van ran to the back of
the building in case any suspect tried to escape.

Daniels had Doug Martin on his team, a narcotics investigator with the Ithaca Police Department, a man he'd learned
to respect highly after working with him on narco cases as
part of the Tompkins County Drug Task Force. Daniels had
assigned Martin the job of taking the outer storm door off
the duplex if they found it locked. Although Joanna White had
told them that Michael locked both doors, their habit was to

try it first. Daniels ripped the handle off as he grabbed the doorknob, but the door was locked. Martin was behind him with a halligan tool, a crowbar with one end pointed and the other end flat, that's considered the quickest way to lift open an outside door or to break a padlock.

As Martin tried to drive the pointed end of the tool into the lock, he was too far away from the edge of the door. When he pulled, the door just bent out while the lock stayed in place. "Damn," he said and smashed the glass out on the upper half of the door, ripping the lock open with the halligan. Martin dropped the tool on the ground and stepped back.

Gary Gelinger kept his eyes on the house as he began running forward, holding one side of the battering ram. He saw a man inside the house at the front window pull a curtain back and then quickly let it drop.

Gelinger yelled, "He's at the window," but no one heard him. They were focused on only one thing by then. Gelinger and Joe Brainard ran roaring behind Martin with the battering ram. They hit the inner door near the lock and it sprung open. There was enough daylight to see their way inside. Dropping the ram, they quickly followed the others, who were going "forty miles an hour," running close together behind the heels of Doug Vredenburgh, who held a shotgun.

Every man wore something that identified him as a policeman. Vredenburgh wore a bright blue and gold fluorescent vest with *POLICE* written across the front. Daniels and Michael Lohan had shields they used in New York City raids hanging over their chests. Daniels carried a twelve shot, nine millimeter, semi-automatic, the standard weapon for narcotics units. Others held the same type of semi-automatic and some carried .357 magnum revolvers.

Yelling "police," they ran full speed through the small front room heading for Michael's bedroom on the second floor. It was Martin's job to make sure the Doberman they knew Michael Kinge owned didn't interfere. If it did, he would have to shoot it. The big black dog came out of the kitchen growling. Martin yelled "stop" and pointed his gun at the dog; the dog backed up, still growling while the team ran through the front room and upstairs.

Joe Brainard, the team floater, dashed upstairs first to protect the men coming up. Vredenburgh roared after him with Daniels and Mike Lohan right behind. Still shouting "police," they turned to the right. The bedroom door was open.

"Don't do it, drop the gun!" Vredenburgh yelled as they entered the bedroom. They saw Michael Kinge sitting on the other side of the bed with a 20-gauge sawed-off shotgun stuck between his legs, the tip of the barrel under his chin.

Vredenburgh took a low position at the foot of the bed, pointing his Ithaca shotgun at the suspect. Daniels, the second man in, took a high position on the left side of the bed and Mike Lohan kneeled down in the doorway. Daniels cut in, "We're from the state police and we have a search warrant, you lay down your gun and everything'll be all right." Kinge's back was toward Vredenburgh and Daniels, his head turned toward the men rushing in.

Before Martin had a chance to sweep the downstairs, he heard voices upstairs, screaming, "don't do it, don't do it." He ran to the top of the stairs, and tapped Mike Lohan on the leg to let him know he was there. Lohan took one or two steps into the room and Martin stood in the doorway with his gun pointed at Kinge.

The left side of Martin's face and left arm were inside the room. He held a nine millimeter Glock in his left hand. Martin had to hold fire, because he was afraid of hitting Vredenburgh or Daniels. He watched as Daniels put his knee on the bed and reached over to Kinge to grab the barrel of his gun.

A thought flashed through Daniels' mind. He's lured us in here. Kinge is staging a suicide, thinking we might relax enough for him to take us out or, at least, do enough damage so he could get out. Kinge knew the police officers wouldn't shoot him in the back.

"It's all over," Daniels yelled. "Just give me the gun and things will be okay."

Daniels reached for the gun. Kinge whirled around and fired. He had reduced the trigger pull on his weapon which, along with the jerkiness from being excited, caused the gun to go off on the side of his face. Vredenburgh, who was on his knees, came up and hit the suspect with three shots fired in rapid succession.

Once Kinge was hit, he kept turning, turning toward the officers, getting up to a standing position and staying upright after he was hit several times.

Martin intently watched the suspect. Everything seemed to churn in slow motion. He wondered how Kinge could still be erect after being hit with a shotgun. He expected him to fly against the wall, but instead Martin saw him falling backward, two holes in Kinge's T-shirt. "Maybe he's got a bullet proof vest on," Martin mumbled. When Kinge's gun dropped out of his hand, Martin saw a rifle barrel leaning up against the wall behind Kinge. He's not really hurt, thought Martin. He's going to fall down and grab that rifle. Martin followed Kinge with his gun and when Martin could clear Daniels and Vredenburgh from his firing path, he shot one round at Kinge's head. He missed and something plastic flew up in the air. Almost simultaneously, Daniels shot Kinge in the chest. Kinge spun completely around and fell backward on the floor. Nine shots had been fired in a matter of seconds. Suddenly the room was silent. Then Martin heard a shot downstairs. It sounded like a cannon going off.

Doug Vredenburgh slumped over at the end of the bed. For a second Daniels had the terrible thought that his best friend had been hurt by the plan he'd put together. Then Vredenburgh got up and smiled.

"My God, Doug. You scared the hell out of me," Daniels said. Vredenburgh laughed, "I was just taking a deep breath."

"Next time, talk to me first, will ya? Don't ever do that to me again."

Turning to the others, Daniels shouted, "Cease fire." He and Vredenburgh checked Kinge's body. "He's dead." For several moments, the officers stared at the body of Tony Kinge, the man who had caused so much tragedy.

Then they had the rest of their plan to carry out. Vredenburgh stayed with Kinge. The others searched rooms, closets, and hallways for the baby and to make sure there was no one else hiding anywhere.

Meanwhile, Gary Gelinger and Joe Brainard had been securing the first floor. Gelinger noticed steam coming from a mug of coffee on the table to the left of the front door. Next to it was a police scanner and a list of police frequencies. From nowhere, the Doberman came toward him, snarling and barking. Gelinger couldn't get past the dog to check the back room. Gelinger shouted to his partner: "I'm gonna have to shoot the dog. I can't get around him."

"Do what you have to do," Brainard yelled.

Gelinger fired his .357 magnum revolver at the dog. The first shot missed him. The dog kept growling and coming towards him. He fired two more rounds and the dog went down. Gelinger walked over and fired one more shot to make sure the animal was dead. The Doberman lay on the floor in the middle of the back room. Gelinger surveyed the room quickly, noticing a dusty professional-looking drill press, a grimy bicycle and some dirty kerosene cans. "God, this place is filthy," he murmured.

"All secure," Brainard yelled from upstairs.

Daniels radioed next door, "Are you secure?"

"We've got our subject in custody," he was told.

Daniels then radioed McElligott. "They can move the cars in now." He didn't tell McElligott their suspect was dead.

At headquarters, Kelly began his questioning again after giving another pack of cigarettes to Joanna. She still refused offers of food and coffee. A few minutes later, an investigator knocked on the door and asked Courtright to step outside. He went into the hallway and learned that the first information he'd received about the entries was wrong. Michael Kinge had been fatally shot in the raid.

"Jesus, now I've got to go in and tell her that news," Courtright said morosely.

He felt very badly about the situation, not only because their prime suspect could never talk, but also because Courtright would have to retract his first statement. Besides making him feel like a fool, changing what he had said might lessen their credibility in Joanna's eyes and Courtright hated to tell her that the man she'd lived with, the father of her child, had been killed in a gun battle with police. No matter what Kinge had been like, it was a painful message to bring. A wave of sympathy went over him for this frail, pathetic young woman.

He took Joanna's hand and said quietly, "I have bad news for you." She crumpled up in the chair as if accepting a blow. "The first information I received about Tony was incorrect. He's been shot in the raid." Courtright tried to explain that Tony had a gun pointed at the officers and refused to lay down his weapon, so the police had no choice.

Joanna became hysterical. She rocked back and forth sobbing and between rapid, short breaths of air she uttered pathetic-sounding squeals. Kelly brought her a glass of water and put a box of tissues on the table. Courtright held her hand while she cried.

"What about my baby? Is he okay?" she finally blurted out.

They assured her that Jimmy was safe.

"When can I see him? I've gotta have my baby," she pleaded.

Courtright told her he wasn't sure if she'd be free that day or not. It depended on what she had to tell them. Slowly she began to calm down. Kelly brought her a can of soda and Courtright asked her to tell them about Tony. He could tell that Joanna wasn't convinced Tony was dead.

She said Tony couldn't find work and that she had to support them most of the time.

"Why won't you let me go, now that Tony's been shot?" she asked.

Courtright looked her directly in the eyes, his voice hardened, "Because you haven't told us the truth yet about Tony and the Harris murders. You know a lot more than you've told us, so we'll sit here all day and night until you stop lying and tell us the truth about what happened on December 22."

It was clear to the police that Joanna was frightened to death over the thought of being arrested. Courtright kept telling her that what would happen to her depended on what she told them. "Ultimately it will be up to the district attorney." The officers couldn't say if charges would be brought against her because they knew so little about her at that point.

Piece by piece, through persistent questioning over several hours, they got Joanna to tell them what happened on Friday afternoon, December 22, and the following morning. According to Joanna she drove Tony, wearing a dark blue parka which had a hood, with his bicycle in the back of her truck, to Genung Road at about 3:30 P.M. She described the route they took, but said she didn't know the name of the road where she dropped him off. Tony told her he was going to "work." He carried a knapsack, which usually had a gun in it, since he always wanted to protect himself.

Around 7:00 A.M. the next morning, Tony arrived at Ithacare, Joanna's workplace. He wanted keys to the truck so he could wait inside until she got off work at 7:30 A.M. The bicycle was in the back of the truck when she came out. She related how they went by the banks on Triphammer Road and the Pyramid Mall before driving home. When Courtright asked about the credit cards, Joanna said she noticed them on the kitchen table that morning. One card had Warren Harris's name on it. She heard the early news on the radio that night about the Harris family being murdered. Later on that night,

Tony brought in a VCR, a television and a pair of sneakers and said he'd gone Christmas shopping with his mother. Joanna said she was afraid to ask Tony about the murders.

As she talked to Kelly and Courtright, Joanna repeated several times that Tony had threatened her about going to the cops. He said he'd kill her if she said anything about the Harris murders to anyone. According to Joanna, after the cops spoke to Tony through the window of their apartment, asking if he'd seen anything strange going on along Etna Road the night of the Harris murders, he made her telephone the state police from work and tell them that she knew Tony was home baby-sitting on December 22. The investigators asked if Tony had ever been physically abusive to her. She said he hadn't, but he was constantly threatening her.

Courtright and Kelly were writing on their yellow pads when they weren't asking questions. Joanna's hands trembled as she chain-smoked. She was fidgety, sitting on the edge of the seat and moving back again, crossing her legs, first one way and then another. She took sips from a soda but still said she didn't want anything to eat although there were donuts on the table and Kelly had brought in a bag of chips. At this point, Joanna was giving them information and repeating whatever they asked for. Finally, she seemed to accept the fact that Tony was dead. Now she began cooperating with her interrogators, probably hoping this would get her released sooner.

Later in the afternoon the two investigators had Joanna direct them along the exact route she and Tony had taken from their Etna Road apartment to Genung Road on December 22. Kelly wrote down notes as Courtright drove.

When they returned to the barracks, a six-page statement was typed out, including the portion that verified Joanna had been advised of her Miranda rights after the officers picked her up at Ithacare that morning. After reading the document, Joanna placed her initials beside the rights statement and signed the paper.

Courtright excused himself and went to find David McElligott. He was at his desk and Courtright gave him the gist of Joanna's statement. The two agreed that she'd provided important details to nail Michael Kinge as the Harrises' killer. McElligott was satisfied that Joanna's peripheral role in the crimes did not warrant holding her at the time. The two men went back to tell Joanna she would be released. For the first time she gave a wan smile.

It was dark by the time investigators drove Joanna to her parents' home on Hanshaw Road. They told her to contact social services the following day to get her little son back.

Eighteen

In Custody

Don Vredenburgh joined the state police in 1966, followed by his brother, Doug. Don had been an investigator since 1974, first with the VFW squad (Violent Felony Warrant) and now attached to the narcotics unit out of Binghamton. Art Daniels liked the way Don handled himself in tense situations. He could rely on Vredenburgh to stay cool and not make mistakes. Don also had years of experience doing forced entries.

A tall man to begin with, Don's broad chest and thick neck made him seem even larger. He resembled a bodybuilder, and his hands were huge. Like many of his buddies in the undercover unit, Don kept his hair nearly shoulder length, had a mustache, and constantly wore old jeans and sneakers. Only the clear-rimmed glasses which showed his gentle brown eyes detracted from his tough-man image.

While Daniels' team went in for Tony, Vredenburgh's team planned to go through the back door. They wanted the shortest route to Shirley Kinge's upstairs apartment. The team knew that the layout of her side of the duplex was the reverse of Tony's. They expected Mrs. Kinge to be sleeping and by going in the back door, they had only two or three steps to the staircase.

As soon as the van with Don Vredenburgh's team pulled up in front of the Kinge house to the left of the other van, the men rushed out and ran to the back of the building. They followed their driver, Dave Beers, who was assigned the job of positioning himself at the rear door to prevent any escapes. The idea was to hit so quickly that no one inside would have a chance to do anything. Each man had a specific assignment. Vredenburgh tried the outer storm door to see if it was locked. It was, so his partner behind him, Joe Carmody, with a halligan tool, knocked the glass out. The force broke the lock and the door flew open. Vredenburgh slammed the inner door with his right shoulder and it sprung open. This time they didn't need the ram.

The rest of the team began clearing out the downstairs. There were boxes all over the floor, which the officers had to climb over or push away to conduct their search. Nothing unusual turned up. They unlocked the front door for other investigators to enter as soon as the place was secure.

They had borrowed vests, knowing that Michael Kinge had a .22 caliber gun that shot small bullets, which could go through their ordinary protective vests.

The weight of the 30-pound flak vest on Vredenburgh slowed him down a little as he took the first steps up the staircase. At the top, Vredenburgh spotted Shirley's Doberman. He roared coming up the last few steps, yelling "police" all the way. Following behind Vredenburgh Crosier saw the baby sleeping in the room next to Shirley's. He alerted trooper Charlene Hippensteil, who had been waiting outside, because they knew a female officer would be needed to take care of the female suspect. As the trooper rushed to get inside the front door, Hippensteil slipped on the ice-covered steps, spraining her wrist as she tried to brace against falling. The trooper got up quickly and almost missed a step as she ran inside and up the stairs. Eisenberg's team, there to take care of the baby, followed Hippensteil into the duplex. They all headed up to the room where the baby was.

Meanwhile Vredenburgh kept his eyes on the dog, which turned as soon as it saw Vredenburgh and scooted into Shirley's bedroom to the immediate right of the stairs. Vredenburgh followed the animal into the bedroom, pointing his handgun at the dog and then at Shirley, who sat up in bed, shocked at what was happening.

"Police! Police! Stay where you are! Show me your hands! We have a search warrant," Vredenburgh yelled. He had a very deep voice and when he raised it, the sound resonated off the walls.

"Don't kill the baby," Shirley screamed.

"We aren't gonna harm the baby," Vredenburgh added.

Shirley had the covers pulled up to her neck. Vredenburgh shouted again, "Show me your hands!" He moved toward her, still pointing his gun at her body.

"State Police," Vredenburgh shouted.

He knew who Shirley Kinge was, having seen many surveillance photographs of her. But Vredenburgh had to ask. He never forgot the time he asked a suspect, "Are you Mike?" and he said yes but turned out to be the wrong Mike.

When she answered that it was her name, Shirley Kinge dropped the covers, and put her hands up. Vredenburgh stood beside her. He saw that she just had panties on, but he paid no attention. Pulling back the covers, Vredenburgh rummaged inside the bed to see if she had any weapons. There weren't any. "You can put the covers back up," he said. She didn't ask him any questions.

Croiser, who was also in the room, watched the dog. Though the animal wasn't growling and didn't appear to be vicious, Croiser knew the reputation of Dobermans. He wanted to get the dog out of there. Croiser then told Shirley to put some clothes on. She got out of bed and wrapped a blanket around her body. Then she helped the officers usher the dog into the bathroom across the hallway. Afterward, Shirley got back in bed.

Trooper Hippensteil came into the room and asked Shirley Kinge where her clothes were. Shirley pointed to a chair. Hippensteil lifted the slacks and sweatshirt, felt for pockets, shook the garments, and then told her to dress. Croiser turned his back to the suspect as he stood in the doorway. Vredenburgh made a quick run through the rest of the upstairs and saw that Joe Carmody had found Sallie Reese in the bedroom that faced the front of the house.

Carmody had turned left at the top of the stairs as Vredenburgh and Croiser went to the right. He found Sallie Reese in a room a step or two from the stairs. She was in bed.

"Police!" he shouted.

"What's this all about?" Sallie asked, pulling the blankets tightly around her neck.

"Get up and get dressed. You have to come with us," Carmody told Reese. Standing at the foot of the bed, he showed her his identification.

Reese, who was nude, got out of bed and tried to hold the blanket as she walked over to a closet. Carmody turned his back while she dressed and then escorted her downstairs where he turned the woman over to Investigator Charlie Porter.

It had only been about 10 minutes but seemed much longer as McElligott sat in his car, waiting to hear the all-clear signal. His window was down and he felt the cold winter air sting his face. He worried that he might have sent his team to their death. Smoking cigarette after cigarette he stared at the trooper standing a few feet away at the intersection of Etna and Hanshaw Roads. The trooper rocked back on his heels and came down again. "He hears a gunshot," McElligott murmured. He remembered seeing servicemen at military funerals go back on their heels in unison when the guns went off. Maybe it's instinctive, McElligott mused, like dogs who seek cover before the storm hits, sensing the approaching thunder and lightning.

Daniels radioed to have the cars move in. McElligott turned the key and started the motor. Getting out of his car he saw Daniels taking off his vest. McElligott hadn't expected to see anyone.

"Why aren't you with Kinge?" McElligott asked.

"We had to shoot him, boss. It was us or him."

Conflicting thoughts rushed through McElligott's mind. *My God, how's it going to come out? Was the shooting absolutely justified?* If not, he'd be in a hell of a lot of trouble. For two days McElligott had been reviewing what to say and what not to say to Michael Kinge when he interrogated him. Now relief mixed with disappointment. McElligott clenched his teeth. They'd never know what really happened that night at the Harrises.

Daniels escorted McElligott up to the second floor where Kinge lay on the floor face-up. At first, McElligott didn't see his weapon. His face reddened. Then Daniels pointed to the shotgun on the floor above the victim's head. McElligott sighed heavily, he was glad to see it.

After they told McElligott what happened during the raid, he realized that one of his men could just as easily be lying on the floor as Kinge. If any one of them had been shot, McElligott would feel responsible and probably never forgive himself.

Knowing all they'd been through, McElligott wanted to get the entry team back to the barracks immediately for a debriefing session.

Meanwhile, with only the baby on his mind, Eisenberg ignored the commotion going on and headed for the room where the crib was. Going over to it he wrapped the little boy in a blue and white blanket that lay in the bed, then lifted him. The baby snuggled against Eisenberg. The social workers opened drawers, looking for baby clothes and diapers to take with them. In less than ten minutes, the baby was inside their car and headed for the Ithaca barracks.

Karl Chandler came in the front door as Don Vredenburgh was handcuffing Shirley, standing by the staircase. Chandler looked at Shirley, spoke a word or two to Vredenburgh and Hippensteil, then muttered, "Let's go." There was plenty of work ahead of them and Chandler didn't like to waste time. He also wanted to get out of there before the media swarmed in. Vredenburgh and Hippensteil were on either side of Shirley as they walked from the house to the unmarked car, a four-door maroon Buick, parked in front. Hippensteil got in the back with Shirley, Chandler entered the driver's side with Vredenburgh next to him in the front seat.

As they began the drive to the Cortland station where the officers planned to question the suspects, McElligott was in his own car driving some of his team back. He was reviewing in his mind what to say in the debriefing session. He'd remember, he promised himself, to tell the team he was proud that they had solved the crime in forty-seven days. And he would keep his disappointment to himself at having a dead suspect.

Major Farrand stayed at the scene to talk with the district attorney, who arrived a few minutes later. As the men who were on the raid detail rode back to the station in the vans, their moods were mixed—still keyed up from the entries but feeling relieved it was over. On the way back to the barracks the officers who hit the Shirley Kinge side, found out their prime suspect, Michael Kinge, had been killed. They'd been in the same building, but they were so focused on their individual assignments that they hadn't heard the shots fired next door.

* * *

Karl Chandler's car arrived in Cortland at 7:45 A.M. He watched Vredenburgh and Hippensteil escort the handcuffed Shirley Kinge into the station and turn her over to Chandler and Investigator George Clum. Clum removed Kinge's handcuffs and took her into one of the offices where they planned to interview her. "Please take a chair across from the desk that Chandler is sitting behind," he said to Kinge.

Chandler asked, "Would you like some coffee?" Kinge shook her head. "We've a lot to ask you," he went on, but first he recited the Miranda warnings. Kinge looked away from him. When she turned back her face showed no emotion. She asked for a cigarette.

"We've been investigating the Harris homicide for weeks now and from what we've turned up, you are a suspect, Mrs. Kinge," Chandler began, handing her a pack of cigarettes. "We want some answers from you about what you did on December 22 and 23."

Shirley didn't say a word.

Chandler asked again: "What can you tell us about what happened during the time when the Harris family was murdered? We have a lot of information, Mrs. Kinge, that points the finger at you as a suspect."

"Where is Tony? Has he been arrested?" she asked

"We want to know from you, Mrs. Kinge, what happened December 22 and 23."

Shirley bent her head down and said all she knew about the Harris murders was what she read in the paper or saw on television.

"I had nothing to do with it," she said in a barely audible voice. As she raised her head up, her eyes had a stony glaze that didn't seem to be focused on anything in the room.

"We have reason to believe that you're heavily involved, Mrs. Kinge, in those brutal murders. We want some answers," Chandler kept pressing.

Both investigators had notepads in front of them. Clum

had started writing as soon as the questioning began. It had been planned that Chandler would do all the questioning. Clum was to get everything of importance down on paper.

"What's happened to Tony? Where is he?" Shirley asked again.

Chandler reasoned that she was probably scared of her son, thinking about what he'd do to her if she told anything. Nevertheless, he decided not to reveal that Michael Kinge was dead right away. In court it might appear that he was using the news as a shock device to get her to talk.

"We're interested in your role in this thing, Mrs. Kinge," Chandler said, avoiding the topic of her son.

"I don't know anything about it," she insisted.

"Where were you on the night of December 22, Mrs. Kinge?"

Shirley stared into space and said she was home all night.

They weren't getting anywhere. Chandler figured she had decided not to talk, believing that the police had nothing against her as well as fearing her son.

Because of this, Chandler began outlining the investigation to her. He mentioned the people they'd talked to who had led them to both suspects. They told her how handwriting from The Peregrine House receipts had been compared to the Harris Visa card receipts used on December 23 after the Harrises were dead.

"I have documentation that you were the person who used the Harris credit card, Shirley," Chandler said, a steel edge to his voice.

Chandler stared at her. He couldn't tell if her eyes were open or closed. She had big shaded lenses on her glasses.

"You're not going to sleep on me, are you Shirley?"

She didn't answer him.

Chandler asked Hippensteil to take the suspect to the ladies room. She refused all offers of food. They were drinking coffee in Styrofoam cups. They asked her again if she'd like some coffee and when there was a pause in the questioning, Clum left the room for refills. No, she didn't want any coffee, Shirley told them. She just wanted cigarettes. He bought her a pack of cigarettes and asked someone to go out for donuts.

Shirley told them that Tony said he'd kill himself before he'd let the cops take him.

Then Chandler pressed her again on what she knew about the night of the murder and the next day. He repeated that they had the goods on her. She asked him again about her son. Chandler looked at his watch. It was 9:50 A.M. They had been questioning Shirley for nearly two hours. Chandler was weary of getting nowhere with her. Maybe the news would change her outlook. He told Kinge, "Your son Tony is dead."

She let out a loud cry and slumped to the floor in front of her chair, continuing to wail as she dropped her head down and reared it back up again.

Her cries of grief resounded through the building. Vredenburgh and Hippensteil, who were at the opposite end of the station to the interviewing room, heard them. Clum stuck his head out of the door and called for Hippensteil. When Shirley stopped wailing the room became silent.

Shirley didn't ask Chandler any questions about how Tony died. Earlier she'd mentioned that Tony said he'd kill himself before he'd let the cops take him. She may think he committed suicide, Chandler thought. She asked if she could see the body. Chandler told her no. It went through his mind that she might think they were playing a trick on her, that Tony really was not dead and that they were using the ploy to get her to talk. She seemed afraid of her son and what might happen to her if she told the cops anything she knew.

Shirley's face was swollen from crying. She began taking great wrenching breaths. Hippensteil brought her a Styrofoam cup of cold water and when the trooper couldn't find any tissues in the station, she grabbed wads of toilet paper from the bathroom, bringing them to Shirley to wipe her face. Hippensteil knelt down and put the cup of water to the woman's mouth. Then the trooper helped Shirley off the floor and into the chair. A moment later, Shirley pointed to the cup and Hippensteil gave her more water.

"He's dead?" Shirley asked hoarsely.

"Yes," was the reply.

"Michael was a beautiful child until he turned fifteen—when he became a monster," Shirley said in a monotone.

Hippensteil escorted Kinge to the ladies room to calm down. While Shirley was out of the room, Chandler took a long drag on his cigarette. He thought of the way the suspect showed her grief—crying a lot, but without actual tears. It might just be a good act. She might be planning how she's going to save her skin. She can blame everything now on a dead man.

Hippensteil returned Shirley Kinge to the room, and Chandler began his questioning again. "We want to know what you did on December 22 and 23." He leaned over the desk with his arms crossed and glared at Shirley, who sat across from him.

At this point, Shirley seemed relieved and began to talk.

According to the investigators, Shirley told them she was home all day December 22, maybe she went out to the store, but that's all. Joanna had asked her to watch the baby all night, which she did. Shirley told Chandler and Clum that she didn't know if Tony was home that day or night. She didn't see him. Joanna came in to get the baby about 7:30 or 8:15 Saturday morning. The first time she saw Tony was late that afternoon when he came over and asked her to go Christmas shopping with him. Shirley said she didn't want to go, she hated shopping, but Tony said he'd buy the gas. They went to Marine Midland Bank on Triphammer Road, where the machine ate Tony's card while he tried to get cash. Tony told her that the card had his prints on it and if the police found out, he'd be in trouble. Shirley told him that the bank would probably just mail the card back, but Tony said that she just didn't understand. When they got to the Auburn mall, she explained that Tony handed her a credit card and said use it. He gave her an address and phone number to go with the card. Tony said he'd gotten the card from a guy near the Commons.

Chandler asked how she used the credit card. Shirley went through the purchases she made in Auburn and at the Camillus mall: the white Reebok sneakers, the $400 diamond stud earrings and two sweaters.

"Where are the sneakers and earrings now?" Chandler asked.

"The sneakers are at home and I threw the earrings away."

"Why did you throw the earrings out but not the sneakers?"

"I figured anybody could have sneakers."

"What did you do with the sweaters?"

"I gave those to my mother."

"Is that all you purchased with the Harris credit cards?"

She nodded. "That's all I got."

"Our investigation shows that two bras and six pairs of ladies underpants were bought with the Harris credit card at Hess's Department Store in the Camillus Mall," Chandler said.

"No, I didn't buy those things," Shirley replied.

They asked what she did when they got home from shopping. "I fed the dog and took her out." Shirley paused. "Then my mother told me some people in Dryden had been killed. I asked what their names were and she said Harris. That's when I made the connection."

"What connection?" asked Chandler.

"That Tony had been out there."

"I told Tony the next day why didn't he tell me. He said he knew I'd react this way."

"What way were you reacting?"

"Outraged."

"Did you ask him why he went way out to Ellis Hollow Road to the Harrises?"

"I asked him how he got onto these people, but he never answered me. I asked why he did it and why he got me involved. He never gave an answer. He said I didn't know those people, so why should I care? He just looked at me."

"What weapons did you know Tony to have?"

"I don't know if he had any," she said quietly.

"What did he tell you he'd do if police came?"

"He said he'd kill himself."

"Did you ask him why he went back and burned the bodies?"

"He said he burned the bodies to destroy whatever evidence he may have left behind."

"Did you ask him why he killed them?"

"Yes, and he said he'd done it so they couldn't identify him. He went to rob them. He said if any of us went to the police, we could just forget it. I said why don't you come over here and blow me away while I'm sleeping."

"Did you take him seriously? Did you think he'd kill you and the others?"

"No, I didn't think he would've harmed me. But after the cops came to the door, I asked him if he wanted me to keep the baby, and he said, no, the baby might offer some kind of protection."

These were all oral admissions. The investigators had to get them down in a typed statement. They called Hippensteil in to escort Shirley to the restroom. Someone brought in some sandwiches, and a few of the donuts that Chandler and Clum had been eating were still in a box on the table. Shirley just drank coffee and smoked.

From 11:10 A.M. to 1:55 P.M. Chandler typed out a statement in question and answer form. His document began by saying that Shirley Kinge had been advised of her Miranda rights. The investigator commented that Shirley never asked for a lawyer during questioning nor did she exercise her right to remain silent.

When the six-page statement was completed, Shirley said

she couldn't sign it, because she didn't have her reading glasses. She had to read the statement first. Chandler left the room to call the Ithaca station to arrange for her glasses to be delivered to Cortland. Meanwhile, Shirley asked Clum about David Savage. Clum said he didn't know any David Savage (Clum had not been a party to any of the planning of the undercover work). Shirley told Clum that David Savage was probably the cop who knew her from The Peregrine House and framed her. She said she'd been followed for days by a yellow Cadillac.

While they waited, Hippensteil read the document to Shirley. Chandler asked Kinge if it was accurate. She said that it was.

Still waiting for Shirley's glasses to arrive, Chandler started to question her with more intensity. He asked her about being at the Harris crime scene and her possible responsibility in the homicide or in helping to start the fire. Chandler told the woman that she had been sighted in the Harris family van on Ellis Hollow Road a few minutes after the fire alarm went off.

"I wasn't ever in that house or on that property. That was Tony's mess," Shirley kept repeating.

"Shirley, we've gotten your fingerprints off a gasoline can found inside the house," Chandler told her.

"I was never in that house, I tell you."

"Shirley, there is no explanation for the prints on the gas can. It says to us that you had to be there and, in fact, were a party to setting the fire."

Shirley stared into space over Chandler's head and took another drag on her cigarette.

Chandler was becoming more agitated. "For Christ's sake, Shirley. We've had four people brutally murdered inside their home. What in the hell do you think you're doing sitting here and telling me lies? I know you were in that house." Chandler couldn't hold back any longer. He wondered why she didn't confess since they had her fingerprints.

"Well, if my prints are on the can, it's because I borrowed a can from a neighbor across the street one time when Jo had run out of gas and possibly Tony took that can to the scene to burn the house down."

"What kind of gasoline cans do you own, Shirley? Describe them to me," Chandler said.

She began to describe two 5-gallon cans she said were hers.

"What kind of can did you borrow from your neighbor?"

Shirley described it as a two and a half gallon can that was red, rectangular in shape and had "gasoline" written, possibly at an angle, across the can.

"Was there anything else about the can that you remember?"

"Yeah. It had a spout on it."

"Do you know of any other gas cans you may have handled?"

"No, none," she said.

Chandler typed in her responses about the gas cans.

By that time her reading glasses arrived. Chandler handed her the statement again.

"No, I won't sign," she said.

"You said it was accurate, Shirley."

She glared at him and said, "no."

It went through Chandler's mind that it might have dawned on Shirley that police could easily check out her story with the neighbor and find out if the neighbor's gasoline can matched Shirley's description of it.

After Shirley refused to sign, a tired and fed up Chandler got out of his chair and said: "Okay, that's it. We're going to Syracuse for the lineup."

David McElligott planned that Ted Palmer would head up the team to organize a lineup in Syracuse's public safety building on South State Street. He hoped that some of the clerks who waited on Shirley Kinge in the Auburn and Camillus malls would recognize her and give a positive identification that could be used in court. A couple of investigators called the witnesses during the morning and arranged for them to be picked up and taken to the Syracuse facility in the early afternoon. They also made arrangements for Professor Stuphin to be driven up from Ithaca to view the lineup.

Arriving in Syracuse, Palmer had to move fast since he didn't know how long Chandler would take questioning the suspect in Cortland. He had to find at least five black females similar in size and age to Shirley Kinge to stand in the lineup with her. A corrections officer escorted him downstairs to the women's jail. He walked through the halls, searching the cells for possible look-alikes. The black women in the jail were much younger than their suspect. He picked out two inmates he thought were close enough to use. The officer asked the women if they'd stand in the lineup (the reward was an extra phone call that day) and both agreed. Now Palmer had to round up three more black females. He discussed with the officer other means of finding the women. It was suggested that he might have to go out on the street and approach the public. Palmer didn't like that idea since he knew McElligott wanted to keep what they were doing low-key and out of the public eye.

Palmer decided on an unorthodox approach. He combed the offices in the building and found a secretary on the third floor who seemed close to Shirley Kinge's age and build. He didn't like doing it, but he approached the woman. In his calm, matter-of-fact voice he explained the unusual situation and asked for her cooperation. She agreed to help. Then he was informed that the two inmates he had just picked out in the jail had been bailed and released. Which meant he needed four females again and time was running short. Palmer asked the local authorities for help; they came through. Several black female officers from local law enforcement agencies agreed to be in the lineup.

McElligott saw that the entry team members were de-briefed separately and statements written up. He had to make sure the raid was thoroughly documented to satisfy legal questions and the skeptics. It was clear to him the team had no choice in the shoot-out with someone like Michael Kinge, who hated cops and had vowed he wouldn't be taken in.

The ballistics expert from Albany arrived and conducted a test on the weapons found in Michael Kinge's apartment to determine the Harris murder weapon. They had found a sawed-off Charter Arms rifle in the upstairs closet, a sawed-off .20 gauge pump shotgun and the sawed-off shotgun he had fired during the raid. All the guns were fully loaded. McElligott couldn't help thinking. You don't need more than one bullet to blow your head off. You certainly don't need an arsenal.

However, the ballistics expert Henry Miller was not known for hurrying. It would take time to do the analysis work, he first told McElligott. But someone must have pressured Miller because a few hours later on the seventh, he returned to the laboratory in Albany and phoned McElligott. He said the Charter Arms was the murder weapon. When Miller fired a bullet out of the Charter Arms gun, the same grooves and scraping marks matched the bullet fragments that had been extracted from all of the Harris bodies.

McElligott added Miller's records together with what they already had: a black Nasbar bicycle, cords, ropes and laces matching ropes and laces taken from the crime scene, along with burglar tools, materials to make silencers, and magazines on how to make weapons had all been found in Michael Kinge's apartment. The TV and VCR bought with the Harris credit cards were there. McElligott was sure they had gotten the killer. And he had the evidence to prove it.

Don Vredenburgh and Charlene Hippensteil drove Shirley to Syracuse's public safety building. They left Cortland at 3:00 P.M. and arrived there thirty minutes later. Shirley asked to smoke in the car, but the officers said no. Those were the only words she said during the trip. In fact, the only thing Vredenburgh heard Shirley Kinge request since he arrested her that morning was could she have a cigarette.

Hippensteil immediately took Shirley downstairs, where she changed into dark blue jail coveralls, the inmates' uniform and what all the women wore for the lineup. There was a number on the wall above the head of each female for identification purposes (suspects are allowed to choose their own numbers in the interest of fairness since the courts look at the lineup procedure as a highly appealable issue). The suspects were told to look straight ahead at the one-way mirror that extended from the ceiling to the floor. The witnesses viewed the lineup in a room behind the mirror. Palmer discovered after it was too late that the number Shirley Kinge chose for the lineup was the same number the investigators had arbitrarily assigned her on the photograph sheet of possible suspects drawn up two weeks earlier. He hoped the coincidence wouldn't cause them trouble in the courtroom.

The witnesses were kept in a room and given instructions not to talk about the case as they waited to view the lineup. Some women were nervous and others grew tired of waiting. One witness was worried about her child arriving home on the school bus before she got home. Palmer brought in whatever soda they requested and a bag of potato chips. He had to keep them relatively happy, so they wouldn't get disgusted and leave.

Palmer escorted one witness at a time into the viewing room. He started at one end of the lineup of six women and asked each woman to step forward as her number was called. Deborah Mannise from the 16 Plus store at the Camillus Mall was the first to see the five women in the lineup. Mannise told the investigators when they first interviewed her that she couldn't remember anything about the two-sweater transaction on December 23 that was charged on Dolores Harris's Visa card. But the police still had to try and see if she might recognize Kinge in a lineup. Mannise looked at all the women carefully for a minute or two. "I'm not able to identify anyone," she said.

They brought out Malinda Ouderkirk, a salesperson in the Lingerie Department at Hess's Department Store at the Camillus Mall. Ouderkirk recalled waiting on a person she described as a middle-aged black woman the evening of December 23. Business had been slow that night so she helped the customer pick out some bras and underpants that were on sale. The woman, Ouderkirk had said, charged the items on a Visa card, with the signature of Dolores Harris. Ouderkirk took less than a minute to view the lineup. Then she pointed to Shirley Kinge and made a positive identification.

Kathleen Wood, who was working at Reed's Jewelry Store on December 23, remembered a black woman buying $400 diamond stud earrings. Wood worked with investigators to help create a drawing of the customer's face. On two occasions they showed her mugshots. She looked at hundreds of black females without picking out anyone. On February 4 when she was shown a photograph sheet of suspects, Wood tentatively identified Shirley Kinge.

Now Wood studied the women in the lineup. She pointed out Kinge, but said she couldn't be certain, because the suspect had her eyes closed. When it was Professor Stuphin's turn he said he couldn't identify anyone because he wasn't sure. Palmer knew that for various reasons some people have trouble pointing the finger at anyone even if they have strong opinions. The lineup had produced one positive identification and a tentative one.

Vredenburgh and Hippensteil left Syracuse with Shirley Kinge at 4:30 P.M. and arrived in Ithaca at 5:35 P.M. Television cameras and reporters gathered in the police barracks parking lot. As soon as the officer's car stopped, the media swarmed around the vehicle, shouting questions. Shirley protested, saying she didn't want to be seen.

"Put your jacket over your head," Hippensteil told Shirley.

"We'll take you in and escort you into the back entrance." It was only a few feet away. Kinge was led into the Zone Sergeant's office where a Secret Service agent asked her to complete handwriting samples. Then she was fingerprinted and photographed.

Nineteen
The Lineup

George Dentes looked like a high school science teacher. From a distance his bald crown and rimless glasses made him appear older than he was. Up close his youthful face was fair and unblemished, a sort of face that gave the impression of living by the rules. A man you could trust. A Scout Master.

Dentes was born in Ithaca of Greek parents: his mother was a teacher and second-generation Greek while his father immigrated from Greece as a young teenager, living first in Elmira, and after serving in the armed forces in World War II came to Ithaca where he moved up from selling roasted nuts from a cart to owning his own tavern downtown. Dentes graduated from Ithaca High School a decade after Bill Sullivan. His technical background (an engineering degree) led him to specialize in patent law with a New York City firm after he finished Cornell University Law School. But Dentes found patent law too dull. The work of a public prosecutor appealed to him, because he liked trial work and wanted to do some kind of public service. In 1981, Dentes was hired as an assistant district attorney in Manhattan, where he carved out a reputation.

When he prosecuted cases, Dentes was a man who knew the facts thoroughly and worked out his strategy from beginning to end, so that when he faced the jury he spoke with confidence and conviction.

Although Dentes had only been a prosecutor in Ithaca a little over a month he knew he had the chance to make or break his reputation with this case. It was the type of major assignment most D.A.'s never see.

Dentes was keenly aware of the community's outrage over the Harrises' brutal murders and while he wouldn't use the term "revenge," he knew the public wanted to see action taken and justice done.

The D.A. called Dryden's Town Court Justice, Ed Sweetland, at noon to tell him they had a suspect in custody for the Harris murders and ask if he could be ready for an arraignment later that day. Dentes wasn't sure how long it would take for investigators to question Shirley Kinge. He told Sweetland the best prediction was that they would be in Dryden between 4:00 and 8:00 P.M.

Dentes had already written pages of charges against the Kinges and background information about them on the personal computer in his office. Although he had been on the job as district attorney only a little over a month, Dentes was prepared for the Kinge arraignment. McElligott had kept him informed every step of the way, talking with him on the phone or in person every day.

At one o'clock, after Major Farrand informed Dentes about the forced entry proceedings that morning on Etna Road, Thomas Constantine, New York State Police Superintendent, arrived from Albany. They set up a press conference in a garage behind the Varna barracks. Over sixty media representatives, including twelve television crews, jammed the room to hear details about the shoot-out and arrest. Six officials sat behind microphones at the front of the makeshift conference room: New York State Police Superintendent Constantine; District Attorney George Dentes; Major Farrand, acting commander of Troop C; Ithaca Police Chief Harlin McEwen; Captain Carl Shaver of Troop C's Bureau of Criminal Investigation; and Wayne Alford, special agent in charge of the FBI Albany division. McElligott was asked to attend the conference but declined. He wanted to be in on the action not the talk.

Constantine began by reading from a prepared statement in which he gave a condensed version of the case from the time the Harris family was found murdered to the events that occurred early that day on Etna Road. Throughout his message Constantine referred to the prime suspect as Anthony Turner (others used the name as well, stating that Turner had used various aliases). He mentioned the excellent reputation George Dentes had as a prosecutor. Robert Morgenthau, New York City's District Attorney, had told him so, and Constantine praised the entire investigative work done on the case.

Major Farrand then fielded questions from excited reporters who were shouting over each other: He said they didn't know at that point if Turner had died from the shotgun he fired or from rounds by the officers; they were still processing the scene to find the murder weapon; it was still an ongoing investigation. Farrand didn't want to comment on how long the Etna Road surveillance had been going on; he did say Shirley Kinge was being held on charges connected with the crime; her arraignment would be in Dryden sometime that day.

McElligott asked John Beno if he'd like to be the uniformed trooper to take Shirley Kinge to the arraignment. It seemed fitting that Beno, who had discovered the homicides, be involved with bringing one of the perpetrators to justice.

As Shirley Kinge was escorted from the car in the parking lot to the Town of Dryden courtroom on Main Street around 7:15 P.M., a Syracuse television reporter yelled at her. "Did you do it, Shirley? Did you do it?" There was no reply.

Beno was seated to Shirley's left with Dentes and McElligott sitting to the right of her on the courtroom bench. While they waited for the judge to appear, a reporter came in and sat behind them with his laptop computer, muttering to a colleague next to him about how he had run out of gas and after he fetched some gasoline, had spilled a lot of the fuel over himself when he was pouring it into the gas tank. Beno got a whiff of the strong odor and the hair on the back of his neck stood up. Maybe, he thought, remembering the smell of gasoline at the crime scene, that's a sign we've got the right person.

The proceedings in the court room began at 7:40 P.M. Judge Sweetland took twelve minutes to read the six pages of charges against Shirley Kinge. They included several counts of murder. Sweetland asked the defendant if she needed a court-appointed lawyer. She said, "no," her mother would get an attorney to represent her.

In consultation with the district attorney, Sweetland set a preliminary hearing to be conducted the following week, on February 13 at 10:00 A.M. He told the court that the charges against the defendant were severe enough to hold her in Tompkins County jail without bail (a town court cannot set bail in a murder case). The district attorney must present evidence in the hearing on, at least, one of the felony charges to continue to hold the defendant for prosecution.

As the news got around Ithaca some blacks expressed the hope that Shirley Kinge's arrest would ease tensions. A black mother on Ithaca's southside commented, "It's nice to know that the next knock on my door won't be because my son was seen in a place where people of color normally are not." Others felt differently.

One resident told a reporter, "When a white commits a crime, it's quickly forgotten, but when a black does, it lingers."

A white neighbor of the Kinges from whom Joanna and

Tony had borrowed gasoline for their truck many times, told a reporter that she thought Tony Turner was a very nice man and a good neighbor. Within a few days, the woman received threatening hate mail.

John Taylor, a man who once lived in the duplex next to Kinge (before Sallie Reese and Shirley Kinge moved there), said he was "blown away" when he heard the news. "He seemed like a law-abiding citizen to me." Taylor thought it (the murders) might have been connected to drugs.

Dave Hollenbeck from Dryden said, "They must have had an awful sense of false bravado to be staying this close to the area."

By the end of the day on February 7, Shirley Kinge was in jail; her mother, Sallie Reese, was questioned by Investigator Charlie Porter as well as Trooper Linda Brady and taken to an Ithaca emergency shelter on West Court Street for the night. The baby, Jimmy, was in foster care; Joanna White was with her parents. And Michael Kinge was dead.

Twenty

Preliminaries

Bill Sullivan said he didn't want the case. He told Bob Stolp that he was exhausted from a recent trial and needed to catch up on work in the office. Stolp, Tompkins County's Administrator for Assigned Counsel, said he wasn't having any luck getting legal representation for Shirley Kinge. He pressured Sullivan to take the case. "Otherwise," Stolp told Sullivan, "I'll have to go outside the county to make sure the defendant's legal rights are protected." Sullivan finally agreed to talk with Shirley Kinge at the Tompkins County jail. Stolp hung up the phone, feeling confident that he had his man.

Sullivan believed the county should take care of its own, and besides, he thrived on controversy in and out of the courtroom and was attracted to unpopular causes. Sullivan was known as the hot lawyer for defendants accused of serious crimes, because he fought like a tenacious bull for his clients, not giving up until the dust settled on the last day in court. When questioned about his career and how he decided to handle a particular case, Sullivan would say he was motivated to protect the rights of the innocent, something about which he felt very passionately. His biggest thrill came, he said, when an innocent person was acquitted.

Sullivan immersed himself in a case so much that he took on the defendant's cause as his own. Every last detail got his attention. He talked about a case to almost anyone who would listen and he solicited other opinions, asking attorney friends how they'd handle whatever problem he was grappling with at the moment.

The appearance of the man revealed his style. Sullivan started the day with his silvery gray hair neatly combed and by noon it was as disheveled as his rumpled business suit and tie. He was of average size, a bit overweight, but as agile as a boxer. And his ready smile showed a man who indulged in life. He often mingled with reporters as he enjoyed a hot dog from a vendor on the Commons during a lunch break from court proceedings. More than anything, he loved to talk and he was charismatic. The young journalists and television personnel loved to get him going. Personalities like Sullivan were their bread and butter.

After Sullivan graduated from Ithaca High School in 1961, he went to Notre Dame University and received his law degree from Buffalo State. Then he came home to begin his career and stayed; first as an Assistant District Attorney under Matt McHugh; then he was elected District Attorney on the Republican ticket in 1972 for a three-year term. In 1975 he lost the race to Joseph Joch, a Cornell-educated lawyer and new Ithaca resident who the Democrats put on the ballot at the last minute. After losing, Sullivan went into private practice, where he'd been ever since.

His law offices on North Aurora Street beside Casadilla Creek occupied the downstairs of the white, frame house of his childhood. It was an unpretentious setting. Little had been done to modernize the quarters. It was obvious that Sullivan was not concerned with the appearance of the place. Every room was crammed full of steel cabinets, file folders, and cartons of paper, much of it stacked on the floor. Decoration was confined to images of Abraham Lincoln: a painting of the President hung over the boarded-up fireplace in the former dining room (now the receptionist's office); bookends of a seated Abe and a sculptured face of Lincoln stood on the mantelpiece. Sullivan felt at home there as he greeted people in stocking feet and ushered them through the maze of accumulated materials to the back of the house where he had his office.

After several meetings with Shirley Kinge at the county jail, Sullivan decided to take her case. On Sunday night, the lawyer announced to the public that he would represent Shirley Kinge. At best, Sullivan told the press, the district attorney had flimsy evidence to implicate his client in the Harris murders. At worst, it was a lynch mob that had decided somebody had to pay for those brutal slayings of a nice white family. In truth, Sullivan realized that defending the mother of the man who killed the Harrises could be the biggest challenge he'd faced so far.

As the news of the Etna Road shoot-out and arrest of Shirley Kinge hit the air waves and newspapers, sighs of relief could be felt in the Ithaca area, especially in Ellis Hollow. Residents who had wondered if the police would ever solve the case now only had words of praise for the investigators. The Ellis Hollow community could now begin its emotional healing, said one resident. People expressed amazement that the killers could remain so close to the crime scene and the investigation's command post. When some locals learned who Michael Kinge and his mother were, they seemed relieved to know they were outsiders. They fit their image of criminal types immigrating to the quiet town from New York City.

Some in the black community criticized the police going in and killing the suspect. They said it looked like an assassination to them. The cops went in with revenge in mind, not justice. *Why didn't they throw in a smoke bomb to get the suspect out or use a bullhorn?* They thought it was another case of black suspects treated differently from whites.

It was reported later that police had ruled out tear gas because of the potential danger to the small child and women inside. Tear gas also could destroy crucial evidence. The police knew the suspect owned an arsenal of weapons and had vowed not to go back to prison.

Don Lake broke down and cried at his desk after McElligott called Lake at work and told him the news. When Mary Harris's daughter met her at the airport in Ft. Myers, Florida, that day, the daughter told her they'd found the killers. Mary Harris was shocked and surprised. She'd been on the verge of notifying the television program *Unsolved Mysteries* to say they could come in and start filming when investigators asked her to hold off a few days. She hadn't dreamed the police were so close to solving the crime.

Tom Constantine praised McElligott and his team for their good work. Constantine told Harding he'd done an outstanding job with the fingerprints. McElligott was proud of the team. Everyone had made a contribution. That's the way crimes were solved, but he felt that if there had been any heroes, they were the guys on the entry teams who risked their lives to bring in the suspects.

David Harding had to be elated. With Michael Kinge dead, he couldn't deny his mother was involved in the crime. It was Shirley Kinge's word against Harding's and he had proof. He had the fingerprints he claimed were lifted from the gas can found inside the Harrises' house. Harding was the only fingerprint expert on the case. Lishansky, whom Harding had trained, was his partner and Harding knew Lieutenant Harvey would believe in him.

Harding would be a hero to the district attorney and the state police before this thing was over, despite McElligott. Harding knew he hadn't scored with the boss, who seemed to distrust and question him at every turn, but he wasn't going to let McElligott spoil the sweet smell of success.

The preliminary hearing on Shirley Kinge began at 10:00 A.M. February 13 in Dryden's cramped courtroom on Main Street. The Justice, Edwin Sweetland, had been a town justice for sixteen years. Before that he had been a maintenance supervisor at Cornell's veterinary school. It was his job to decide if there was "reasonable cause to believe that a felony had been committed" and, if so, to hold the accused in jail.

A few minutes after the hearing started, Sullivan asked the judge to close the proceedings to the press and public because he was concerned that the evidence presented in the case could affect his client's ability to get a fair trial.

"It's not unusual for evidence to be presented that is illegal and prejudicial if made part of the record," Sullivan said.

George Dentes and members of the press immediately protested Sullivan's request. Someone shouted out, "That's illegal." But Sweetland decided in Sullivan's favor: He ordered the press crowd of some thirty people and about ten spectators to clear the room.

Press members and much of the public were furious, claiming it was illegal to close the courtroom. Some vowed to have their lawyers make formal complaints. A Dryden resident felt cheated when told she had to leave. Another local observer said she was mad because "we think something's being hidden." Many from the media remained outside the glass doors of the courtroom, catching tidbits of the hearing that seeped through.

The prosecution brought the three witnesses on the arson count, one of the six charges against the defendant: Trooper John Beno, who discovered the first body in the Harris home on December 23, and state police investigators Randy Stark and David Harding (Stark did not testify). Several sets of reproduced fingerprints were presented and a photograph of a gasoline can was passed around.

When Harding testified, McElligott noticed he was strangely evasive. At first Sullivan asked him routine questions, such as what year he had graduated from college. Harding said he couldn't recall. Sullivan asked Harding the date that he finished his training in identification work and again Harding replied he didn't remember.

McElligott's eyebrows shot up as the defense was forced to press Harding for answers.

"Where is the photography of the fingerprints on the gas can before you lifted them?" Sullivan asked Harding. At the time of the Harris murders, police did not have a one-on-one camera, which can take a picture of the print on the surface and what is next to it. With a regular camera it is not possible to identify the print from the picture, only its location on the surface.

Sullivan accused Harding of lying about the evidence. He had a long-held suspicion that police didn't always tell the truth on the stand.

McElligott didn't take his eyes off of Harding. He didn't like Harding's demeanor on the stand. McElligott knew Sullivan was a smart lawyer who shouldn't be played with. Besides, it wasn't appropriate for Harding to dodge his questions. What the hell was wrong with Harding?

When it was the prosecutor's turn, George Dentes mentioned the defendant's ownership of property on the subject of setting appropriate level of bail. "How in the world does she qualify for assigned counsel?" he asked, annoyance plain in his voice.

"Second, isn't twenty-five thousand dollars bail, in light of those very substantial real estate holdings, quite little for a person of her means?" Dentes continued. He pointed out that court-appointed lawyers were paid by the county.

Sullivan alleged that the prosecutor had overstated Kinge's financial status. He suggested that the property wasn't worth that much and Dentes was aware of that. He requested five hundred dollars bail while Dentes asked that Kinge be held without bail.

Sweetland asked for written proof of Kinge's poverty status after hearing Dentes' arguments against assigned counsel. "We do need to have Mrs. Kinge fill out an indigence form and submit it to the court for further evaluation to know whether or not the assignment should be made through the office of assigned counsel or contracted with her attorney by herself."

Sweetland, however, did not change his mind. He held to his ruling that Shirley Kinge receive assigned counsel, at least for now, knowing that it was ultimately up to a higher court to make the final determination.

As his questioning of Harding continued, Sullivan insinuated that Harding's undercover work, tricking Kinge into addressing envelopes for him so he could get handwriting samples and handing her a coffee mug for fingerprints, was a kind of entrapment. It was perfectly legal, but mentioning it might gain his client some sympathy.

During the hour and a half lunch break, some of the journalists left. *The Ithaca Journal*'s managing editor, Jacqueline Powers, had informed the law firm that represented the paper about the closed session. Mark Wheeler, one of the firm's attorneys, appeared in the Dryden courtroom at 3:00 P.M. and presented a written document asking Sweetland to halt the hearing, claiming that the judge had violated case law on procedures to close a hearing. Wheeler said he was seeking an "order to show cause" that would require the hearing to stop while he made legal arguments against closing.

Sweetland glanced at the first page of the four-page document, shook his head, and continued the hearing. He told Wheeler to leave the room.

Outside the courtroom, Wheeler said that if a judge closes a hearing he must cite his reasons and hear arguments on the issue at the time. He added it is Sullivan's burden to demonstrate beyond a mere possibility that evidence presented in the proceeding could affect his client's ability to get a fair trial. Another lawyer representing *The Ithaca Journal*, Edward Hooks, said he planned to take further steps to have Sweetland's decision reversed. He had prepared Article 78 papers to present to the state Supreme Court. Part of that brief would request that *The Journal* be provided access to the transcript of the preliminary hearing.

At the end of the five-hour hearing, Judge Sweetland, looking tired but resolute, ruled there was sufficient evidence to hold Shirley Kinge on the charge of arson in the Harris home. Arson was one of the lesser of the six charges brought against her. Dentes had presented only that charge at the hearing.

It was up to the prosecution to present the charges to a county grand jury as the next legal step. That body decides if there is enough evidence to take the case to trial in criminal court. By law the prosecution must bring the case to a grand jury within the next forty-five days.

Bail was set for Kinge at twenty-five thousand dollars in cash or a fifty thousand dollar bail bond.

Outside the courtroom, George Dentes refused to discuss any of the proceedings with the news media. Sullivan spoke into several microphones as members of the press gathered around him, "There is no reasonable cause to believe Shirley Kinge committed any offense in connection with the Harris murders."

Sullivan also told the press that he intended to ask a superior court judge to reduce the bail because his client did not have that kind of money. Dentes planned to ask the county judge to revoke bail.

A Syracuse bail bondsman said that writing a four hundred and fifty thousand dollar bond was very rare. He said that Kinge would need land with at least one hundred thousand dollars worth of equity on it for him to even consider writing a bond for her. The Watertown property Shirley owned had a market value of only ten to fifteen thousand dollars.

McElligott cornered Harding as he got out of the car at the

barracks parking lot upon returning from the Dryden court-room.

"I don't like the way you conducted yourself on the stand, Dave. Don't be fencing with Sullivan because you'll lose," McElligott said, his temper rising.

Harding shrugged, "It'll be fine, boss. You got nothing to worry about."

"You'd better mark those prints and put them in evidence right away. I don't like you carrying them around."

"I've got to blow them up first," Harding answered.

"Is there anything wrong with those prints, Dave?" McElligott asked sharply. "If so I wanta know right now," McElligott looked directly, challengingly into Harding's eyes.

Harding spoke softly, "I would never do anything like that in a case of this magnitude." Harding turned away from McElligott and walked into the barracks.

McElligott was not reassured by Harding's answers. He didn't like the way Harding had testified, not one bit. He found his friend, Charlie Porter, doing some paperwork in one of the offices and spouted off to him.

"I don't like Harding's smart-ass tactics. He's not there to challenge the goddamn defense. He's there to answer questions. And I still have an uneasy feeling about those prints and him," McElligott said.

Porter told his friend not to get so worked-up. It was probably nothing to worry about.

McElligott tried to bury the episode in the back of his mind. It is possible that McElligott was being unfair to Harding, but he couldn't help it. He just didn't like the guy.

The case moved from Dryden Town Court into Tompkins County Court after the preliminary hearing. At the request of the district attorney and the defendant, William C. Barrett, Tompkins County Court Judge, convened a bail hearing two days later on February 15 at 2:30 P.M. Barrett, gray haired and distinguished looking, was nearing the end of his first ten-year term as a county judge and he intended to run for a second term in the fall.

George Dentes argued that the court should not set bail for Shirley Kinge. He spoke of the defendant's financial resources and her lack of ties to the community. Dentes claimed that Kinge's land was worth about thirty-five thousand dollars and the 1989 Suburu was valued at fourteen thousand dollars. Furthermore, the extremely heinous crimes for which Kinge was charged should prohibit bail considerations. Dentes told the court that while the defendant did not have a criminal record, she did tell investigators about an alleged larceny charge against her in South Carolina. Dentes said in that case she'd fled the state after appearing in court three times on that charge. If convicted on the Harris crime charges, Kinge would face a possible "life sentence" or at least a substantial part of her life in jail. Knowing this, Dentes argued, wouldn't she flee if let out on bail?

Dentes' brief included several pieces of physical evidence that the prosecution had in its arsenal against Shirley Kinge: a gas can bearing the defendant's fingerprints, found in the Harris home; the gun used to kill the Harrises, found in Michael Kinge's apartment; and some of the items purchased after the murders with the Harrises' stolen credit cards, found in both Shirley's and Michael's apartment.

Shirley Kinge, wearing a beige winter jacket and matching sunglasses, sat motionless while Dentes presented his arguments. After Sullivan made his counter-arguments on the fairness of setting a reasonable bail for the defendant, he announced to the judge that his client wanted to speak for herself. It was the first public statement Kinge had made since her arrest.

Kinge told the judge, "The only thing I have to ask, I do want to stay here and I'd like to get this over with." She began crying and bent her head down for a moment. "I'm very sorry," she continued in a quivering voice, "I need to bury my son."

Michael Kinge's body was still with the Onondaga County Medical Examiner's office.

After all arguments had been presented, Judge Barrett sat quietly looking at the papers in front of him. After several minutes, Barrett announced that he was revoking the defendant's bail, citing the seriousness of the charges brought against Kinge and stating that he was not convinced she would remain in the area if released.

Sullivan told reporters after the hearing that he would fight Barrett's action by asking a different court to review the bail decision. He said his client was very troubled when speaking in court. "She's also concerned by the fact that she's black in this community. She knows this community has been very, very angry about the crimes with which she's charged and didn't do. There's no basis not to set bail in this case," Sullivan continued. "The evidence, if it's not nonexistent, is certainly near invisible."

When reporters asked Dentes if Michael Kinge's girl-friend, Joanna White, would be charged in the Harris crimes, he replied, "We have no reason to suspect anyone else." Not long afterward, the Associated Press released information, found in court records, stating that White had driven Kinge within two miles of the Harris home on the day of the murders.

On February 20, in the old Tompkins County Courthouse on East Court Street, three attorneys representing different regional media brought their arguments concerning the legality of closing the February 13 hearing in Dryden before Judge Robert Rose, a New York State Supreme Court Judge. Sweetland's attorney presented his client's reasons for closing the session. Sweetland's attorney told the court that the judge was only trying to protect the rights of the accused and was concerned that the suspect get a fair trial.

Rose, after listening to both sides, ruled that the Dryden

Town Justice, Edwin Sweetland, should not have barred the media from Shirley Kinge's preliminary hearing. He said that the Dryden justice "improperly closed the door on petitioners' First Amendment rights." Rose ordered that the transcripts from the closed preliminary hearing be made available to the media and the public. Sweetland's argument that he was acting to protect defendant's right to a fair trial was dismissed on the grounds that he did not cite specific reasons for his concern. Rose said it wasn't enough to mention an article of criminal procedure law and say that closure was in the best interest of all.

Furthermore, Rose decided the refusal to hear arguments from press attorneys who tried to plead their case was improper. "Our law in this state provides a presumption of open criminal proceedings."

The burden, Rose explained, was on Sullivan to prove two elements: "substantial probability" that an open hearing would violate Kinge's rights and that any alternative to closure could not adequately safeguard her rights. The alternatives are the voir dire process of jury selection, or a change of venue, which means moving the trial out of town.

After the ruling, Sullivan complained to reporters that the entire case had been a media circus of rumors and misinformation supplied by police and the district attorney. He said the result of the publicity had been a "campaign of hatred toward Shirley Kinge and her family."

Edward Hooks, representing *The Ithaca Journal*, commented, "It is rather ironic that the first time the press has an opportunity to listen to facts, to listen to evidence, that Sullivan wanted the hearing closed."

The twenty-three members of the grand jury convened on February 27 to hear the evidence in three cases, including the Kinge case.

Bill Sullivan said in a letter to the district attorney that it was not fair for the same grand jury to hear all three cases. "Notwithstanding any instructions that you or the court might otherwise give to the grand jury, these evidentiary considerations in the other cases will make it impossible for Mrs. Kinge to receive a fair hearing before any grand jury hearing any evidence regarding the Lane and Vann cases," Sullivan claimed.

He criticized Dentes for questioning Kinge's right to assigned counsel and for releasing information to the press and public that had prejudiced people against Kinge. Sullivan requested a voir dire, a questioning, of the twenty-three people serving on the grand jury because of extensive publicity. He suggested that they had not been selected randomly.

In the same letter to Dentes, Sullivan said he had been informed that the district attorney intended to call before the grand jury one or more of the people who killed Michael Kinge in the February 7 raid. "In my brief investigation to date, a number of persons have suggested that there may be criminal responsibility on the part of those who took the life of Michael Kinge . . . Shirley Kinge asks that those directly and/or indirectly responsible for the death of Michael Kinge have an opportunity to defend their actions in the criminal courts, in the same way that you seem to be intent upon having Shirley Kinge defend herself with respect to the deaths of the Harris family." He also charged that from Sallie Reese's testimony, four hundred dollars in cash hidden under a mattress was missing from the Etna Road apartment after police invaded their home on February 7.

Sullivan did not pursue the propriety of the grand jury selection, an issue he had raised with the district attorney in one of his motion papers.

Dentes was getting a taste of Sullivan's tactics. This strategy consisted of a series of quick word punches, often inflammatory, to set his opponent up and weaken the other person's defenses in a myriad of ways; any one of which was hard to separate and attack. In contrast, Dentes' style was cool and concise, delivered with logical blows. The fight ahead would be a test of the will and the power of two very different trial lawyers.

The emotionally wringing Harris case came to a head when, on March 21, Shirley Kinge was indicted on twelve felony counts of burglary, arson, forgery, hindering prosecution and possession of stolen property. The grand jury did not find enough evidence to indict her on the four second-degree murder counts. They also investigated the death of Michael Kinge involving police officers during the February 7 shoot-out and decided the killing was justified.

It was later reported that police officers had found a four hundred dollar check in the Etna Road apartment at the time of the raid and had left it there. Sallie Reese conceded that the check hadn't been cashed; she had found it when she returned to the duplex.

Judge Barrett postponed Shirley Kinge's arraignment until March 30, after being notified that the county was investigating the value of Kinge's Watertown property in order to determine if she qualified for assigned counsel. Meanwhile, Barrett asked Sullivan to continue to represent Kinge as a "friend of the court."

Sullivan continued to speak up, telling the media that he thought the charges against his client were "bogus," that what evidence they had for arson was circumstantial at best and that the indictment was a product of the media's prejudicial hate campaign being influenced by the district attorney. In contrast to Sullivan's outspoken style, Dentes often declined to speak to reporters or would refer them to his statements in the public record.

Kinge's property in Jefferson County, which only had a gravel road access with no public maintenance, was assessed at ten thousand dollars. About three dozen people sat in Tompkins County's main courtroom on March 30, to listen to attorneys debate Kinge's right to free counsel. Sullivan estimated that to hire a private attorney would cost between $25,000 to $30,000 if the county did not provide one for the defendant. He said the delays had hurt his client, but wouldn't specify how. Sullivan said the costs that the prosecution had already spent on the case with fifty investigators had to be nearly $500,000, so by the time the work is over, "Mrs. Kinge will be the first million-dollar lady in Tompkins County and they're complaining that counsel be appointed for her," he vehemently complained.

After an hour of arguments back and forth, Judge Barrett closed the discussion, saying they were wasting their time talking about land upstate. He announced his decision to uphold the lower court's determination and appointed Sullivan as the defendant's counsel. He ended the session with the formal indictment, handed up by the grand jury. Shirley Kinge was charged on twelve felony counts.

After the arraignment, Sullivan said that he planned to file charges of misconduct against the district attorney for even questioning Kinge's eligibility for a free attorney. He told reporters that he decided against contesting bail for his client because she had received death threats in jail and, therefore, felt safer behind bars.

The $32,708 reward fund was divided among seven informants, some of whom wished to remain anonymous, who had helped break the Harris case. The amount each tipster received was based on the timeliness and weight of the information he or she provided. Representatives from the two major contributors (Bob Dean of the Deanco Corporation and a representative from Wilcox Press) along with Captain Shaver and McElligott made the judgment calls on who should receive money and what amount.

McElligott had the pleasant duty of finding Connie Littleton, who he thought deserved a reward more than anyone, and awarding her with a share of the reward money. Littleton had acted against her employers' advice and gone to the Varna barracks to do what she thought was right. Her information about the Kinges had, more than any other informer's tips, set the police on the right track. She had the "courage of her convictions," McElligott liked to say.

McElligott found Littleton, now obviously pregnant, working in a diner downtown. She was suspicious when McElligott asked her to sign an identification document. She hadn't known about any reward.

The next day, McElligott and another investigator returned to the diner, took her aside and showed her the money inside a bank bag. She gazed with awe at ten thousand dollars. Crying with excitement and appreciation, she said she could buy things for her baby now, and thanked the two men over and over. Her pleasure warmed McElligott's heart.

Even with Shirley Kinge in custody, Michael Kinge (a/k/a Tony Turner) dead, and rewards dispersed, neither the town nor its citizens were able to return to their former tranquillity. The grisly crime, which had snuffed out a family everyone had known and liked, continued to haunt those left.

Ellis Hollow residents, friends of the Harrises, and relatives from Syracuse got together that spring, trying to heal their pain and deep sorrow. A Grey Goose sale was held on April 7, with the profits going into the community center's general fund. The boys in Marc Harris' Boy Scout troop and his ice hockey teammates organized a garage sale in May, where many of the family's household and personal items were sold to the public. Those proceeds were divided between the two youth groups.

Townspeople rebuilt the fire-damaged Harris home. The family had decided to turn the house into a day care center, an idea suggested by Kevin and Barbara White, who were close friends of the Harrises. By the second week in May, Pat Jennings, who had moved into the house after it was repaired with her teenage son, began accepting applications for the Montessori program.

There were some Harris friends who could not face the tragedy head-on. They sealed it off and buried it in their subconscious, refusing to deal with it. Therapists in town were still seeing clients in late spring who were deeply troubled by the December violence. One resident was so disturbed by the murders that nothing helped relieve her anxiety and she finally moved out of the state.

Friends and family members decided to release their grief and pain by writing about the Harrises they knew. These remembrances were bound into a small paperback by Barbara and Kevin White with the title: *The Harris Family—Those who have Given of Themselves to Others Live Forever Within the Hearts of Those They Touched.*

Twenty-one
Advance Maneuvers

As the last vestiges of winter melted, spring appeared and then summer took its place. During this period, Bill Sullivan inundated the prosecution with legal motions, citing sections of criminal law, quoting the Constitution and famous case decisions, to challenge the district attorney in his handling of procedures against Sullivan's client, Shirley Kinge. Papers were rushed back and forth between Sullivan's office and the courthouse. He accused Dentes of withholding exculpatory evidence from the grand jury by failing to call Joanna White as a witness.

Though investigators had said no more arrests were planned after Shirley Kinge was taken into custody, on July 12 they charged Joanna White with criminal facilitation in the fourth degree. Sullivan argued that White had information that "exculpates" Shirley Kinge and that the People charged White to prevent her from testifying for Kinge at the trial. His claims were made in a ninety-seven page document in which he demanded a Bill of Particulars from the prosecutor because Sullivan said he could not adequately prepare or conduct the defense without such details.

"Once again," George Dentes sent back in reply, "the defendant has filed papers replete with claptrap and devoid of law. Although jammed with ninety-seven pages of computer boilerplate, no where is it made that defendant can't adequately prepare his defense." He reminded the defense that his office had served the defendant with the prosecution's demands for alibi witness information, and that at the final conference held with Judge Barrett when parties were to submit their witness lists, the defendant filed no witness list.

Sullivan's charge that the prosecution withheld exculpatory evidence from the grand jury by failing to call Joanna White as a witness was baseless, Dentes said. White's peripheral involvement in the crimes justified refusing to give her immunity. Dentes reminded the defense that he supplied them with a copy of Joanna White's statement to police and so far the defendant hadn't pointed to anything in the statement that exonerated Shirley Kinge.

According to the defense, the prosecution waited to arrest Joanna White in order to avoid having the state's witnesses put on the stand in the Shirley Kinge trial and cross-examined before appearing in the more serious allegations against Shirley Kinge. At one time, in preparation for the Kinge trial, Dentes had thought Joanna White would be a prosecution witness, but after she refused to take a lie-detector test unless her attorney was present, they dropped her as a potential witness. The state police officer who administered the polygraph test told the district attorney that a third person in the room could possibly influence the test results. They offered to make tape recordings of the session so that James Kerrigan, White's attorney, would have complete knowledge of what was said and done during the testing, but the offer was refused.

The District Attorney responded to the defense assertion that the prosecution had not supplied enough information by noting that the People had already presented the defense with more than 1,000 pages of documents.

Sullivan held a press conference on the courthouse steps

July 13, in front of local and Syracuse television cameras: "The man upstairs [Dentes] with the big stick is threatening her [J. White]. That's wrong, absolutely wrong. He has no sense of justice."

According to Sullivan, David McElligott said that Joanna White was prepared to testify on Shirley Kinge's behalf. Kinge supposedly told Joanna that she would never have used the credit cards had she known that Michael had anything to do with the Harris burglary or homicide.

"The D.A. never called her [as a witness in the grand jury] and I know why he didn't call her," Sullivan said, speaking into the microphones. "Because it would blow his case out of the water. It looks to me like he's grasping at straws right now." Sullivan claimed that with a misdemeanor charge pending over her, White wouldn't be able to testify for Michael or Shirley Kinge without jeopardizing her own case.

White's court-appointed attorney, James Kerrigan, questioned at the arraignment in Dryden court why bail ($5,000 cash or $10,000 bond) was necessary for his client on such a low level charge. Judge Sweetland responded that bail was set at Dentes' request.

Kerrigan told reporters after the arraignment that he knew what "games were being played here." He accused Dentes of not showing up at the hearing so he wouldn't have to defend White's arrest before the press. He echoed Sullivan's charge that Dentes and the state police were trying all aspects of the Kinge case in the media to bias potential jurors.

Sullivan tried to have the case against Shirley Kinge dropped for insufficient evidence and improper procedures by the prosecution. Although the lawyer claimed that his client might not receive a fair trial in Tompkins County, he did not request moving the trial to another place. Sullivan seemed to feel he stood the best chance at home. The local climate was far more liberal than in other upstate communities.

The wheels of justice in Tompkins County continued

grinding with the selection of jurors for the Kinge trial beginning on July 23. Six women and six men were chosen, including two African-Americans (one to serve as a regular member of the panel and one as an alternate).

Twenty-two
The People Decide

The main courtroom on the second floor of the Tompkins County courthouse has high-ceilings rimmed by cream-colored plaster that had been carved like a wreath, and five hanging gold chandeliers, each adorned with a perched eagle on top. It was there, on Monday, August 13, 1992, a hot summer day, that the trial began.

Two police officers stood outside the courtroom with a metal detector. Handbags, briefcases and other personal items were checked before the hoard of spectators and reporters were allowed entrance.

Reporters had already begun their ongoing coverage on the local Ithaca channel. Syracuse, Binghamton and Elmira channels would cover the trial on their nightly news report. Television cameras hummed all around the room.

The Prosecutor, George Dentes, entered the courtroom dressed neatly in dark blue suit and tie, smiling and speaking in a low voice to the personnel and assistants sitting near him at the prosecution table.

In his opening remarks, Dentes stated publicly for the first time that Shirley Kinge was in the Harris home the night of the brutal murders. Dentes spoke as a person who had been personally moved by the brutality of the crimes against the Harris family and who intended to see that justice was done. He outlined what he planned to prove during the trial: that Shirley Kinge was with her son, Michael Kinge, at the Harris home.

"The defendant joined him there sometime in the evening and returned there in the morning," he began, alleging that the fifty-five year old woman dumped a gasoline can on a downstairs floor while hurrying to get out of the dead family's home after an alarm went off. Shirley Kinge "lost her cool, dropped that can, and didn't have the time to wipe off her prints," Dentes said.

He told the jurors in a sincere voice that he would prove that Kinge was at the scene of the crime and therefore guilty of the twelve felony counts of burglary, arson, forgery, hindering prosecution, and criminal possession of stolen property with which she was charged.

Bill Sullivan strode to the front of the courtroom to make an impassioned opening plea.

"Ladies and gentlemen of the jury, we've heard this morning from the D.A. a recital of what he expects to prove. I suggest to you that what he expects to prove and what he may prove are two different things. In this regard we all start from the premise that Judge Barrett referred to earlier, the premise, at the time right now, Mrs. Kinge as she sits before you is not guilty."

Sullivan asked the jury to keep in mind that the evidence presented by the prosecution would in many instances be circumstantial and witnesses would give their opinions about events, but there would be no proof. "I suggest you might hear something less than half-truths as the testimony is given, and from people, I suggest, that ought to know better."

In the closing moments of his remarks Sullivan insisted that Shirley Kinge had not been in the Harris home either

December 22 or 23. "That leaves the charge of possession of a credit card in Tompkins County, a stolen credit card, criminal possession of stolen property. We suggest with respect to the charge as well the D.A.'s proof will fail. At the end of the case we ask that you return verdicts of not guilty with respect to each of the twelve counts of the indictment."

Looking attractive and forlorn, Shirley Kinge, wearing a new black wig purchased for the trial, a dark suit, and tailored white blouse, sat with her eyes riveted on Sullivan. The rest of her face showed nothing of what she must have been feeling. In front of her was a pad of paper on which she occasionally jotted down notes. In the audience, Shirley's seventy-three year old mother watched along with a small crowd of spectators, most of whom were reporters.

McElligott, as with many of the investigators, was subpoenaed to appear as a witness. He had assisted Dentes in the lining up of his witnesses. He gathered evidence that the D.A. needed to present as exhibits during the trial.

Dentes called eight witnesses during the first day to introduce the details of the six and a half week investigation to the public. Sullivan relentlessly cross-examined some of the witnesses. He reduced one witness, a friend of Marc Harris, to tears in his demand for exactness on the weather conditions the day of the murder. When the prosecution passed around photographs of the crime scene, showing one partially burned victim, Shirley Kinge, her face still expressionless, stood up to get a better look at the exhibits.

McElligott watched the proceedings on a monitor on the second floor of the courthouse and chatted with a reporter, one of the few he liked. Sullivan found out where McElligott was and made a motion to bar him from watching the trial. He wanted to eliminate the chance that McElligott might prompt a witness after hearing something in the courtroom. Judge Barrett granted the motion.

McElligott shrugged and moved to Dentes' office on the top floor of the courthouse. He'd been on opposite sides in court with Sullivan many times. He knew the defense attorney was just doing his job.

Dentes and McElligott went out to lunch with a witness, but never discussed the testimony. Dentes would not allow it. McElligott respected the new D.A.'s integrity. Not every district attorney was that strict.

McElligott, like the local police officers, was beginning to admire the way Dentes worked. He was an honest, strictly by the rules D.A., who seemed to be on their side. Not a political animal as were some district attorneys he had dealt with in the past.

As the days wore on, the contrast between the emotional style of Bill Sullivan and the cool disciplined court demeanor of George Dentes became plainer to those watching the Shirley Kinge trial. Sullivan entered the courtroom carrying a bulging briefcase and a stack of folders under his arm. At the podium he spoke loudly, sometimes screaming his point, gesturing with his hands like an evangelist. He often held up the proceedings while thumbing through his papers to find something. Sullivan attempted to prove that Shirley Kinge couldn't have been in the Harris house, that she was a scapegoat who had been sacrificed to appease those who wanted to satisfy a hungry public.

Dentes rarely carried papers. He quietly, logically presented his evidence in a low key but sincere manner. He attempted to prove Shirley Kinge was in the Harris house when the fire was set there. He used the gas can fingerprints as a focal point. The Kinges' neighbor, Janet Hayworth, from whom Shirley said they often borrowed a gas can, testified that she never owned a rectangular container like the one found in the Harris home. Because the credit cards were used out of the county, the prosecutor had to prove jurisdiction as well as the crimes, which could be done by showing that the defendant had the intent to use the credit cards in Tompkins County.

Dentes tried to prove that the gas can with the lifted fingerprints belonged to the Harrises by showing the similarities between the living room gas can known as People's Exhibit 87, and a nearly identical can police found in the Harrises' garage, People's Exhibit 264.

David Harding was on the stand for four days. He testified that after he got prints off the can, he took a photograph, wiped the can clean again, then took a picture of it positioned next to the garage can. Sullivan attacked Harding for wiping the gas can clean after taking off the prints and for not saving the tape he removed from the can.

In a quiet but firm voice, Harding explained that he had wiped the dirt and grease off the can in order to see the writing on it, to make it easier to identify that can along with the other gas can found at the crime scene, both owned by the Harrises. The prosecution wanted the witnesses who were aware the Harrises owned two gasoline cans to identify both of them. The defense argued that Michael Kinge brought a gasoline can from his home to the Harrises.

When they went to lunch, McElligott asked Harding how he was doing on the stand.

"Great, great," the younger officer said.

McElligott had no way of hearing Harding's testimony since he was confined to Dentes' office and barred from watching the monitor. He also knew that the DA wouldn't discuss witnesses while they were testifying.

A colleague later told McElligott of Harding's court testimony about how he wiped the gas can clean. That was news to McElligott. It had been hectic those first days in February when they were planning the forced entry. He could have missed it. He had let Dentes know that he wasn't satisfied with the way Harding handled the fingerprints, but despite his discomfort with Harding's manner and the man himself, there was nothing to prove the fingerprints weren't okay. Although McElligott couldn't help adding that there was really nothing to prove they were, either.

While McElligott understood Harding was trying to make

the cans easily identifiable, it could also be thought of as sloppy police work if not something worse. He told Dentes, "I'm beginning to believe there's something rotten about Harding, and that maybe the woman was never in the house." But to be fair, McElligott admitted Harding's record seemed impeccable. Dentes had to agree.

In his cross-examination, Sullivan, who had a bad cold and a sore raspy throat, hammered away at Harding's unorthodox methods. While he tried to wear Harding down with his flood of questions and contentious remarks, it was the jury who was getting tired and reaching its limit. Nevertheless, Sullivan was beginning to make some headway into Harding's armor when Judge Barrett interrupted to say that the defense counsel was obviously not feeling well, and asked if he would prefer to close for the day.

Dentes decided not to put McElligott on the stand after Karl Chandler's detailed testimony. He didn't like to be redundant.

Sullivan's defense hammered away at what he termed the circumstantial evidence of the prosecution—namely the defendant's fingerprints on the Harrises' gasoline can found at the crime scene. He said Kinge could not be tried for the credit card abuse because the cards were used outside Tompkins County and were never meant to be used within the county. In defending Kinge, Sullivan tried to paint a picture of a poor but intelligent woman who never had a criminal record, who worked hard for a living all her life and because she was a mother, had tried to help her son and his family. Now she was being tried for her son's crimes.

"Why would a smart lady use credit cards knowing they belonged to people just murdered?" he asked the jury. "Wouldn't that be stupid?"

Sallie Reese provided an alibi for the defendant when she testified that her daughter was home baby-sitting the night the Harrises were killed. She was still at home the next morning, according to Reese, when the family's house was set on fire. Reese told the court that Shirley normally baby-sat her grandson at night when the baby's mother was working. She added that she would often look after the child during the daytime when Shirley was working.

During his cross-examination of Reese, Dentes pressured her about a statement Reese gave to police February 7, in which she said that she, not Shirley Kinge, regularly watched the baby. Reese responded, "Someone waves a gun in your face, you're going to remember things."

When Sullivan objected to some of the prosecutor's questions not being relevant, Dentes pointed to Reese and said, "She was the babysitter in that house, Your Honor. That's the relevance."

Only a portion of Dr. Charles Ewing's testimony was heard by the jury. Sullivan introduced Ewing, a forensic psychologist from Buffalo, as an expert witness to testify that Shirley Kinge was on the verge of a nervous breakdown by the time the police raided her apartment. The defense wanted to show that police used classic psychological tactics such as withholding information about her son's death until two hours into the interview to get Kinge's confession to some of the crimes.

However, Dentes voiced objection to the testimony based on a New York State evidence rule that prohibits an expert from venturing opinions on matters within the ken of laymen. Dentes argued that the jury was capable of reaching its own conclusion regarding the defendant's mental state at the time of the police questioning. Judge Barrett sustained the objection.

After the court day was over, Sullivan made sure the press heard all of Ewing's opinions based on four hours of interviewing his client.

During that week, one panel member was booted off the jury at Sullivan's request. Sullivan said he had heard the juror was discussing the case out of court. The juror denied the accusation, but using abundant caution, Judge Barrett dismissed her.

Without putting his defendant on the stand, Sullivan rested his case on November 9. When questioned about his decision, Sullivan replied it was his evaluation that the district attorney did not prove his case and it was not necessary for Shirley Kinge to testify.

Some court observers doubted that explanation. *Could it be that Sullivan needed to protect his client from herself when on the stand?*

The defense began its closing statement on November 13. Sullivan told the jury that Dentes had failed to prove Shirley Kinge was at the murder scene.

"The prosecutor has taken on the burden of proving that Michael Kinge murdered the Harris family," Kinge's attorney said. "He has proved that Michael Kinge murdered Warren Harris, Dolores Harris, Shelby Harris and Marc Harris. But Shirley Kinge," Sullivan added with an edge to his voice, "is not on trial for being Michael Kinge's mother, and her relationship with her son is where her alleged connection to crimes committed in the Harris house ends."

Sullivan tried to demonstrate that the prosecution failed to show beyond any reasonable doubt who owned the gas can on which his client's fingerprints were found. He told the jury that Michael Kinge was a professional criminal who would not be stupid enough to have his mother come in, handle a gas can, and then pour gasoline over the place.

As Sullivan made his arguments he pounded the podium with his fist and his voice got louder and louder, rising to a crescendo. In five and a half hours, and then the entire next morning, he quoted poets, case law, the Constitution and Abraham Lincoln. His whole life had been wrapped up in the case for nearly a year and it was obvious that he believed Shirley Kinge was innocent.

George Dentes, however, felt just as strongly that Kinge was guilty. "The defendant left her calling card, by which I mean her fingerprints," Dentes told the jury in his summation. "The rock-hard core, the terra firma, is that her fingerprints were on the gas can. There's no innocent explanation."

Dentes tried to debunk the story Shirley Kinge gave police after being arrested—that she had never been in the Harris home, might have touched a gas can that belonged to a neighbor before the crime, and that her son didn't give her the credit cards to use until the evening of the day that the bodies of the Harris family were discovered. He reminded the jury that Shirley Kinge confessed to using the Harrises' credit card on three occasions, only denying the fourth "Dolores Harris" purchase of underwear.

Dentes told the jury that the Kinges' haste in leaving the Harris home after the alarm went off was such that the gasoline downstairs was not even ignited. "Somebody went through that house meticulously. A team of cleaners, I suggest to you," Dentes said as he reminded the jury that the Kinges had worked together as cleaners in the area.

Dentes suggested that Shirley Kinge went into the interrogation after her arrest with two plans in mind: Plan A was "nobody talks, everybody walks." He argued that Kinge waited until she knew her son was dead before using Plan B, which was to blame everything on him. "She denies everything she thinks she can," Dentes said. "She was never broken. She was never coerced. She told as much as she wanted to tell."

Shirley Kinge intended to use the credit cards in Tompkins County, Dentes insisted. It was important for the prosecution to convince the jury that the defendant intended to use the credit cards locally, otherwise she could not be convicted of the crimes by a Tompkins County jury since the purchases were made in Cayuga and Onondaga counties.

Finally, Dentes asked the jury to concentrate on the issues

and not be distracted by Sullivan's emotional arguments. "You've got to keep your eye on the ball," Dentes told them.

The Shirley Kinge trial was distinguished by its longevity. Stretching over four months, it was the longest criminal trial on record in Tompkins County. In fact, it had taken approximately twice as long to try the case as it did to solve the crime. Finally, the trial came to an end.

Judge Barrett dismissed the two alternate jurors before jury deliberations began. One alternate juror who sat in during the entire trial told reporters that it had been very difficult to be tied up so long. She'd just retired from Cornell University and had planned to do a lot of other things. She said she'd become well-acquainted with the panel members and felt confident in their ability, "They're very lucky to have the group they have," she remarked to a reporter.

At 3:00 P.M., November 15, the jury started their deliberations as to Shirley Kinge's guilt or innocence. Judge Barrett had instructed them for an hour about the legal issues surrounding the charges against Shirley Kinge and what they must do to reach a verdict. They weren't in session long before the foreman sent out a note asking to see the two gas cans that were removed from the Harris home. One of them was People's Exhibit #87, and allegedly bore Kinge's fingerprints.

While the jury deliberated, Sullivan spent most of the time pacing up and down the corridor outside the main courtroom while Shirley Kinge and a sheriff deputy quietly waited in a nearby room. When no decision had been reached by 10 P.M., the panel was sequestered overnight in the downtown Ramada Inn.

On Friday afternoon, November 16, the jury announced it had reached its verdict. The courtroom was packed with media and spectators as the jury foreman, John Turner, read off the verdicts. Charge by charge, he pronounced Shirley Kinge "guilty."

Sullivan, his hands clasped together in front of him, bent his head down and closed his eyes while Shirley Kinge, sitting next to him, stared straight ahead. Picking his head up Sullivan requested that the jurors announce their verdicts individually. As the bailiff read off their names, each one pronounced the word guilty.

A sheriff's deputy escorted Shirley down the aisle to the back of the courtroom. She stopped beside her mother, who got up to embrace her daughter before Shirley was again handcuffed in the back room and returned to the county jail.

Sallie Reese left the courtroom in tears. When reporters asked for her opinion of the verdict, she angrily responded, "It's called truth, it's called justice, it's called the American way," she said bitterly.

Some other court spectators also reacted with anger at the verdict. Mary Dunkel, who had befriended Sallie Reese during the trial, told reporters, "I think the adversarial system becomes a case of ego, to win at any cost." Another spectator who was in the courtroom every day wrote a statement two days before the verdict which read in part: "The alleged perpetrator is dead, but the public may still seek vengeance from someone to satisfy some hidden river of 'blood lust' which lurks beneath the surface."

One local black activist, Gregory Rolle, predicted the verdict would leave the area more racially divided. He said, "A lot of black people will see why living in fear is justifiable."

But there were many residents, black and white, who felt the jury's decision was fair and justified. Others felt the community had been cheated out of real justice. At a South Cayuga Street bar, one patron expressed the frustration of many, commenting, "What really stinks is that nobody, except maybe Shirley Kinge, really knows what happened the night that family was killed. It's always going to be a mystery, something we'll talk about here for years to come. It's our curse."

The verdict was a relief, but not a surprise to David Harding. He stood on the courthouse steps next to George Dentes as the district attorney spoke to reporters, television cameras rolling. Dentes called Harding a hero. He praised Harding for the work he and other investigators had done. Harding smiled broadly, his brown hair glinting in the few rays of sunlight. It was their day. Harding's future in the state police never looked brighter.

McElligott had the day off when the verdict was announced. Charlie Porter called him at home and gave McElligott the news. On television that night, McElligott saw the district attorney speaking to reporters. When he spotted Harding smiling at the camera, McElligott muttered, "What in the hell is he doing there?"

On January 30, 1991, Shirley Kinge faced Judge Barrett for sentencing. Laymon Herring, a portly ebony skinned man with a stubby beard, his hair arranged in tight corn rows, sat in the courtroom that day. He stood out in the crowd of spectators. The sixty-year-old Herring had befriended Shirley Kinge while she was in jail. Herring said he started to fall in love with Shirley when he watched her on television after she was arrested.

"When she first got arrested, she sort of moved me. Her hair was just blowing in the wind and she was just so sad and angry at the same time. She's a beautiful person," he told reporters.

Since the end of her trial in November, he had made regular visits to see Shirley Kinge in jail. At first, Shirley thought he was kidding, but he won her over and now they were engaged to be married. She called Laymon from jail several times a week. Shirley said they planned to eventually live in Florida.

Laymon told the media that he edited and published a monthly newspaper in Syracuse, geared toward minority issues. One local observer disagreed and described Herring as a publicity-seeker who hadn't published anything in over a year, a person who liked to stir things up in the name of injustice without regard for truth.

The main courtroom was filled. Harris family members were in the audience, David Harding and Robert Lishansky sat across from them, and more African-Americans were in the crowd than had been present during the trial.

Shirley Kinge read a two-page statement to the court in which she described how unfairly she was treated by the police and the prosecutor. She charged that the prosecutor had unfairly challenged one of the only two black jurors, preventing the person from sitting on the jury (she was appointed fourth alternate). And most of all, she castigated the prosecution. "During the trial, the prosecutor called several witnesses who were loose with the truth. One of these witnesses flat out lied about fingerprints, about conversations with me and about other things, like wiping the can clean to make it shine." Shirley Kinge went on, "The unfair tactics of the prosecutor and the police did not stop there. He did everything he could to keep the truth away from the jury."

Kinge admitted using the stolen credit cards and said she was ready to be punished for that crime. At the end of the statement, the convicted woman told the court she shared the outrage over the actions of her son in taking the lives of the Harris family. She said the community had suffered and so had she by losing her son and her liberty. "I'm sorry that my justice has to wait for another day."

It was a moving and articulate statement, but many felt it was untrue while others said that it was curious Kinge never mentioned the Harris family members when she talked about the suffering of those left behind.

Judge Barrett was not swayed by Kinge's speech. Through a complicated calculation of imposing separate sentences on each count, he ordered the maximum sentence of fifteen to thirty years in prison. As Shirley Kinge, dressed in her black suit and white turtleneck, faced the bench, she stood motionless and listened. To many spectators she appeared superhuman or not human at all. Perhaps for Shirley Kinge, however, it was the only way she could cope with the rage that burned inside her.

Sallie Reese glared into the cameras outside the courtroom, and when asked what she planned to do next, replied, "Get the hell out of here."

Joanna White had been out on $5,000 bail since the day after her arrest. At a suppression hearing held on February 19, 1991, to decide what evidence could be used in White's unscheduled trial, James Kerrigan, her court-appointed attorney, argued that police failed to adequately inform his client of her constitutional rights before questioning.

White told the court that police threatened her during questioning, saying that she would never see her child again if she tried to get an attorney during the interrogation. White said she pleaded with the officers to use tear gas and not to make an armed raid on her home, because she feared for the safety of her family.

Bob Courtright and Tom Kelly, the two investigators who picked up Joanna White and questioned her, told the court another story. Her Miranda rights were read to her in the car going over to the police barracks, they said. The officers testified they told White she would see her son at the end of the questioning. At the time, however, they had no idea how long it would take to get the information they needed from her. At no time did White request a lawyer or refuse to talk, they said. She went willingly, and in fact, never asked why they wanted to talk with her when they appeared at Ithacare early that morning.

The big question at the suppression hearing was whether

White knew she wasn't initially in custody. Legally, that meant she could have refused to go to the state police barracks and answer their questions.

It was up to Judge Barrett to decide if Joanna White's six-page statement could be used as prosecution evidence in her trial. After hearing from both sides on the question of whether or not the defendant was properly advised of her rights before questioning and if police used legally correct tactics, Judge Barrett ruled against suppressing Joanna White's statement as evidence in trial. He later made the document public.

Jim Kerrigan, White's lawyer, knew the chances of winning an acquittal for his client were next to nil with White's statement allowed as evidence. She had admitted driving Michael Kinge near the crime scene and lying to police about his whereabouts on the night of the crimes. The best Kerrigan could do for her was to try and make a deal with the prosecutor.

The lawyer worked out a plea bargain arrangement with Dentes. In exchange for White pleading guilty to two charges of criminal facilitation and hindering prosecution, Dentes would recommend a sentence of one to three years. For the crimes that Joanna White was charged with, sentencing could be up to seven years in state prison. The need for a trial was eliminated. Harris family members were relieved not to have to go through another trial, and the county would save money.

Dentes said he would recommend that Joanna White serve one to three years in state prison. Judge Barrett agreed not to impose a stricter sentence.

Judge Barrett conducted the sentencing on May 20, 1991, in the small courtroom next to his chambers on the first floor of the Tompkins County courthouse. The few chairs, usually used for family court cases, were filled with family members and reporters. Some leaned against the walls.

Joanna White came into the room wearing a long-waisted lavender and white print dress that stopped above the knee.

She wore no jewelry, and low-heeled pumps. White had a stoic quality, her back rigidly straight, her head high, as she walked with her attorney. But her poise crumbled when she gave a brief statement to the judge. White sounded like a frightened young woman, her voice trembling as she apologized to the Harris family.

"To the Harris family, I'd like to say I'm sorry if I caused them to suffer any longer. I had no choice but to do what Michael told me to do." White's voice cracked as she said in a low voice, "I hope to go on to a better life and raise my son."

Kerrigan asked the judge for leniency. He said that Michael Kinge had used verbal abuse and threats to intimidate White into lying to the police. In White's defense, Kerrigan explained that she lived with Kinge and their son amid an arsenal of weapons and burglary tools. She drove Kinge to Ellis Hollow, but she had no idea that crimes of this magnitude were going to be committed.

Dentes told the court that state prison time for what White had done was appropriate. She was the one who purchased the .22-caliber rifle that Kinge modified and eventually used to kill the Harrises. She knew he was a convicted felon. But Dentes also noted that White had provided the police with detailed information about where Kinge kept his weapons and about the layout of the duplex just before they raided it, information that probably saved the lives of police officers.

Judge Barrett split his decision between the two opposing recommendations. He sentenced White to serve one year in Tompkins County jail. With "good time," that would mean no more than eight months of actual prison time. Barrett said her crimes were too serious not to warrant some incarceration.

There was no visible reaction from White as she stood before the bench and heard the judge's decision. Her mother, who watched with the other spectators, dabbed the tears on her face with a handkerchief. After the proceedings, she embraced her daughter. They walked to a room down the corridor where White's sisters and friends waited for a last visit before she went to jail. One woman in the group yelled at a reporter who was firing questions at Joanna.

George Dentes told the press he wasn't disappointed in the sentence. "By pleading guilty," he said to the reporter who questioned him about the abuse charge Kerrigan made, "it seemed to indicate she wasn't so confident in that defense that she was willing to go to trial on it."

As White, now in handcuffs, was escorted out of the courthouse on that sunny May day when the redbud and cherry trees bloomed in profusion, the air glistened and the sky overhead was cloudless. The young woman stood erect, looking straight ahead as she walked down the steps of the courthouse. A crowd of reporters, television camera people and observers watched a sad-faced Joanna White climb into the police van which then drove away.

At that point it seemed the saga that had started when the Harris family was found murdered and their bodies burned two days before Christmas had finally ended. Those responsible for the crimes were either dead or behind bars.

Twenty-three
Mistaken Notion

Feeling that he was ready for the big time, Harding decided to join an antiterrorist squad within the Central Intelligence Agency (CIA). His record looked great on paper, and he seemed to have all the qualifications. On January 14, 1991, Harding was going to the CIA office in the Washington, D.C., area for a routine polygraph interview as part of his application.

By that February, as Shirley Kinge started serving her thirty-year sentence at New York State Maximum Security Prison for Women in Bedford Hills, David Harding's recognition as a hero for his part in solving the Harris murders also began. He received a superintendent's commendation and was asked to speak at a seminar with David McElligott and Karl Chandler during an international homicide school in Albany. Harding was asked to lecture at sociology classes about the Harris case. His colleagues expressed their admiration of him. It was assumed he would be moving up in the police ranks.

Not everything was going right, however. Harding's ex-

wife was threatening him with lawsuits over not paying full
alimony or child support on time. His father, who had remained with him at the little farm outside Waverly when
Harding's wife and children moved out, had died. That had
been a hard loss for him. Harding sold the house and property that he and his wife had bought at the beginning of their
marriage and moved into an apartment in an old Victorian
house in Waverly.

He was moved out of the identification unit in Sidney to
the Binghamton station at his request. He wanted to be closer
to Waverly, the village only four miles from where he'd been
born.

By local standards David Harding had come a long way
from the farm on Dry Brook Road in Waverly that his father
had owned before his marriage broke up. When David was a
preschooler, the family moved out of town to one hundred
acres off this back-road in Chemung County and raised six
children in the modest nineteenth-century farmhouse. John
Harding had once had a good-sized operation. They still
were only four miles from Waverly, the closest village, but
the hills and forests around them and poor roads made the
place seem a very long way from anything.

Chemung County is located on the southern tier of New
York State that borders Pennsylvania. The area is sparsely
populated. Much of the rural landscape looks impoverished,
with barns that need painting and rundown houses and trail-
ers. Across the state line in Sayre, Pennsylvania, is the highly
regarded Robert Packer Hospital and the home of Guthrie
Clinics as well as industries like Ingersoll-Rand in nearby
Athens, making those towns the center of activity in the "valley," a term used by locals referring to the border towns that
sit in the valley between the Susquehanna and Chemung rivers.

Waverly became prosperous as a terminus for the Erie

and Lehigh Railroads in the 1800s, with foundries and all the other businesses that grow up around railroad yards. It was now a quiet village with a main street in decline, pretty much a bedroom community for residents who commute to Binghamton, Endicott, Johnson City or Elmira along route 17, the Southern Tier Expressway.

John Harding couldn't make it on farming alone, which was true for most farmers in the area. Both he and his wife held full-time jobs in nearby towns to support the family. Despite this, they began selling off parcels of land in 1970. They raised a few hogs and owned quarter horses that were used in barrel racing and other events in weekly rodeos run by a professional. The Hardings rented out the corral space and bleachers they had built. The venture brought in a little extra money, and John, who wanted to provide some fun for his children, built an inground swimming pool next to the house.

The family regularly attended a small fundamentalist church. The oldest son became a minister and moved to Canada. A daughter, Diane, was in charge of the church nursery every Sunday. John Harding refused to buy the Sunday papers because it was the Lord's day, he said. Many of their neighbors were members of similar small churches that dotted the countryside. Locals called the area "Methodist Valley."

Appearances were very important. The Hardings kept their troubles to themselves. Everybody thought of them as nice, churchgoing people. One neighbor remembered when he told John he didn't work his kids enough, John said there was plenty of time for them to work.

It must have been a bickering household to grow up in, with David's mother constantly leaving and his father, John, always going to track her down and convince her to come back. John would never tell her he was sorry or take any blame for their troubles. They couldn't talk to each other, his wife remembered years later. It was either John's way or no way.

David, next to the youngest in the family, learned early how to please and charm others to get his way or to be noticed. He developed the kind of personality and good manners that drew others to him.

While Harding was a student at Waverly High School he was known as a kid who got good grades, played hard enough on the junior varsity football team to impress the coach, and even worked at a greenhouse after school to earn enough money to buy a car. By the time he was a senior, though, Harding's work schedule kept him from participating in school activities and maintaining many close friendships. Still, he appeared to teachers as a very mature and serious young man.

David was a senior in high school when he persuaded Henry Thomas, the local deputy sheriff, to let him ride around with him during his night shift. The deputy was impressed with Harding's seriousness and marveled at how fast Harding picked up whatever Thomas told him about the work. Thomas felt Harding would make an outstanding policeman, especially liking David's attitude. Harding said that wanting to help people was the reason he wanted to be a cop. The deputy advised David never to forget that police work had to do with people and not statistics. Thomas also advised Harding to get a college degree before applying for the state police.

David already knew what he wanted to do with his life. In the 1976 high school yearbook, an entry read, "Dave Harding leaves for the police academy." He was the only student in the yearbook senior pictures wearing sunglasses, perhaps already wanting to look the part of a detective.

He had a great urge to succeed. He especially wanted to be in a profession that was respected. And in the beginning he had a romantic notion about police work. There was something glamorous about it that appealed to Harding. He'd heard that the state police paid well and if you worked hard you had a chance to go up the career ladder.

Unlike most of his classmates, David knew he had to do well in college to get ahead. He applied himself to his work, first at Tompkins-Cortland Community College with an associate's degree in criminal justice, and then two more years for a bachelor's degree from Elmira College. Doing better than most others in his classes added to his confidence.

He married his high school sweetheart, who was from a well-respected and affluent family. They owned the big supermarket in town. This was a first step up the social ladder. He began working for the Waverly school district while completing college. By 1982, at age twenty-four, Harding became the full-time director of the Home-School Justice Program, where he set up programs for kids in trouble or near it. He started peer counseling for students with substance abuse problems. When he left the job in 1985 to join the state police, he was showered with praise and notes of appreciation from parents and teachers about the excellent job he had done.

During his time with the school program, Harding was in charge of federal and state grant monies that covered most of the budget for which he was responsible. It was easy to take some of the cash for himself without anyone noticing it. Harding rationalized to himself that he wasn't being paid enough for the amount of work he did.

After Harding was accepted by the state police, he drove to Ed Kelly's house. Harding knew Kelly had been with the force a long time. Harding introduced himself as a new recruit in the state police. Kelly was in his front yard planting a cherry tree. He had heard of Dave Harding around town. The two men talked for a while, and Kelly was impressed with the young man. Kelly was happy to welcome him into the state police, he told Harding.

Looking towards moving up kept Harding on friendly terms with Kelly, who was high up in the organization and might be able to help David in the future.

Harding started the six-month course at the police academy in Albany, New York, in September 1985. He had a jump on many of the recruits with his four-year degree in criminal justice and solid work experience. The training was tough, but Harding bore down, determined to do well, and came out near the top of his class. He didn't mind working hard. He'd watched his father put in long hours and knew it was essential to getting anywhere. Harding's teachers chose him to deliver the valedictory address at the academy graduation exercises.

After Harding started the police academy he was notified by the Waverly School District that they had discovered $1,000 unaccounted for in the budget he had managed. They accused him of embezzlement but had not gone to authorities. Harding had left such a good impression on them and had performed so well in the position he held, and being a hometown boy, that he was treated more like a wayward son than a thief.

Harding went home the next weekend and pleaded with his former boss not to reveal his wrongdoing to the state police. His future would be ruined, he said. Harding would pay back what he had taken. He had intended to pay them back all along. Immediately, Harding sent the district a check and they agreed to keep silent. Harding maneuvered out of the bad situation with polished guile.

By the time Harding graduated from the academy his instructors and peers predicted a bright future for him in police work. Many thought he had the intelligence and personality to go far in the elite force.

The lifestyle Harding took on soon after joining the state police showed that he was sure of his future. He and his wife bought a spacious house with a small farm for his father to run. David drove a Park Avenue Buick and filled a closet with three-piece suits, ties, shirts and shoes. Not expensive clothes, but fashionable.

He spent less than a year as a road trooper, unlike most officers who work the highways several years before moving up. The next step—undercover drug and theft investigations—was more to his liking. Convinced he needed a specialty to stand out among his peers, Harding took the highly technical training in evidence identification work and became an expert in fingerprints. He was also an experienced photographer.

At the time of the Harris murders, Harding had just been promoted to investigator and was the top ID man in Troop C, having completed the necessary training a year before. He was thirty-one years old.

But the long hours he spent on the job and his liking for women finally caught up with him. He went through a bitter divorce that filled him with rage and self-pity.

Even though people were calling him a hero, Harding fluctuated between bouts of self-pity and delusions of grandeur. He told friends he was writing a book or screenplay about the Harris murders. That he was planning to sell it to a Hollywood producer. His story would feature him as the hero in the investigation. Maybe Harding said he could play his own part. He had always wanted to be in the movies.

At just about that time, Harding and an old high school friend decided to go into business together. Being a CIA overseas operative had fallen through for Harding. Now he'd have to show the hometown crowd he could be a successful businessman.

Harding figured he was smart enough to juggle two careers. He was used to working long hours. And he wanted to make big money. He called the venture "Harding Enterprises," with a slogan of, "We'll make your dream a reality." The partners started looking for land to buy where they could first build a Go-Cart racetrack and add a miniature golf course later. Harding bought a vanity New York State license plate for his pickup truck that read: HAINC (Harding Incorporated).

Harding made sure his colleagues and superiors knew he wanted to be assigned to the Owego station when something opened up. Owego was closer to the Waverly area where his business interests were. The nearness to home and a lower work load at a small, rural station fit his changed priorities.

Even though people around Harding were applauding his heroism, it seemed to David McElligott that every time he ran into Harding the younger man was whining about something. McElligott listened as Harding complained with tears in his eyes about not being able to see his children when he wanted. His ex-wife was heartless, just wanted his money, and caused the divorce, Harding said. Though even McElligott had heard of Harding's infidelities. He then talked about writing letters to his daughters every day because their mother wouldn't let him talk to them.

"Be real nice to her," McElligott advised. "Don't cry about it."

Shortly afterward, McElligott heard that Harding had stopped drinking, which was a good thing, McElligott thought. Everybody knew alcohol made Harding crazy enough to want to fight everybody in sight.

One day McElligott walked into an office at the Varna station and saw Harding moping over in the corner. "How you doing, Big-time?" McElligott asked. As he watched Harding, it triggered McElligott's feelings that he didn't like this man, that there was something wrong with Harding's basic character. McElligott wished he knew exactly what.

"I lost my father a year ago today," Harding answered, tears rolled down his face.

"Well, I lost my father thirty-five years ago and you know

what I do, I come out every day and make him proud of me. You don't sit around and cry about it," McElligott said. He told Harding his kids were born about twenty-seven years after his father died and they still loved him. "My nine-year-old son says in his nightly prayers, 'God bless grandfather because I like him, love him and miss him.'"

McElligott's dislike of Harding was growing. He was tired of Harding's childish behavior, and McElligott had little patience with people who brought their troubles to work.

Harding started teaching a course in the Criminal Justice Program as an adjunct professor at Tompkins Cortland Community College, where he had received an associate degree. He thrived in the role. He walked back and forth in front of the class as he shook his finger to make a point. He boasted of how he found Shirley Kinge's fingerprints on a gasoline can in the Harris home. It was the only evidence, Harding said with a broad smile, that connected her to the crime.

"Fingerprints don't lie," Harding told the class. "Forensic evidence and physical evidence is what convicts people."

It was at this time that Harding met Joe O'Brien, another adjunct professor in the same program. O'Brien was an ex-FBI agent who had published a book about his Mafia undercover work. Harding told O'Brien he'd read the book, and then asked if he would help Harding get contacts in the publishing world. Harding told O'Brien he was writing a book about the Harris murders. O'Brien was impressed, saying that he'd be glad to put Harding in touch with his agent.

The contact was to be yet another ego enhancer.

Harding liked squeezing in many commitments and projects. The frantic activity proved to Harding that he was in demand.

During this period, Troop C decided to add a third investigator to the BCI unit in Owego. That was good news for

Harding. He expected to be transferred to the small, low-profile location to do routine investigative work. Harding had made it clear to his bosses that he wanted a spot in Owego.

McElligott was responsible for the Owego BCI, but stationed thirty-five miles away in Ithaca, he could not closely supervise the two investigators on staff there. The Owego men, therefore, had to be very reliable and self-suffcient. Among other things, Harding's personality had bothered McElligott for a long time. He didn't think Harding was stable enough to handle the independence. He was too emotional. And though McElligott had tried to forget his feeling about Harding's testimony at the Shirley Kinge preliminary hearing, he hadn't been able to. If something was wrong with those prints and Harding had lied to him, McElligott would expose him. More than anything, McElligott hated rotten cops.

McElligott went to the captain and explained some of his misgivings about Harding. He explained that he had no proof but he wanted to watch Harding closely. McElligott asked that Harding not be assigned to Owego. Because of the conversation, Harding was passed over and remained in Binghamton.

Not long afterward, a suspicious David Harding called the captain and asked why he hadn't been given the Owego assignment. *Did David McElligott block it?* The captain took full responsibility for the decision, but Harding learned from others that it was McElligott who had been the stumbling block.

McElligott's autocratic style had always rubbed Harding the wrong way. His surefire directness intimidated Harding. In fact, he was scared of the man. The Owego opening had appealed to Harding because he could be on his own. He could be a big fish in a small pond. With Harding's technical background in identification work and the reputation he had in Troop C, the other investigators would look to him for leadership.

The word got back to McElligott that Harding was boiling mad over not getting the Owego job. It was then that McElligott realized his strong feelings about Harding went beyond a clash of personalities. McElligott had begun to think Harding was more than unstable. There was no telling what Harding might do. He was dangerous. McElligott decided to protect himself and started wearing a gun all the time.

Harding knew where McElligott lived. He drove by McElligott's house on the way to work at the Binghamton station every day.

On St. Patrick's Day McElligott was investigating a homicide on which Harding was assigned as one of the ID men. Before McElligott returned to the station, Hank Brown called from Binghamton to say Harding had injured his back en route to the crime scene. Harding had discovered a flat tire and as he lifted the spare out, Harding claimed to have pulled something and was in terrible pain. McElligott doubted the story, but at least he knew Harding would go on sick leave and be out of McElligott's way if not off his mind. As the days passed, McElligott relaxed a little more and got back to work.

On disability from the state police at full pay due to his back injury, reportedly a fragmented disk, Harding still worked hard making preparations for the Go-Cart track, "Lil' Daytona," to open for the summer season. He found a good location in Athens, Pennsylvania, set between two heavily traveled roads. Harding told a trooper friend that he'd be making a thousand dollars a day on the track because it would be so popular with kids and adults. Apparently, there was very little to do for recreation in the area.

At first, Harding consistently showed he had a back problem every time he was out in public. After all, someone might see him and report to his superiors. As time went on, however, Harding got careless at the racetrack and began

hauling heavy cars from his truck in plain view of spectators.

Rumors about Harding's health got back to the department, and though McElligott heard them, he held his tongue.
McElligott was more interested in waiting for Harding to
make a major slip, one where McElligott could catch and expose him.

Twenty-four
Lies and Truth

It had been the usual busy morning for Francis DeFrancesco on May 26, 1992. Just as he was finishing up the paper work, his secretary announced on the phone intercom that a local FBI agent wanted to speak with him. DeFrancesco was chief of the inspection section of the New York State Police in Albany. It was his job to see that the professional standards of the five thousand employees were upheld. Suspected wrongdoing and disciplining the offenders when necessary, were his section's assignments. DeFrancesco had been with the state police for thirty years, starting out as a road trooper; he now held one of the top positions in the organization. He'd been in this job for five years.

Suddenly, the phone rang. DeFrancesco heard an agitated voice. Agent Josh Billings outlined an incident that had occurred eighteen months before and had just been brought to his unit's attention by the headquarters of the Justice Department. The time lag, so the agent had been told, was due to an internal congestion problem.

"I'm to pass on to you that one of your people made an

admission to the CIA during an interview that he'd falsified evidence in a criminal case," the agent told DeFrancesco.

"Who made the admission?" DeFrancesco asked.

"I don't have any more information about the thing. You'll have to call the CIA for details."

DeFrancesco asked who he should call at the CIA and got the name of a spokesperson and a telephone number in Virginia. Worried, he called the agency immediately.

The CIA spokesperson put him in touch with the general counsel for the agency, who corroborated what DeFrancesco had been told by the FBI agent. The spokesperson explained that the job applicant made criminal admissions during a routine polygraph interview. He had faked fingerprints in some case. The person was David L. Harding. The Kinge case flashed through DeFrancesco's mind.

They discussed how DeFrancesco could get additional information about the taped interview. He wanted to send officers from his staff down to Virginia right away to listen to the tape and to speak with the interviewer. DeFrancesco explained that Harding had been involved with a number of cases and one in particular had a high profile.

The CIA agreed to rush a security clearance on Ed Kelly and Richard Solomon, the two inspectors DeFrancesco decided to send down.

DeFrancesco knew David Harding and his sterling reputation. His division was responsible for an annual awards ceremony that recognized outstanding achievements of individual troopers. Harding had been nominated for that award for his work on the Harris murder case, but he wasn't selected. DeFrancesco thought Harding was an outstanding police officer with a bright future. Harding seemed a good role model for beginning troopers.

While they waited for Kelly and Solomon to be cleared by the CIA, about twenty inspectors began studying the

Troop C cases in which Harding was involved. Since the investigators didn't know the names of either the defendant or the victim in the evidence tampering case to which Harding admitted, they were in for a long, painstaking job. They had been told it was a 1988 homicide involving an old man. At least that was a beginning.

On June 17, Kelly and Solomon were cleared and the next day, the two men drove down to CIA headquarters outside of Washington, D.C. There, Kelly and Solomon were permitted to listen to the three and a half hour tape of Harding's polygraph interview and to take notes. The CIA policy did not allow tape reproductions because they wanted to keep the methods that examiners use to ask sensitive questions under strict control. They also did not allow Kelly and Solomon to talk with the examiner whose identity the CIA preferred to keep confidential.

Formerly, the CIA had conducted background checks on all their recruits as part of the preliminary selection process, which was a very expensive undertaking. Then they would hold polygraph interviews, but they found that some who passed the field exam were flunking the polygraph, so they switched it around and put the polygraph at the beginning of the process. The polygraph interview focused on specific questions regarding allegiance to country and lifestyle and was intended to uncover serious violations of the law, drug use, and financial instability. The object was to determine if the applicant could be trusted to handle classified information. Every employee of the CIA had to take the polygraph.

The Security Office, housed away from the CIA compound, is responsible for conducting the polygraphs. The examiners have no law enforcement authority. The interviews are all recorded on a master forty-track reel that may cover a three-day period of consecutive interviews. The recorder has a video window on it which displays the reel time as the interview is taking place to a hundredth of a second. In Harding's case, the reel on which Harding's interview was recorded covered three calendar days.

The examiners are trained in probing techniques that delve into a candidate's character. Before he was interviewed, Harding signed a release which stated that the interview was confidential except in matters of violations to national security or admissions of criminal activity. The form stated that the CIA was obligated to notify the Justice Department if an applicant admitted to breaking the law. The release included his rights under the Fifth Amendment of the United States Constitution. Kelly and Solomon heard the interviewer give similar oral instructions to Harding on the tape.

Early in the test the examiner made in-depth inquiries to see if Harding was involved with individuals or nations that are considered a threat to the security of the United States. Harding was clean in that respect. He had never wandered far from the rural area of New York State where he was born. It was in the last thirty minutes of the tape, when the examiner moved on to questions of lifestyle, and character issues, that Harding's answers changed. When the examiner asked if he had ever broken the law, Harding hesitated and cleared his throat. The examiner pressed, repeating the question.

Harding, lowering his voice, said, "There was a case in 1988, a homicide, involving an eighty-one year old man who was beaten over the head with a lead pipe. We could place the suspect on the property, but we couldn't place him in the house. I took a print and said it came from the victim's house, but it came from the property of the defendant's residence."

"I pulled this trick two or three times," Harding added. Amazed, Kelly looked at Solomon, whose face reddened.

There were other admissions Harding made on the tape that further disturbed both men. They hit Ed Kelly in a more personal way, since he was the person Harding had come to early in Harding's career. Although Kelly didn't have contact with Harding on the job, Kelly had heard Harding was doing very well in Troop C. He had been proud that another Waverly resident was making a name for himself in the state police. Kelly knew Harding had personal problems, a nasty divorce and his father's death had been a blow. It was hard keeping anything a secret in the small village of Waverly, but Kelly had believed that on the job, Harding was a superstar.

The two investigators played the last thirty minutes of the tape over and over to make sure they had all the facts down precisely. They listened intently as the interviewer asked Harding if he had ever stolen from a friend. Before Harding answered, he was told the significance of lying to a friend. "If you lie to a friend, you can't be trusted for anything. How can a colleague trust you if you can't even be trusted by a friend?"

Harding nodded yes; he once stole a baseball glove from his best friend. His tone of voice changed again. It got flatter. Harding sighed, sounding more languid and depressed. At one point he said, "I can't believe I'm telling you these things." Harding admitted to the interviewer that "I'm indictable as I sit here today."

"That's not my concern, David," the examiner said. "What I want to do is get you through the interview."

Harding said he didn't think the superintendent, the head of the New York Police, would agree with him. The interviewer asked, "Is there anything else?" Yes, there was a lot more.

Harding told about stealing a bicycle when he was five, lying during his divorce proceedings, holding back alimony money, stealing money from the school district where he was employed before joining the state police, stealing money meant for a drug sting, taking weight off seized drugs to give a guy a break and adding weight at other times. By the time Kelly and Solomon finished listening to the last half hour of the polygraph interview, they had written down a shocking eight-page confession.

Stunned, the two men drove back to Albany and conferred with DeFrancesco, McElligott and Chandler. Harding was still on sick leave; so they didn't have to worry about public safety. They had time to conduct a thorough investigation before confronting him. Their first priority had to be to find out about the 1988 case of the old man hit over the head with a lead pipe in which Harding had admitted to faking a print. At this point they knew very little. The next day inspectors went through all the homicide case files that Harding had worked on in 1988. It took the whole day and they still didn't find anything. They decided to try looking at all major cases—burglaries, robberies, assaults—after 1987.

By Tuesday afternoon, June 23, they'd found a robbery and assault case that occurred August, 1988, in Tompkins County where the assailant, Mark Prentice, hit an old man over the head with a lead pipe. Harding had supplied fingerprint evidence in the case, but the investigators didn't know if there had been a trial. They had to do more digging. DeFrancesco wanted it all verified by the crime laboratory before the police faced Harding with all the evidence against him.

However, late that day DeFrancesco found out that Harding was involved with the Eichele murder case in Broome County. William Eichele was accused of killing Judith Dashev, whose body was found in a ditch with her head wrapped in silver duct tape. Harding had supplied Eichele's fingerprint, which Harding said he had lifted from the duct tape.

Hearing this, DeFrancesco knew they had to move fast. He called the Broome County District Attorney, Gerold Mollen, to ask Mollen if he had that case ready for trial.

"Oh, no. That's in trial now," Mollen said. "My chief assistant, Kevin Dooley, is prosecuting the case."

DeFrancesco asked what participation David Harding had in the trial.

Mollen replied, "Dave's scheduled to testify as a witness tomorrow."

DeFrancesco told Mollen, "We have to talk with you." DeFrancesco took a deep breath and let it out. "We have a problem with Harding. Don't put him on the stand," DeFrancesco said.

"Can't we talk about it on the phone?" Mollen asked.

"No." DeFrancesco replied grimly, "I'm sending Ed Kelly down tomorrow morning to meet with you."

After talking to McElligott, Kelly, Solomon, and Dan Martin drove down to Binghamton on Tuesday night. Martin worked directly under DeFrancesco as deputy chief inspector in charge of the professional standards unit.

The three men met with Mollen and Dooley at a Howard Johnson's on Wednesday morning. They decided to meet in the restaurant because Harding was in the D.A.'s office waiting to testify. Harding knew Kelly was with internal affairs and might suspect something if Kelly was seen in the building.

Kelly told Mollen and Dooley they had an allegation about Harding tampering with evidence, something he admitted to during a CIA polygraph interview. The investigators' search so far had turned up the Mark Prentice assault and robbery case in Tompkins County in 1988. They were fairly certain but not positive it was the one.

Dooley told them, as far as he knew, the Eichele print Harding had lifted was good. "But you've got to interview Dave and find out," he said in an agitated voice. "I can't wait till you guys get more proof. Interview him right away. I've got a jury sitting in there. I've got to know if those prints are good or not," Dooley insisted.

"But we aren't ready to interview Dave. We don't have all the information we need to confront him yet," Martin told the district attorney.

"You've got to interview him now. This trial has to move forward," Mollen fired back. ·

Because of the time problem, Kelly, Solomon and Martin decided to ask George Dentes, the Tompkins County District Attorney, to come down from Ithaca. It turned out he was scheduled to meet with a Broome County District Attorney and a judge that morning.

Dentes and McElligott drove down to see the judge together. When they arrived at the courthouse, Mollen asked to see Dentes privately. McElligott waited in the front office.

He hadn't been there very long when he saw David Harding coming down the hall. Harding looked suntanned and McElligott noticed his hair was longer in the back.

When Harding got close, McElligott stood up, "How are you doing?" McElligott asked. The two men shook hands in a perfunctory way. Dave Harding's smile seemed forced, but he appeared to assume McElligott was testifying in another case. Harding picked up a newspaper and walked back down the hall to Dooley's office.

Harding waited outside the office all Wednesday morning. A secretary said the trial had been held up, Harding's testimony was postponed, but she didn't know why. When he finally walked into the D.A.'s office after noon, Harding was caught off guard. He was expecting to go over his testimony with Dooley and found gathered there Gary Mollen, Ed Kelly, and two men he didn't know, Dan Martin and Richard Solomon. They had decided to interview Harding about the CIA admission that day.

Kelly introduced Harding to Martin and Solomon from internal affairs and immediately began asking Harding about the CIA revelation. Harding denied the accusations about the faked Prentice print. He said it wasn't true. Then everyone left the room except Kelly and Solomon.

Harding appeared fidgety and unresponsive. His face had turned ashen. He looked down and wouldn't meet Kelly's stare. Kelly asked Solomon to leave the room, thinking Dave might open up with someone he knew. After a while, with only Kelly questioning him, Harding admitted he'd faked the one print, but that was all. When Kelly confronted him with other admissions of misconduct he'd heard on the CIA tape, Harding told him none of the others were true. According to Harding, he was trying to make the kind of impression he felt the CIA was looking for in their overseas operatives. "They weren't looking for choir boys or Boy Scouts," Harding told Kelly.

The Eichele print was good, Harding insisted. Harding told Kelly he wanted to come clean on the Prentice case. He wanted to admit his mistakes but he didn't want the Eichele prosecution to suffer.

By this time Harding appeared emotionally overwrought; he began pleading with Kelly to disclose what would happen to Harding in his career. The state police was his life, Harding said emotionally. He broke down several times as he paced back and forth, fingering the beads of a rosary. Harding said his recent conversion to Catholicism was getting him through some bad times. He mentioned the breakup of his marriage and that he still missed his dead father. Ed Kelly looked at Harding with disgust, "I'm glad your father isn't around to see you."

Kelly told Harding he didn't know what would happen to him. Kelly couldn't make those predictions. He brought Dan Martin in and Harding asked him the same question.

"It's not my decision," Martin said. "But I assume you'll never work for the state police again."

The rest of the day, Dooley prepared Harding for the cross-examination of his testimony on the Eichele print. The defense would be notified about the dummy Prentice print. Harding would have to be very forthright on the stand about the procedures he took in lifting the Eichele print in order to convince the jury that this one was good. Harding, agony on his face, nodded. He asked Dooley what was going to happen to him. Would he be charged? Dooley said that was up to Mr. Dentes since Prentice was a Tompkins County case.

McElligott drove Dentes back to Ithaca after they had seen the judge that afternoon. Dentes was unusually quiet during the trip home.

That night McElligott received a call from Richard Kaiden, a senior investigator in Binghamton.

"Something's up in the troop. Something to do with the Eichele trial," Kaiden said.

"What makes you think there's something up?" McElligott asked.

"They postponed the Eichele trial and the D.A. wouldn't tell me why. He sounded real up-tight."

"Keep me posted, buddy," McElligott said as they hung up.

Harding went back to Binghamton on Thursday morning to testify in the Eichele trial.

On that same morning, Kaiden called McElligott again.

"Inspectors are in town. Somebody's in trouble," Kaiden said.

"I wonder who it is—uniform or bureau? Probably something to do with drugs," McElligott said.

Later that day, Kaiden called McElligott for a third time.

"You wanna know who's the guy in trouble?"

"Yeah, tell me," McElligott said.

"It's Harding," Kaiden announced.

McElligott, who had been waiting for this for a long time, felt his heart skip a beat. The connection became silent for a long moment. Then McElligott asked, "What did he do?"

"Something to do with perjury," Kaiden told him.

"Goddamn, it's the Kinge case," McElligott fired back.

"No, it's something here. It's got to do with the Eichele case. Damn it, I know those prints are good," Kaiden said. He was an unwavering believer in the guys who worked under him. Kaiden went on. "He couldn't have faked those prints." It was Kaiden's case. He had a personal stake in it.

Bits of information were coming together in McElligott's mind. "When did he make his match—before or after Eichele's arrest?" McElligott asked.

"About a week after the arrest, I think," Kaiden answered.

McElligott knew then that more revelations would follow. It was just a matter of time. The first news broke the next day in the media. Harding had admitted, during a CIA interview, that he lied about a fingerprint in the Mark Prentice case in 1988.

McElligott realized his worst suspicions had been right on the money. He thought about how Harding appeared to be such a devoted father to his two daughters, how much he complained about not seeing them enough, and yet he wanted to join the CIA to be sent all over the world.

Kevin Dooley, the Broome County Assistant District Attorney trying the Eichele case, met with Judge Patrick Matthews in his chambers Thursday morning to tell him of the Harding problem. The judge said under the circumstances of admitted perjury, it would be entirely improper for Harding to testify in the Eichele case.

Harding still swore to Dooley that the print he had taken was good. He wanted to help Dooley out in the case. Harding would come back on Friday regardless, he told Dooley.

Late Thursday, Harding contacted Gary Allen, who had been his supervisor at one time and was now a retired senior investigator living in Tompkins County. Harding said he didn't know what to do. He sounded so distraught that Allen drove over to Waverly. Harding didn't tell him the full story of his troubles with the state police, but it was obvious to Allen that Harding needed legal counsel. He contacted Earl Butler in Vestal, New York, who agreed to be Harding's lawyer.

At 1:00 P.M. on Friday, June 26, the foundation of Harding's reputation crumbled to the ground. The former star investigator was notified that he had been suspended without pay from the state police.

Twenty-five
Shelling Paradise

Towns, like individuals, have personalities: the warmth of Atlanta, the excitement of New York City, the sophistication of Paris, the majesty of London. When traumas occur, towns also accumulate stress points. If the total of these strains exceeds the tolerable limits, they can contribute to a character breakdown. Such was the case with the town of Ithaca when its stunned citizens heard that their hero, David Harding, the man who had quelled the fears and anxieties provoked by the Harris murders, the man who discovered the evidence that satisfied their collective need for justice and sent Shirley Kinge to prison, was now accused of evidence tampering.

Like a choral refrain, the repetitive chant of questions about Harding's crucial fingerprint evidence rose to a crescendo. The Harrises' neighbors and friends, as much as they hated to see the case reopened, knew that justice required giving Shirley Kinge another trial.

The townspeople's confidence, their cohesiveness, their spirit, which after so much emotional turmoil had finally begun to heal, dissembled once again.

While they tried to cope with this new blow, more questions surfaced about Harding himself. Why did he lie and tamper with evidence when he was already advancing rapidly in his career? Was it to stand out as a "whiz kid," was it for self-promotion or to get ahead faster than his peers? DeFrancesco remarked to the press how unusual and sad this kind of integrity investigation was. In most cases, police corruption was motivated by financial gain, not for career advancement as the Harding affair seemed.

Later DeFrancesco told a news conference at the state police barracks in Kirkwood, New York, outside of Binghamton, "This is a disgraceful situation. There are no two ways to look at it." He explained that a team of fifteen fingerprint and other technical experts, inside and out of the state police, would do a total review of Harding's work. The team of state inspectors received advice from FBI forensic experts about what to look for in the cases, how to spot suspicious evidence, and what they should do with that questionable evidence to get it ready for the FBI crime laboratory.

"There are other allegations concerning his conduct that I'm not going to get into at this time," DeFrancesco added.

Bill Sullivan announced he would seek a new trial for Shirley Kinge largely because of the Harding revelation. He said that without Harding's testimony, Kinge could not have been convicted.

"It's my view that the jury in the Kinge trial must feel terribly betrayed by the conduct of Mr. Harding. It puts the whole system at risk and in jeopardy," Sullivan said with emotion.

Sullivan had been working at two levels in his continued defense of Kinge. He had filed a notice of appeal immediately after Kinge's conviction and until the announcement about Harding, had been preparing a case for direct appeal to be heard before the New York State Court of Appeals.

An inspector expressed to McElligott his compassion at how hurt McElligott must feel after working so closely with Harding, implying the two men were friends.

McElligott looked straight into the man's eyes. There it

was again. He was caught between saying nothing to uphold department loyalty and telling the truth out of honesty to himself. It was the essential dilemma in which sooner or later each person finds himself. This time, McElligott chose to serve his own conscience.

"Let's get this fuckin' straight. As I've said before he don't like me and I don't like him. He's a jerk," McElligott said decisively.

A sealed, eleven-count indictment against Harding was handed up Tuesday, July 14, in Tompkins County Court. Unsealed Wednesday morning, the indictment charged Harding with four counts of first-degree perjury, six counts of tampering with physical evidence, and one count of first-degree making a sworn, false statement. All the charges were related to the Mark Prentice case in which Prentice was charged with striking an eighty-one year old man in the head with a metal pipe during a robbery in August of 1988.

Harding had testified during the Prentice trial that he'd found the defendant's fingerprint on the kitchen sink in the victim's home and on a Budweiser bottle on the ground outside. His testimony connected Prentice to the scene of the beating and robbery. Prentice pleaded guilty to his six-count indictment two days into the trial. Harding now admitted he lifted the prints from a Labatts bottle discovered in a garage at the defendant's home.

Troopers knocked on Harding's door in Waverly at 12:30 A.M. on Wednesday, July 15, and told him he was under arrest on charges of evidence tampering and perjury. Harding asked them would it be okay if he took care of some family business first?

The troopers agreed to wait for him at the front door. One trooper remained there and the other stood by the patrol car parked in the gravel driveway. Ten minutes later a smiling Harding came out; he had changed into a dark blue double-breasted suit and striped silk tie. When the trooper reported the incident to cops who knew Harding, they said Harding probably figured the media would be around and he wanted to look good on camera.

Harding was held in a secure area in Tompkins County Jail overnight. County deputies thought he might be a target for inmate violence.

His arraignment was scheduled for Wednesday morning before County Judge Betty Friedlander. Harding didn't enter a plea at that time, because his lawyer wasn't with him. Judge Friedlander set that Friday morning as the time for Harding to return to court with counsel. She released him on his own recognizance based on George Dentes' recommendation.

Though Harding's personal guilt was the first thing to be decided, his arrest ignited the most serious scandal to engulf the New York State Police in its seventy-five year history. It brought out long-standing gripes and resentments some people had harbored toward the elite force for years. Newspaper editorials rapped the agency hard. They scorned the idea of the agency investigating itself. One editorial proposed that an outside group be hired to investigate the problems within the state police. Other troopers across the state had recently been accused of misconduct in the media.

Defense lawyers told reporters they weren't surprised the Harding revelation came to light. They claimed state investigators were elitist, even arrogant, and when they appeared as witnesses juries tended to believe them more often because of their badges and the tradition they represent, rather than as a result of the evidence or arguments they present.

Major Robert Farrand, the Troop C commander, reminded the press that Harding was "just one guy" out of more than four thousand people serving in the state police. State Police Superintendent Thomas Constantine said that charges of evidence tampering "strike at the very heart of the criminal justice system," and promised that evidence in every case Harding had ever handled would be reassessed.

DeFrancesco called the preliminary charges the first step in the overall investigation of Harding's involvement in about fifty cases, spanning his seven-year career. The best the state police could hope for was that Harding had committed one gross error and the rest of his cases would come up clean.

At a press conference that afternoon, State Police officials said the alleged misconduct disgraced the state organization. They described Harding as an aberration and dismissed suggestions that evidence tempering could be widespread.

In 1983 Harding had taken a course in bloodstain analysis under Herbert MacDonell, a forensic expert from Corning, New York. He couldn't remember Harding well but did recall that Harding had received an "A" in the course. When he was interviewed, MacDonell said he'd heard of many evidence tampering cases in his more than thirty years in the field. "Some investigators feel they've got to have a conviction," the expert, who was now in private practice as a teacher and investigator, said.

Harding's colleagues wondered why he had jeopardized his promising career with such a flagrant violation. And why would he admit perjury to the CIA? The story that the intelligence agency wanted no "Boy Scouts," that they were looking for tough guys who could pull off feats in or outside the law, sounded naive, or just plain stupid. Did Harding really think the CIA hired crooks?

Twenty-six
Vainglory

The Tompkins County courthouse was buzzing with television cameras and press people even before Harding arrived on Friday morning, July 17. Most of the reporters knew Harding from the celebrated Shirley Kinge trial. On that occasion they'd had him on camera every day while Harding was testifying and the press could always count on Harding to talk. Some imagined, with the tables turned, he might not be so ready to gab with media folks. After all, this time he was being indicted on serious charges.

The reporters had nothing to worry about. From the time he was spotted walking from the parking lot into the building, Harding greeted reporters with a smile, looking relaxed in his blue suit with silk tie and matching pocket handkerchief. He looked more like a star attending an awards ceremony than a suspended police officer facing the consequences of perjury.

Harding walked over to where the media gathered in the courtroom before proceedings began. "If you want me to cry my eyes out, I won't. There's no reason for me to," David Harding told the reporters. He talked to them about his clothes after someone remarked how sharp he looked. Another reporter asked Harding about his hair, recently turned blond and grown longer in the back. Harding told the reporter he had been cast as the adult son of one of the women baseball players in the film *A League of Their Own*, and the director suggested that Harding dye his hair for the part. "There I am, center-screen for a couple of seconds," he said with obvious pride.

Harding appeared to relish telling the group about the fun he had making the movie in Cooperstown, New York, the previous summer. He was asked about the movie script he was writing on the Harris murders and Harding said it was going very well. When asked about the charges against him, Harding said he couldn't talk about it.

The actual arraignment was almost anticlimactic. Harding pleaded not guilty to multiple charges of perjury and evidence tampering, stemming from the 1988 assault and robbery trial of Mark Prentice. Judge Betty Friedlander once again followed George Dentes' recommendation and allowed Harding to remain free without bail. A trial date would be set later.

Outside the courthouse after the arraignment, Earl Butler, Harding's attorney, blasted state police officials for holding a press conference Wednesday afternoon. Butler said the comments were premature, coming before Harding had been given a fair trial. He indicated state police were trying to gloss over their own internal problems.

"It is unwarranted that he's a lightning rod for everything that's wrong with the state police," Butler said.

Butler refused to say if Harding had implicated other troopers in the evidence tampering charges.

As soon as he heard about Harding, Bill Sullivan began to seek a new trial for Shirley Kinge. He said, "She thinks two and a half years is a long time to be jailed for something she didn't do."

George Dentes pointed out that Kinge would still serve

time for four forgery counts even if the rest of the conviction were undermined.

"There won't be an apology from me, that's for sure," Dentes said. "It's not like she's a totally innocent person sitting in the can."

Dentes and McElligott saw each other a few days after their trip back from Binghamton. Dentes told McElligott that as of yet, nothing had been uncovered to indicate that Harding had fabricated evidence in the Kinge trial.

McElligott felt differently. "George, every goddamn case he touched is suspect in my book. The whole Kinge case is gonna blow up in our faces because of that lying bastard," McElligott said in an agitated voice. Dentes told him that if there was one chance in a thousand that Shirley Kinge was sent to prison unjustly, he wouldn't be able to sleep at night until that wrong was made right. "We should move her out now, George," McElligott advised.

But Dentes objected, saying that nothing was proven yet that Harding had tampered in the Kinge case.

McElligott shook his head vehemently. "That woman was never in that house. That's just my opinion, like I said before," McElligott said.

Lil' Daytona racetrack was getting a lot of publicity in Athens and Sayre, Pennsylvania, when David Harding and his partner opened for business later that July. Long lines of children and adults waited for their turn to drive a miniature racing car around the track. Harding began boasting that he'd opened a gold mine on Elmira Street, where the traffic going by was said to be eight thousand cars a day from Binghamton, Elmira, Johnson City and Endicott.

As for the indictment against him, Harding figured it was not a big problem, because it would be his word against what someone said he had related to the CIA. No way would the secretive agency release the interview tape, which was the only real proof that he admitted fabricating evidence. And it was his word against Ed Kelly's regarding what was said in the Broome County courthouse in June.

The future would tell if Harding had judged correctly, but his indictment on charges of perjury in a Tompkins County assault case had already caused a great stir. County Judge Betty Friedlander, who was hearing the case against Harding, felt it was appropriate to appoint a special prosecutor to handle the Harding case to avoid a possible conflict of interest by the district attorney. She explained that the district attorney's office was in the position of prosecuting the defendant for perjury while having to defend his testimony in other cases. Friedlander felt a private attorney would best serve the public interest, because the defendant had been around central New York and district attorneys knew him.

Dentes responded to Friedlander's proposal with a firm rebuttal. He argued that to appoint a special prosecutor now would not only be premature but pointless.

"The issue is always the same—did the defendant lie in the particular case before the court or did he not?—and that can be argued just as well, and just as ethically, by one district attorney as by any one or more surrogate prosecutors," Dentes insisted.

In the same statement, Dentes said he expected to strike an agreement with Shirley Kinge's lawyer unless the state police verified the evidence that David Harding provided against Kinge.

At the request of the state police, the FBI laboratory in Washington, D.C., had begun to study the fingerprint evidence in the Kinge case, making that case a priority over the fifty others in which Harding had been involved as an identification specialist.

The agreement, Dentes announced, could involve dropping or reducing some charges against Kinge. Remaining charges might be satisfied by the two and a half years she had already served in prison and Kinge could be released.

Curt and brief for one of the rare times in his career, Bill Sullivan said no deal had been struck.

Sullivan added, he would have to bring Shirley Kinge any offer the prosecutor made and if she accepted the offer, it would go into effect.

Sullivan filed a 139-page motion on August 13 asking the court to drop all charges against his client Shirley Kinge in the Harris family murders. In his motion, Sullivan claimed the Tompkins County court jury that had convicted Kinge heard incomplete, unreliable and possibly tainted evidence. He also accused George Dentes of misconduct in regard to blocking evidence from Joanna White that would have bolstered Kinge's alibi. Sullivan claimed Dentes kept quiet the part of White's statement in which she said that Shirley Kinge was home all night December 22, 1989, baby-sitting her son, and when White returned the next morning there was no indication that Kinge had moved her car during the night. Snow covered the car and there were no footprints going to or coming from the house. Sullivan announced that White was willing to testify on Kinge's behalf in a retrial.

Sullivan blasted Harding's testimony against Kinge, calling it "hardly believable . . . in light of the recently uncovered facts." Sullivan went on, "I was troubled by his testimony as it came in at the time of the trial . . . I'm more troubled by it now."

Shirley Kinge's long pent-up anger surfaced in a succinct sworn statement Sullivan took from her when he visited the Bedford Hills prison. "I categorically and unequivocally deny that I was at the Harris home or was otherwise involved in any manner in respect to any of those crimes," she said. Kinge admitted using the stolen credit card, but she said she did not know Dolores Harris had been murdered until Kinge watched a late television news report after her December 23, 1989, shopping trip. Sullivan claimed that Joanna White had told police Kinge nearly had a heart attack when she discovered her son had killed the family.

George Dentes stated at a defense motion hearing on August 25 that a state police investigator's alleged admission that he falsified fingerprint evidence in another, unrelated case, "constitutes sufficient new evidence" for a retrial. Dentes said he agreed to the retrial because it was just. He added that a new trial didn't mean Harding's testimony in the Kinge trial was false.

Judge Barrett ruled at the end of the hearing that, based on the Harding allegations, Shirley Kinge deserved a new trial.

When he talked to Dentes, Karl Chandler expressed his outrage at the Harding news with a few strong swear words and let it go. But it nagged at McElligott. McElligott told Chandler he wished he'd socked it to Harding that day after the preliminary hearing when McElligott had heard Harding give less than forthright answers to Sullivan's questions. "I should have sat him down right then and hammered away, like he was a suspect. I knew he was rotten."

The rumors about Harding were bringing shame to the whole department.

"Why should my record suffer because of that lying s.o.b.?" McElligott asked. Although from the first, McElligott had tried to get the others to see the truth about Harding, McElligott was nevertheless perceived by the community to be the officer who ran the Harris murder investigation, and therefore took a lot of heat. Inside, McElligott felt responsible for having failed and accepted the public's criticism but he hated the cloud that hung over Troop C, especially concerning the Harris murder investigation. McElligott firmly believed it was just a matter of time before Harding either admitted he faked the Kinge prints or the laboratory proved he did.

* * *

Despite George Dentes' objections, Judge Friedlander ordered Dentes off the Harding case on August 26 and appointed an Ithaca attorney, Nelson Roth, as special prosecutor. The judge said a conflict of interest would occur if Dentes or any other member of the district attorney's office were to prosecute Harding and simultaneously defend convictions that were obtained, in part, by the investigator's testimony.

Friedlander expressed other concerns about the relationship between Dentes and Harding, saying she saw in Dentes and his assistants, "a troubling inclination to contain the damage done by (Harding's) apparent admissions." Friedlander pointed out that one of Dentes' assistants had stated that the allegations against Harding were limited to the Mark Prentice case, but that view was clearly contradicted by the Broome County Court.

She cited Dentes' recommendation that Harding be released on his own recognizance as an example of a less-than-vigorous prosecution by Dentes' office. Releasing Harding despite the seriousness of his alleged crimes indicated that "manifest inroads in the district attorney's neutrality" had already occurred.

George Dentes bristled at the suggestion that he wasn't a neutral party in the case against David Harding. He filed a caustic reply to Judge Friedlander's decision to pull him off the case as prosecutor. He asked the judge to reconsider her decision to bring in a special prosecutor. Dentes cited instances where Harding had provided evidence in Tompkins County cases under a different district attorney. Dentes informed the judge he had little contact with Harding since the Kinge case and had never known him socially.

"In any event, the Kinge case is not pending before this court. This court has not heard the evidence (against Kinge, who was tried by Judge Barrett) and is not sufficiently informed to make any suggestions about the viability of that prosecution," Dentes wrote in his letter to Friedlander.

The district attorney felt he used the permissible sentencing range to determine the bail decision when recommending that Harding be released on his own recognizance. "Defendants having no prior record and charged with class D nonviolent felonies generally do not go to jail if convicted in Tompkins County," Dentes said.

The friction between Dentes and Friedlander became a public fight, both evaluated the problem differently by virtue of their separate roles in it—as a judge and as a prosecutor. Judge Friedlander wanted to avoid the appearance of a conflict of interest on the part of the district attorney. She had to be careful that a climate of pure objective inquiry pursued these allegations of evidence tampering and perjury by a police officer. She realized the severe damage these charges, if proven, could do to the justice system. Friedlander's overriding concern was to ensure the public that the court's priority was to find the truth in this case and prosecute accordingly.

In a strictly legal sense, George Dentes had been right when he explained his reasons for recommending Harding's release on his own recognizance. However, it was not a very smart move politically. Perhaps this was Dentes' engineering background coming out, following precise details of the law without giving enough thought to the big picture. His opinions were based on the immediate and practical implications. They reflected the investment he and his staff had already made in the Kinge case. The county would save money by appointing another district attorney, because private special prosecutors "are not subject to the monetary limitations that apply to assigned counsel," he had pointed out to Friedlander. Dentes, who had always been so thoroughly honest, was stunned that his motives in the pursuit of justice were being questioned.

Nelson Roth, the new prosecutor Friedlander appointed to look into the allegations against Harding, had offices across the street from the courthouse. It was a handy location since he would be spending many hours in court during the coming months prosecuting the charges against David Harding. Roth had been an attorney in Ithaca since 1978 and was in practice with several partners, doing a variety of legal work.

Soon after Roth was appointed special prosecutor, he asked CIA officials for permission to hear the polygraph tape in which Harding had allegedly admitted to tampering with evidence. After a security clearance came through in September, Roth made a visit to CIA headquarters in Virginia and listened intently to the three and a half hour recording of Harding's interview.

Shirley Kinge appeared before Judge Barrett on September 11, 1992, in the same Tompkins County courtroom where she had been convicted nearly two years before for her part in the Harris family murders. She was freed on twenty-five thousand dollars cash bail after serving two and a half years behind bars. Barrett told Kinge she would have to appear in Tompkins County Court again on November 9 to settle the case. Meanwhile, Kinge went to live with her mother in New Jersey.

Less than a week later, David Harding's attorney, Earl Butler, appeared at a pretrial hearing at his own request, to persuade Judge Friedlander to suppress testimony Harding allegedly made before he was arrested in July. Butler charged that state police tricked his client, luring Harding to the courthouse to testify in a Broome County case, and instead, forcing him to stay in a room answering questions. He contended Harding wasn't even allowed to use the bathroom. "He had no benefit of counsel, and no opportunity to get counsel," Butler said, adding that Harding's Miranda rights were violated.

According to Butler, Harding invented a story because of

the CIA's interviewer's request for proof he was "the kind of man" for which the federal agency was looking. Harding gave certain admissions, Butler asserted, only because inspector Ed Kelly said his disability retirement would be guaranteed if Harding "came clean."

The prosecutor, Nelson Roth, rebutted the claim, saying Kelly did no such thing and that Harding had been free to leave the Broome County District Attorney's office at any time. "Moreover," Roth continued, "based on the defendant's background, training, employment, education, and experience, Harding most assuredly knew his rights and knew he could terminate the conversation and leave at any time."

Roth questioned Harding on the disability issue.

"So, Ed Kelly led you to believe he'd take care of you, get your disability during that first hour on June 24?"

"Yes, sir," answered Harding.

"Yet a higher ranking officer, Mr. Martin, comes in and you asked him specifically the same question about disability and he says a higher authority is gonna have to act on it. Is that right?"

"Yes, sir."

"At that time you didn't believe Ed Kelly could get you the disability, did you?"

"Yes, I did," Harding nodded his head decisively. "Ed Kelly is a very powerful man in the state police. Everybody knows it."

"More powerful than his boss who's standing next to him?"

"Maybe not by rank but certainly in person."

"You understand then, that Ed Kelly would be going over his boss to take care of you?"

"I didn't know what he was going to do."

Inspector Ed Kelly, one of the two witnesses at the hearing, related the events of June 24 and 25 in the Broome County Courthouse very differently from Harding.

Kelly denied he had coerced Harding into talking and asserted he'd said nothing about disability benefits. He admitted to asking Harding about the investigator's back injury but insisted it was only to get at the truth.

Kelly said Harding had denied telling the CIA anything about wrongdoing until he and Kelly were alone, then Harding finally opened up and admitted to faking the Mark Prentice print only. According to Kelly, Harding said no one ordered him to lie about the fingerprints.

The testimony of the other witness, Lieutenant Craig Harvey, seemed to back up Kelly. Harvey told the court of a conversation he had with Harding in which the defendant described his meetings with inspectors in Broome County.

Harvey, who had been Harding's supervisor in the ID section in Sidney, and had also described himself as a friend, told the court that Harding recounted a meeting on June 24 in Broome County courthouse where "he had screwed up." Harvey testified that Harding told him about the CIA polygraph interview in which Harding had opened up and described several incidents of police tampering with which he'd been involved.

After listening to the testimony, Judge Friedlander said she would consider a fact-finding hearing to resolve the dispute surrounding Harding's questioning.

At the same time the FBI laboratory verified the fact that the Mark Prentice prints had been tampered with. The FBI fingerprint expert, John Haliday, determined that the two latent prints that Harding had testified he had found on the victim's kitchen sink and on the Budweiser bottle in the victim's home had, in fact, been lifted from a Labatts bottle Harding recovered from the defendant's property. Haliday said this could be proved by examining the underlying surface from which the prints were lifted. That surface was the Labatts bottle.

After Haliday's explosive testimony, gossip and rumors about the scandal ran through Troop C like a brushfire. The grapevine reported that Harding claimed the guys on the

Prentice investigation knew Prentice was guilty of assaulting the old man, Robert Meeker. According to the defendant, Harding just helped to place him there to get a conviction and to get the man off the streets. He was just trying to protect the public.

"Who in the hell does he think he's kidding?" McElligott angrily retorted. "He's no goddamn vigilante, we're not talking about God and country here. Dave Harding wanted the limelight to get ahead for himself, nobody else," McElligott said disgustedly.

In spite of the public scandal swirling around him, privately McElligott felt better. He was taking care of himself. He had stopped smoking on his birthday in May since his family had been bugging him for years to quit the habit. Now McElligott pulled out the Chapstick in his desk drawer to rub over his lips instead of lighting up. The senior investigator had also stopped eating so much red meat. It used to be steak five times a week, preferably smothered in pork chops. However, despite these personal attainments, McElligott could not help thinking that the changes in the Troop's top brass might motivate him to retire sooner than later. The heat of the scandal would undoubtedly force out some of the officers he liked and change the department in which he had taken such pride.

Harding's lawyer, Ed Butler, agreed with Harding that the CIA would never release the polygraph interview tape for a trial; so the prosecution would necessarily be based on second-hand information. It was going to be Harding's word against another's. Butler would build the defense on that premise.

However, neither Harding nor Butler realized that after Nelson Roth heard the interview tape at the CIA in Virginia, Roth decided he had to prevail upon the CIA to relax their restrictions of confidentiality and permit the tape to be heard in Tompkins County Court. Roth called upon the agency's

sense of fair play. He was aware that the CIA had been sub-
jected to a lot of legitimate criticism recently with the BCI
scandal and that they didn't want to be tarnished by more bad
publicity. Roth had sent them the newspaper articles about
the Harding revelations; so they were aware of the local outrage and the stress the justice system was under.

The CIA agreed to go along with Roth's request. It was the
first time the intelligence agency had cooperated in a state-
run prosecution. Their usual policy was to turn over information concerning criminal activity to the justice department
for lead purposes only. If a case developed, the CIA was
never mentioned.

This time was different; the CIA flew a representative to
Ithaca with a copy of the interview on cassette tape. On October 6 the three and a half hour tape was played in closed
court for Judge Friedlander, the defense counsel, the defendant, and the special prosecutor. Upon leaving, the representative disclosed that the CIA agreed to bring the tape back if
it was needed for trial, but they would maintain custody of it.

The following day, October 7, Judge Friedlander sent
David Harding back to county jail, reversing the earlier decision that had allowed Harding to remain free on his own recognizance. She ruled that a tape recording of Harding's job
interview with the CIA made it more likely the defendant
would be convicted, which increased the possibility he
might flee. He was held on twenty-five thousand dollars cash
or a fifty thousand dollar bail bond.

Harding and Butler were caught off-guard. Now that the
prosecutor and judge knew what Harding had said during
the CIA interview, his defense had to pursue another avenue.

Harding was running out of options. He would surely face
a guilty verdict if tried on the faked Prentice evidence alone,
and the rest of his cases were being rigorously investigated
by the FBI, with special attention to the Shirley Kinge prints.
He knew that the CIA had agreed to send the tape for a jury
to hear, and that the judge would allow the CIA tape in trial

as evidence. A jury would not believe he was coerced into admitting he tampered with evidence, and Roth would put a CIA official on the stand to testify about how polygraph interviews were conducted.

They came up with a new idea. If Harding could prove his superiors had ordered him to move prints and that he wasn't the only police officer engaged in faking evidence, his guilt might be seen in another light. He would be looked upon as the unfortunate cop who was caught in a corrupt system. Harding knew there was a widespread perception that police were under a lot of pressure to solve crimes quickly and to nail suspects with physical evidence in order to prove their guilt.

Harding began to talk to Roth about other investigators. He asserted that others in Troop C were just as guilty as he was, including top officers in the organization. The man to whom he was obviously alluding was the one who Harding blamed most for his downfall, David McElligott.

Harding testified on October 23 during a continuation of pretrial hearings to determine which statements made on June 24 and 25 in the Broome County courthouse would be admissible at his trial. The handsome investigator told Judge Friedlander he was duped by the same interrogation techniques he had used on criminal suspects. Harding swore he didn't recognize those strategies on June 24 when he allegedly admitted tampering with fingerprint evidence. Harding said he assumed the conversation and questions were serious but would be handled within the department. Harding also claimed he had no idea he could be charged with crimes because of his words. Choking back tears, Harding spoke of Ed Kelly as a trusted friend. Harding said he'd always turned to Kelly for advice throughout his career.

Harding quoted Kelly as saying, "David, I always thought of you as a son," he also said Kelly reminded him "that he had always taken care of me in the past."

When Kelly had asked him about the 1991 CIA interview, Harding said he told Kelly, "Ed, that whole story at the CIA was total embellishment bullshit." According to Harding he'd been so eager to get a job with the anti-terrorist unit that he'd oblige them with a laundry list of supposed offenses, so they would think he was a "bad guy."

The only truth of his CIA stories, Harding said, was that he stole cigarettes in high school and once used sting operation money to buy a shirt and meals during an undercover operation.

Harding went on to say that Kelly told him the older officer would try to make sure Harding received a disability package if he was fired by the state police.

He had repeated to Kelly that what he had told the CIA was untrue, but Kelly kept pushing, "And by that time," Harding said, "I was crying pretty good."

However, when Kelly said, "I'm glad your Dad isn't here anymore to see the stuff you've done," Harding became angry.

He asked Kelly, "What do you want from me? You want me to tell you I did it? . . . Alright, I did it."

Harding said Kelly then agreed that the other offenses Harding had admitted to the CIA were untrue, but said, "You moved that (finger) print, you understand."

Kelly, of course, had denied in his testimony the previous week that he forced Harding to say anything.

As the questioning continued, Roth challenged Harding's contention that he was held involuntarily on June 24 and not given his Miranda rights by asking Harding questions about his background. While trying to show Harding was too knowledgeable not to know procedure, Roth got Harding to reveal his college degrees in criminal justice where he learned police procedures. He also brought out that Harding took courses in interviewing, interrogation techniques, and on the Fifth Amendment at the state police academy seven years before and had taught similar courses at the academy.

The prosecutor also tried to discredit Harding by asking

him about other alleged wrongdoing. Roth got Harding to admit that he had lied to the CIA, had cheated his ex-wife out of some money during their divorce settlement, and he had stolen five hundred dollars in funds when he attended Waverly High School.

Though things were going badly, many of Harding's friends still believed in him. They posted bail money late that day and he was released that night, having been in Tompkins County jail for sixteen days.

Twenty-seven
The Last Straw

The phone rang and rang at David McElligott's house. McElligott finally looked up from his papers. It was 10:22 P.M. McElligott trudged over and picked up the phone receiver.

"Hi, Boss-man. This is David."

At first McElligott thought it was somebody kidding him, but soon he realized the voice belonged to Harding.

With a long stretch of telephone cord, McElligott reached for a pad of paper and pen as he talked. He began writing down the conversation.

"Hi, Big-time. How are ya?" McElligott asked.

"All right. You know they suspended Rob?" Harding said.

"Yeah, I'm aware of that," McElligott answered.

"He knows a lot. He could say some stuff that could get us in trouble."

McElligott's face flushed deep red. He roared, "Hey, hey. Hold it. Back up a little bit. What the fuck are you talking about? What do you mean, us?"

"You know, the bad prints on the Harris can," Harding replied flatly.

"Are you telling me here and now that the prints in the Harris house are no good?"

"You know goddamn well they aren't. You told me to put them on."

McElligott's voice combined anger with disgust. "Who in the hell are you talking to, you lousy bastard?"

"You told me to, you kicked me around like an old shoe. You treated me like a whore. You guys told me to do stuff and now I'm going to prison. Well, I'm not going to prison alone," Harding said, his voice rising.

"Listen to me, you bastard," McElligott was yelling now. "You remember a goddamn conversation we had one week after you found those prints and I asked you about where they were?"

Harding repeated his ploy. McElligott responded in expletives with such resounding fury that in replying, Harding's voice shook. Everybody had always said that they'd never want McElligott mad at them, and now Harding knew why.

McElligott slammed the phone down. He called Troop C's commander at home, but the line was busy. He tried Sidney headquarters.

"Is the Captain there?" McElligott asked.

"Yes, he's upstairs with inspection."

It was 10:47 P.M. and McElligott knew inspectors didn't ordinarily work late, but he damn-well was going to try to get one anyway.

Ed Kelly answered the phone.

"Staff Inspector Kelly, this is Senior Investigator McElligott." He told Kelly about Harding's call, concluding, "I don't like it one bit."

"I wouldn't either if I was you," Kelly responded.

"I don't like the implications of what Harding said to me on the phone," McElligott said.

"I'd document it real good."

"I've already documented it. I'm calling you to officially protest," McElligott told Kelly.

Later that night, McElligott was interviewed in person by the inspectors. He didn't go to bed after they left his house. There was no point in it since McElligott couldn't sleep. Throughout the night, he pondered the fact that Harding was getting back at him for having blocked his rise to power at every turn. McElligott showered at dawn, made a fresh pot of coffee, and put on his best shirt. The nightmare for the state police had begun.

Shirley Kinge's long ordeal ended November 16 when she was ordered to pay $640 in restitution after she pled guilty to using a Harris family credit card in December 1989 in Cayuga and Onondaga counties. All Tompkins County charges had been dropped the previous week.

After the hearing, she and her attorney announced they would be bringing a multi-million-dollar civil lawsuit against the New York State Police for wrongful prosecution.

Everybody at the station knew when McElligott was angry. He had been angry before but no one had ever seen him like this. One trooper told a friend McElligott was like a "raving maniac." Someone suggested that maybe he should get a lawyer.

"I don't need any goddamn lawyer! I've done nothing wrong," McElligott, who had been the only one to recognize Harding's real character, shouted.

The troop commander came to see McElligott and said Harding was trying to implicate him. Other inspectors dropped by and asked him to talk with the special prosecutor.

"You mean to say, you're taking Harding's word in this thing?" McElligott asked incredulously.

"We gotta allow the special prosecutor and Albany to see this thing through," they answered.

It was hard for McElligott to keep his seething anger from erupting as he faced Roth and answered the special prosecutor's questions.

When Harding's pending sentences were brought up, McElligott asked Roth, "Can I stand up there and speak for myself? I want everything out in the open. I wanna face that lying son-of-a-bitch."

"No, we'll speak for you," Roth said.

"Well, you better speak damn good. I've got some children who think I'm a hero, not because I've told them that, but because I've been absent from a lot of dinners and missed too many holidays and birthdays just to work on police business: I just want justice."

For McElligott it felt like he had entered The Twilight Zone. Overnight, the confident and respected investigator of so many years had been transformed into an unsavory character being asked to clear his name.

At the end of the interview, McElligott was requested to take polygraph.

"Sure. More than happy to take it. I've got nothing to hide," he said.

The next week a polygraph examiner from Boston came to administer the test.

"Good luck on the polygraph," a friend at work said to McElligott as he left the barracks to take the test in Binghamton.

McElligott scowled. "Obviously, you don't understand a polygraph. I don't need any goddamn luck. I'll tell it the way it is."

After he took the test, McElligott tried to find out who was responsible for the sting. No one would own up to it. He heard it was the chief inspector. It was Roth. It was the district attorney. But it didn't really matter. He'd been hung out to dry by his superiors in the police force he loved. It was the worst day of his life.

However, McElligott could be no less than the honorable cop he'd always been. Using the customary channels to object, he made a vehement protest to the zone commander. "I am insulted by the implications and tactics used to question my integrity," McElligott said.

Dentes was flabbergasted to hear from McElligott that the inspectors had tried to entrap him. Dentes was no longer privy to inside information.

After McElligott took the polygraph test, Robert Towers, an inspector and friend, called to tell McElligott he'd passed. "But Harding flunked the shit out of his," Towers reported.

A little later, Major Farrand called McElligott.

"This is the best news I've ever had, David. You passed the polygraph with flying colors."

"Major, I could have told you that last week," McElligott responded abruptly.

"Look, David, we did you a favor to get you out in the clear."

McElligott, respectful of his superiors as always, did not reply.

Later that day McElligott was told that he was no longer "a target."

"Let me tell you something. Make me a target if you want. There's nothing I've done wrong," McElligott replied.

Retirement was out of the question now, McElligott told Chandler. It would look like Harding had beat him.

The special prosecutor's web was closing tighter around Harding by the day. Every time Nelson Roth interviewed him, Harding changed his story. Roth had confronted Harding earlier about his assertion that the CIA had turned off the tape when they talked about not wanting "choir boys" to apply.

"It's not true," Harding said about the chain of events. "What really happened is they flew me down twice. The first time I had general interviews and meetings with the counter-terrorist unit. It was in those interviews they told me they weren't looking for choir boys. They needed somebody who could get the job done. That's when I admitted evidence tampering. They flew me back for the polygraph interview. In fact, they flew me both times in a private jet."

Roth pressed Harding further, "If you had already told them about it and they brought you back and you were their kind of guy, why did you hold off for three hours before you told them?"

"Well I think the guy knew it," Harding answered.

"I'm sure they did if you told them, David. But that's not my point. If they already knew, why play games with them?"

Harding couldn't give a straight answer.

Roth checked with the CIA and they gave him the flight number of Harding's United Airlines commuter flight from Binghamton to Washington. The records showed he had a round trip ticket as part of a three-day series from January 13 through 15, 1991. Harding flew back on the 14th because he'd been shown the door.

Roth returned to Harding, saying, "I understand you were shown the door at the CIA, David. If they already knew this (evidence tampering), why did they bother to bring you back and then show you the door?" Roth asked.

"They didn't show me the door for what I said on the tape. They already knew about that. They showed me the door because we couldn't agree on a salary," Harding said.

"You negotiated salary with them?" Roth asked.

"Yeah. They were offering me too little."

Roth looked Harding in the eyes. "What were they offering you?"

"I was making in excess of forty thousand dollars in the state police and they were offering me in the low twenties or twenty-three something."

"And you negotiated that with the CIA?"

Harding nodded. "Yes, that's right. I told them if they wanted me to do things like burglarize buildings for them, they gotta pay a whole lot more. We couldn't agree on the terms and that's when they ended the process."

Roth checked the story with the CIA. Their personnel department said Harding had applied for a career service officer position, an entry-level management training program on a GS level. Harding once again had told Roth a series of lies.

Roth and the special investigator now thought the threat of a heavy jail sentence would get Harding to reveal his co-conspirators and to tell them the full extent of his wrongdoing.

They were right. Harding was trapped. He had to work out a deal.

On November 4, 1992, David Harding pled guilty in Tompkins County Court to four separate counts of first-degree perjury under a plea agreement with the special prosecutor. One of those counts was the Shirley Kinge case. Harding admitted he had lied to jurors about the Kinge fingerprint evidence.

During the proceedings in a courtroom crowded with television cameras that kept following defense counsel and the prosecutor up to the bench, Harding got up from his chair. He walked around the table to get a glass of water. The cameras swung back on him. Harding flashed a big smile straight into the camera lens as he sat down again. Though Harding's career was falling apart before his eyes, he still sought the spotlight.

Later, on the courthouse steps after watching Harding plead guilty, Bill Sullivan faced the reporters. "I feel a little sick to my stomach right now." Sullivan didn't say, as he rightfully could have, I told you so.

The same day, Chief Inspector DeFrancesco announced that Robert Lishansky had been suspended without pay over "irregularities" in his processing of fingerprint evidence in the Kinge case. DeFrancesco said the case against Lishansky began when state police internal investigators, in reviewing the major cases on which Harding had worked, became suspicious about a gas can in the Harris case. The FBI lab confirmed their suspicions. Harding's part in pointing out Lishansky's complicity was omitted.

Though still technically free on bail, it was now only a matter of time until Harding was sentenced to jail. His fellow officers in media-battered Troop C hoped they could now get back to police business and away from answering questions about David Harding.

However, on November 14, the owner of Wright Sporting Goods in Waverly reported that David Harding had come to their store and asked if they'd be interested in buying two small guns he had at home. He also wanted to get a large game hunting license. When Harding was told that he had to go through the application process since he did not own a previous license, he asked them, "Can't we take care of this?"

They refused and Harding never came back.

This turned out to be another police slip up. They had failed to confiscate the weapons when they arrested Harding in July. The media again focused on blasting Troop C.

A short time later, Joe O'Brien visited Harding in the Tompkins County jail at the request of Harding's girlfriend, Jill Ryan. Jill was worried about Harding. He was terribly depressed. O'Brien spoke to Harding for a while and came away with the same opinion.

Not long afterward, O'Brien was stunned to see Harding standing on his doorstep November 20. Harding said he had a pile of notes he wanted to give O'Brien for a criminal justice course Harding was scheduled to give during spring semester at Tompkins Cortland Community College. Harding said he wouldn't need them anymore. It wasn't long into the conversation before O'Brien realized Harding was in a highly agitated state.

He railed on and on about how the state police had let him down, that "we cops" know fake evidence is commonplace to get convictions, and that he was pressured by his bosses. Harding claimed that although what he did was illegal, there was absolutely nothing wrong with it.

O'Brien disagreed and told Harding in all of his years in law enforcement, he'd never run across a crooked police officer.

The remarks fueled Harding's rage. His eyes glazed over, his face flushed. Ranting, Harding told O'Brien he was furious with Nelson Roth for handing over Harding's manuscript about the Harris murders to *The New York Times* and then got even more angry because O'Brien wouldn't agree to do anything about it for him.

O'Brien wondered if Harding was armed. He sensed Harding could be dangerous. The former star investigator seemed not only to be losing control, but also his grasp on reality.

After leaving O'Brien, Harding drove to a scheduled meeting with Roth and two state police inspectors. During the lengthy interview the special prosecutor said he had questions about the truthfulness of Harding's statements. He accused Harding of changing his story from day to day. "Big lies and little lies," Roth muttered to himself.

One of the things Roth confronted Harding about was Harding's back injury. Roth said he had seen surveillance photographs of Harding lifting cars at his racetrack.

"I had to get better. I had no choice. I have to eat," Harding replied.

At this interview Roth told Harding that if he found any of Harding's statements to be false, he would have to recommend a substantially longer sentence than the four to fourteen years they had set in the plea agreement. Harding was enraged.

Again he complained bitterly about the handling of his manuscript and when Roth said he was ending the discussion of that subject, Harding kept pursuing it, making threatening remarks. It was a side of Harding that Roth had never seen before.

Later that day, Roth received a call from O'Brien, who told him of Harding's visit and warned Roth of the powder keg that Harding had become. From what O'Brien had heard, Roth could be in danger as well as the other investigators in the probe. O'Brien also thought Harding could be suicidal.

New York state police inspectors already had on file statements from an interview they'd had with retired investigator Gary Allen. Allen was asked how Harding would handle going to prison. "He would go out in a blaze of glory," Allen said. He had added that Ed Kelly should be concerned for his safety.

On November 23, when told about Harding's mental condition, Judge Friedlander revoked Harding's twenty-five thousand dollar bail and sent him back to jail based on the accumulated evidence of emotional instability and threatening remarks.

Captain Joseph Loszynski, the acting troop commander, saw to it that Nelson Roth and his family received twenty-four hour protection. David McElligott arranged the security detail.

One of the investigators who had been present during interviews with Harding and Lishansky told McElligott, "You know, those guys really don't like you."

"I'm goddamn proud of that," McElligott answered.

Twenty-eight
The Real David Harding

At a bail hearing on November 30, attorneys presented two different pictures of David Harding. Butler portrayed him as a repentant whose recent words and actions were misunderstood and misused by his accusers. He was prepared to go to jail.

The prosecutor tried to show the defendant as a lying, desperate man who beat his wife and may have plotted revenge against the people investigating him.

Katherine Lienthall, the Tompkins County Probation Director, testified that when she first interviewed Harding on November 23, he was "confident, calm and pleasant." But two days later, after he had returned to jail, she noticed a change. "His eyes were darting and he was fidgety. He was playing with the buttons on his collar," she said.

As part of her report for the judge, Lienthall had interviewed Harding's ex-wife, who said she had confronted Harding about alleged cocaine use four years earlier. The ex-wife said she had read an entry in Harding's journal about how "the big 'C' keeps me going" and being depressed. She suggested treatment, but Harding told her he could kick his habit on his own.

The probation director went on to say that in the interview with Harding's ex-wife, the woman described an incident in which Harding threw her on a car hood at their home after an argument. Later, they fought again in the house and she said, "he bounced me off a few walls."

Harding had previously told the probation director that his ex-wife might mention cocaine use and a beating but that state police had investigated the allegations and exonerated him.

The defense protested that the prosecutor had based his allegations of Harding's instability on perceptions, not facts. He petitioned the court to release his client from jail before his December 4 sentencing date.

Butler put Dr. Mokarram Jafri, a psychiatrist and a former Broome County Mental Health Director, on the stand. He testified he had interviewed Harding for forty minutes and found nothing wrong with him.

"I couldn't find any single risk factor in him for suicide," Jafri said.

The psychiatrist said that after reading the affidavits that landed Harding back in jail, he determined that the people quoted in them had given no reliable evidence that Harding was dangerous to himself or to others.

Jafri also dismissed the idea that Harding wanted a hunting license so he could legally have a rifle or shotgun to use against investigators. He said people who want to hurt somebody just do it, they don't ask permission or try to get a license.

Jafri's opinions were backed up by a supervisor in the forensic unit of the Tompkins County Mental Health Clinic who testified she had interviewed Harding three times between October 17 and November 25, finding him "grounded in reality."

Butler put Harding on the stand and he denied ever making threats to anyone.

Unsure of Harding's real condition because of the conflicting testimony, Judge Friedlander reserved decision on whether or not to keep Harding in jail.

As Harding left the courthouse, a reporter yelled out, "David, is it right about the cocaine?" Harding answered that he'd never used drugs.

Harding remained in jail until his sentencing date, which had been moved up to December 6, 1992.

The event of seeing David Harding sentenced drew a crowd of loud and gawking court spectators to the second floor courtroom, the scene where Harding had watched so gleefully as Shirley Kinge was sentenced to prison two years before. Judge Friedlander limited the number of television cameras, but David Harding was big news now, having brought the integrity and validity of police testimony into question all over the country. His case was to be covered in newspapers all over, including *The New York Times*, whose reporters sat in the front rows with their microphones and tape recorders.

Harding entered the packed courtroom from the rear, walking at a brisk pace between two sheriff deputies. He was still dressed as fashionably as ever, but this time he was not smiling. A tense silence fell on the audience. The deputies never left the defendant's side.

The prosecutor, Nelson Roth, described the defendant as a person who lies about everything. "David Harding lies about simple and complex things. His lies are so numerous that nothing can be accepted at face value," Roth said.

Seated beside his lawyer with his head bowed and eyes

closed, Harding held clasped hands to his face as if to shield himself from Roth's scathing remarks.

Roth quoted from the report of the probation director who had interviewed Harding and said he showed no remorse.

Part of the report that Roth did not quote in court had convinced Roth that Harding was a pathological liar. The probation director, Marge Whitman, cited cases where the defendant had lied to her. Whitman asked Harding if blond was his natural hair color and he replied yes. She asked if anyone in his family had ever been convicted of a felony and he answered no, but Whitman knew that it was also a lie. A sister had been convicted of manslaughter in the death of a young child.

Roth told the judge that the defendant had technically complied with the plea agreement that was signed when he pled guilty on November 4. It is stated in the plea agreement, Roth explained to the court, that the defendant must cooperate with a special prosecutor, the Broome County District Attorney's Office, and the state police in naming other police officers he knew to have engaged in misconduct. Harding had waived his right to pursue pending or future motions, the right to appeal, and the right to bring post-judgment motions.

Despite this cooperation, Roth continued, "The defendant has undermined public confidence in the criminal justice process in a cold, calculated, and cynical way."

The prosecutor asked for the maximum sentence of no less than four years before parole.

Looking around, Ed Butler, the defense attorney, told the court that he had never seen as much media attention to a case in his entire career. Butler objected to the probation director's inflammatory language and the inclusion of Harding's ex-wife's words as part of Harding's legal history.

Butler mentioned that his client had admitted to perjury, but added that Harding's crimes were nonviolent.

Standing before Judge Friedlander, Harding read a state-

ment to the court that began with an apology "about this entire thing."

After his apologies to the Harris and Lake families, Harding said, "I also apologize to that segment of the people of
the State of New York who feel that their trust has been violated."

Harding said he had worked endlessly to speak for those
who could not, those people whose lives had been cut short
by senseless violence. "It is men and women like myself
who form the barrier between the real people of this world
and the law-abiding members of society."

The former investigator said that his work had resulted in
many commendations and left him "with an immaculate
record until my recent arrest."

Speaking words which sent chills up the spines of many
who watched, Harding asserted, "in these cases where I have
acted unethically, it is because of certainty by myself and
others that the defendant was dangerous to the public and
should be removed from society." His voice rose. "I never
acted with bad intent, nor did I do so for personal gain. My
reward was simply the protection of the public, wherein my
own family resides." Harding added that neither he nor anyone he'd worked with ever attempted to arrest or convict an
innocent person.

The smiles and sense of confidence he'd shown in court
were not to promote himself to the press or public, just his
positive personality coming through in this difficult period,
Harding said.

The former fast-track investigator ended his statement by
saying how proud he was of the great work he'd been a part
of in the state police and that he would like to continue his
service to the people of New York either as part of or in lieu
of incarceration.

When Harding finished speaking, the silence that hung
in the courtroom was so thick it was palpable. For a few minutes Judge Friedlander stared hard at Harding, then said, "I

have to say that your fabrication of evidence and your giving false testimony goes beyond anything that law can adequately sanction because there isn't a crime in the book for willfully destroying or attempting to destroy public confidence in its criminal justice institutions."

Commenting on what Harding and his counsel said in their statements, Friedlander revealed her own deep feelings, "That [what Harding did] is a form of violence to the trust that people have in institutions because that's the only thing that allows institutions to function, is that the public trusts them . . . it's a kind of behavior that the law simply doesn't provide for. So any sanction I'm going to impose today is not proportionate in any way to what you've attempted to do."

Friedlander gave Harding a pair of two-to-six-year sentences, to run consecutively, plus a total of ten thousand dollars in fines covering the Shirley Kinge and Mark Prentice cases, perjury counts in which he had pleaded guilty.

Harding still faced sentencing for first-degree perjury in two other felony cases in another county, where Timothy Vail was convicted of raping and killing a pregnant woman, and William Eichele was accused of killing a woman and dumping her body in a ditch. After this hearing Harding was to be sent to the Elmira Correctional Facility to await further sentencing.

As the television cameras he had once coveted came in for a close-up, a handcuffed David Harding was led out of the courtroom by sheriff deputies. The shot caught Harding looking scared and exhausted, like somebody on the run who had finally been caught. The smile was gone. The head dropped slightly. He looked away from the cameras. His natural brown hair was beginning to show through the blond. The once well-tailored double-breasted suit that he had worn like a model, now looked too big and a little wrinkled on his gaunt body. It was easier to picture him in prison overalls.

* * *

A few weeks later, right before he was sentenced in Broome County, Harding finally admitted to tampering in a fifth case in that county. Harding confessed lying about the fingerprint evidence in the Clive Wildrick murder case in the town of Maine.

When Roth had asked him earlier about this, Harding would not admit to falsifying evidence though admitting his forgery would not have changed his deal with the special prosecutor. The reason he wouldn't in the Wildrick case was that Harding was the only state police investigator involved, which meant that his theory proving a suspect guilty for his superiors or for the brotherhood of the state police couldn't be defended. It was highly unlikely that local police would ask for corrupt assistance. Nor was it consistent with his vigilante pose since it was an open and shut case. Harding's prints were frosting on the cake.

He finally admitted tampering in the case when the FBI finished their analysis and concluded the fingerprints were false.

Harding had told Roth during one of their interviews that he had only sent guilty people to jail.

"What about Shirley Kinge?" Roth asked.

"She's guilty," Harding answered.

"How do you know?" Roth asked.

"I know. I can't tell you how. I just know."

Judge Patrick Matthews spoke strong words full of indignation as David Harding faced him in Broome County Court.

"You had it all. You had education, you had intelligence, you hold a master's degree. But you are so stupid that you can't begin to comprehend the highest concept of American law enforcement. And that is that no man—no man—is above the law. The sad thing is, I don't think you'll ever understand what you did," Matthews said in a voice trembling with emotion.

David Harding's downfall was an exercise in self-illusion. Part of his actions were based on the theory that segments of the population applaud his kind of vigilante effort. In Harding's mind, he believed, "I've put the bad guy away. Crimes are rampant, the courts have shackled law enforcement officials and restrained our activity. I should be congratulated, not condemned and sent to prison." That notion was consistent with his idea that the CIA wanted people to break the law for the right reasons.

In truth, the killer, Michael Kinge, and the police officer, David Harding, had a lot in common. They both believed the end justified any means. They could be charming, they had intelligence, they were risk-takers, egotists, con artists and pathological liars. Kinge, consumed with rage at having nothing and getting nowhere, wanted money so badly it became an addiction for which he was willing to kill and die. Harding, consumed with a need to be in the spotlight, to be in demand, grew to depend on the excitement like an addiction. He had a perverse need to be glorified and was willing to do anything to be a star.

In the end, Michael Kinge was cornered and fatally shot; David Harding was disgraced and barred forever from the profession he said he loved.

Harding was sent to the Clinton Correctional Facility in Dennamora, New York, to serve his term. He was to be isolated in a special unit except for one or two hours each day.

David McElligott, who had known in his gut all along that David Harding wasn't the person his peers and superiors thought he was, now felt justice had finally been done.

The fact that McElligott's family and friends were the only ones who thought of him as a hero was enough. He neither needed nor wanted public acclaim.

McElligott was back doing what he really wanted to do, working every day to solve a kidnapping and murder case that had recently occurred. McElligott knew he had to be frustrated by the investigation not making headway when he initiated a press interview to push the case along. He'd never done that before in his career.

Nevertheless, McElligott was confident they'd solve the case eventually. Before he retired, he hoped.

Afterword

Because of the public's outrage and their own furor over David Harding's crimes, a group of defense lawyers led by William Sullivan petitioned the Governor for a statewide permanent special prosecutor to ensure that the system would be kept honest and to restore confidence in the state's judicial process.

New York State Governor Mario Cuomo appointed Nelson Roth as special prosecutor to investigate the scope of state police misconduct in Troop C.

New procedures for collecting and analyzing evidence were issued by the state police as part of their effort to reform the system and to lessen the effects of the widening scandal, which had become national news. These procedures required photographing fingerprints before lifting them from an object—standard practice for the FBI and most police departments—which would prevent an investigator from lying about where a fingerprint was discovered. The new procedures also required at least two investigators cosign crime scene reports and that at least two supervisors verify the validity of all fingerprints discovered at crime scenes.

The Justice Department and the FBI were looking into why it took more than a year for the CIA to inform the state police about Harding's criminal admissions. Harding and his supporters had told sympathetic listeners that the government's delay proved a conspiracy.

McElligott heard of an interview Leslie Stahl conducted with Harding for CBS's *60 Minutes* in which Harding had named McElligott as one of his bosses who knew what Harding was doing in the Kinge case and approved it. McElligott announced that if Harding's accusations were televised and he wasn't exonerated by the state police on the program, he would quit and go public to defend his name.

60 Minutes was informed that McElligott had passed a polygraph and Harding had failed the test.

The twelve and a half minute segment that aired in March 1993 did not mention McElligott's name. But it showed Harding and Robert Lishansky in separate interviews claiming their supervisor told them to fake fingerprint evidence and they insinuated higher-ups in the state police knew what they were doing. They were referring to Lt. Craig Harvey, the supervisor of Troop C's identification section.

Harvey was arrested on April 30, 1993, on charges he faked evidence to solve a 1986 double-murder case in Delaware County. The state police and special prosecutor claimed Harvey knew that Harding and Lishansky had forged fingerprints, which partially explained why these illegal activities were not uncovered.

Robert Lishansky pled guilty to tampering with evidence in twenty-one cases, and was sentenced to a minimum of six years in state prison.

David Harding, still not willing to accept his own guilt, changed lawyers after he was sent to jail with the hope of reducing his sentence. Harding wanted to prove his superiors ordered him to fabricate evidence.

As for the people who lived in Ithaca and once thought it was a safe community, they experienced shock wave after wave as first the Harris family was randomly murdered in their home, and then the police force who the public looked toward for protection was stained by corruption.

For Ithaca's citizens life would never be the same. It was as if some floodgate had opened and barbarians entered.

But it was the Harris case that would most influence the townspeople. Each night, despite locking themselves behind heavy doors in homes now fortified with security systems and locks, they would anxiously wonder if another killer like Michael Kinge would somehow find a way to get in.

Addendum

What Happened That Night

The following scenario is based on multiple interviews with police staff, state troopers, investigators, the district attorney, accounts in court records, the Justice Department, law libraries, and the author's study of the case.

It tells what they believe happened to the Harrises on December 22 and 23.

Although Michael Kinge keeps himself in good physical shape, he has a hard time pumping his bicycle along the snow-covered, slippery Ellis Hollow Road on the afternoon of December 22. It's freezing cold, getting dark, the road is hilly and he hasn't been on a bicycle for a long time. He rides standing up, like a novice, the wheels wobbling. Kinge wears a heavy knapsack on his back that's loaded down with a fourteen-inch, sawed-off rifle and homemade silencer, clips of ammunition, burglary tools and various types of rope. He's stuffed a ski mask inside a pocket of his jacket. By the time he arrives at the Harris home around 4:30 P.M., he's tired and sweaty.

Perhaps he had picked out the Harris house earlier because it looked upscale or he was aware of the Grey Goose gift shop. He may have targeted the location after riding around with his mother in search of property to buy or rent.

Since Kinge seems to know where he's going and has planned to be there at a particular time, he has probably watched the Harris house to see who comes home and when.

Kinge drops his bicycle halfway down the Harrises' circular driveway. He puts his ski mask on, and walks toward Dodie Harris who has just come out of the front door headed for the Grey Goose. He approaches her and says he has a flat tire on his bicycle, asking if she has an air pump he can use. Dodie directs him to the garage and says Marc will get him their pump.

Wheeling the bicycle over to the garage, Kinge sees Marc walking toward a van that's parked outside the two-car garage.

"Hi. I've got a flat back tire. Your mom said you have a pump?" the stranger asks.

"Oh, sure. We have one over here," Marc answers as he walks to the back of the garage.

The stranger follows Marc. He takes out the gun hidden inside his parka. Marc reaches for the air pump, lifts it, and when he turns toward the stranger, the rifle head is two inches from his face.

Marc lets out a gasp and drops the pump to the floor. He stares at the man in the ski mask.

"You sure as hell better keep quiet and do exactly what I tell you or I'll blow you away, right now."

He jabs the rifle head in Marc's back, ordering the boy to put Kinge's bicycle inside the van. Marc follows orders.

"Now shut the garage door," the stranger barks while keeping his gun pointed at Marc. Marc goes over to the wall where the controls are and flips the switch.

Pushing Marc into the mud room door, Kinge makes his

way through the hall to the kitchen. He gets Marc to tell him that his sister is in her bedroom and his father isn't home. They wait for Dodie to come in the front entrance from the Grey Goose. Shelby is upstairs and doesn't hear anything.

Dodie enters the foyer carrying the tool chest she's promised to deliver that night to Rita Demerest. She places it on the dining table, which is at the end of the spacious kitchen. There are no kitchen lights on except for the dim glow of the pewter light fixture hanging over the table. Taking off her jacket she hangs it on the coat tree in the foyer. Her shoes are wet from the snow. She removes them.

Out of the darkness of the kitchen, the stranger in a ski mask springs out, pushing Marc in front of him, yelling and pointing his gun. "You do one thing and I'll shoot your son right now," the man shouts. Dodie screams and he keeps yelling. "Shut up, you goddamn bitch or I'll shoot you and your son. I want all your money. Everything. You understand?"

Dodie pulls out the cash left from errands and grocery shopping from her pants pocket and throws it to him. The stranger yells that he wants all the cash and she says she doesn't have any from her store because she banked it today. Kinge threatens again that he'll kill her family if she doesn't give him the cash. She's crying and pleads with him that it's her regular routine to bank whatever she earns right away, especially when it's so close to Christmas. Getting hysterical, she reaches for Marc and begs the man not to hurt her children.

"Shut up, bitch. Keep your hands off him! Just do what I tell you if you want your family to live." He keeps the gun pointed at them.

Kinge is furious that there's no more cash around. He doesn't believe that Dodie's banked the store's cash, but it's too risky to check the shop himself. He'll wait for the father to come home. He figures a rich man always carries around a lot of money.

Kinge pushes Marc and Dodie through the kitchen toward the staircase, jabbing the gun in Marc's back.

There's music coming from Shelby's bedroom. She has the radio turned up. They burst into her room; the stranger shouts that he'll kill her if she doesn't do what he says. He has Dodie and Marc stand back to back and orders Shelby to tie their feet together and then their necks with the heavy shoelaces he brought with him. Michael Kinge still has the mask over his face as he swears and yells how she'd better do what he says or he'll kill all of them.

Once tied up Dodie and Marc can't move. Kinge has Shelby sit on a chair in the middle of the room and ties her legs to the rungs with shoestring, and when he runs out of the string, he tells her to cut up a pair of pantyhose. He grabs the scissors that Shelby's just used to wrap her boyfriend's Christmas present. He uses the stocking strips to finish tying her to the chair. Kinge tells her that if she tries to go anywhere, he'll kill her mother and brother.

Then he makes Dodie and Marc hobble down the short hallway to Marc's bedroom. He gets a chair and puts it between the twin beds. After he unties Dodie from Marc, he makes Dodie sit in the chair and he ties her up.

"If you try to make one move, bitch, it's over for your son. He'll be dead meat," the stranger says as he sticks the gun to her chest.

He puts the gun on the end of the bed nearest to the closet, has Marc kneel down on the floor, and ties Marc's arms behind him at the wrists and then to the bedpost.

Kinge pulls Boy Scout uniforms and Marc's dress clothes out of the closet and off the hangers. He opens up the shirt hangers and binds Marc's legs together with the wire and wires him to the bed by his neck. Gagging Dodie or Marc isn't necessary since Kinge knows he can scare them into shutting up. Dodie thinks their best chance is to cooperate with him and tells that to Marc when he starts to yell back at the stranger. Next, Kinge brings Dodie forward, kneels her down on the floor next to Marc and wires her to the opposite bedpost.

He goes back to Shelby's bedroom and unties her. As he stares at the pretty teenager and her lovely body, his sexual fantasies ignite. Kinge's concentration is now divided between robbery and his awakening sex drive. His physical attraction to the white girl is as much fueled by rage as his desire for sex.

Kinge gets Shelby to tell him when her father will be coming home, then pushes her out the door. They walk by Marc's bedroom on the way downstairs. Dodie and Marc are told that if they try to move, he'll kill Shelby. Keeping the gun in Shelby's back or side as they continue to walk, Kinge tells her over and over he'll shoot her mother and brother if she tries anything. Nobody will hear the shots, he says, because of the silencer. They wait in the kitchen for Tony, Shelby's father. Kinge, puffing on a cigarette, looks out the window toward Ellis Hollow Road and blows smoke rings while holding onto Shelby. When he sees a car approach the driveway, he shoves Shelby upstairs.

Tony parks his sedan in the garage, gets out of the car, picks up his briefcase and basketball from the box on the backseat, and walks through the mud room to the kitchen. He sets the ball atop the counter, puts his briefcase on the floor, and takes off his gloves. Part of the family ritual is having Marc bring him his slippers when he gets home from work. Tony calls for Marc. The dog, Annie, comes up to him as usual, but Marc doesn't answer and there's nobody downstairs. He notices there's no dinner cooking and is puzzled because they usually eat soon after Tony gets home. Tony walks through the family room toward the staircase. "Where is everybody? Marc, what about my slippers?"

Tony places his gloves on top of the banister, removes his jacket and hangs it over them. He turns to go upstairs when he sees a stranger in a ski mask come out of the master bedroom at the head of the stairs pointing the gun at him while holding Shelby.

"Your daughter is dead if you don't do exactly what I tell you," the stranger yells at him.

Tony is so stunned that he can't say anything at first.

"I swear, I'll shoot her right now if you don't get your ass up these stairs," the stranger shouts as he grabs Shelby in a tight hold with his left arm.

Running up the stairs, Tony pleads with the stranger not to hurt his family.

The man in the dark ski mask yells for Tony to hand over his cash. Tony pulls out his wallet and the stranger grabs it. After Kinge pulls out a few bills, he screams and swears. Where is all the money? Tony tells Kinge he never carries much on him, that he uses credit cards.

They go into Marc's bedroom, where Kinge makes Shelby put a pillowcase over her father's head and tie him to the chair to which Dodie had been bound. Shelby cries out that she can't tie the knot he wants, but he knows he can't tie Tony up. He has to keep the gun on Tony, who is a big man and his greatest danger. Shelby manages to tie up her father, but the bindings aren't very tight. Kinge repeats that he'll kill Shelby if Tony tries to budge an inch.

Kinge then forces Shelby back to her bedroom and reties her to the chair.

Tony tells Dodie and Marc they have to cooperate. By then Dodie is hysterical. Tony says they just have to do as the stranger says. There's no other way.

Kinge returns to Tony and has him hobble over behind Dodie. He makes Tony kneel on the floor and ties him to the bedpost, wrist to ankle, with coat hanger wire. He binds Tony in a hog-tie position because he's the one who can give him the most trouble. Then Kinge binds him around his neck to the bed. Grabbing pillowcases to cover their heads, Kinge ties the cases with cord.

He goes back to Shelby, her wrists kept bound, and has her take him around the house to show him where the valuables are kept. Kinge finds out there aren't any, except some baseball cards in the closet that he doesn't recognize as being worth anything. He looks over the money he collected and his anger grows. Dodie hands over one hundred and twenty dollars she had left from shopping, while Tony has less than twenty dollars in his wallet. Kinge tears open an envelope in the study and takes the new Visa Gold cards they haven't even signed yet. He and Shelby go back upstairs. Kinge takes Tony's bank card from his wallet and gets Tony to give him his P.I.N. number.

When the phone rings, Kinge has Shelby take him to the telephones outside the kitchen. Kinge has already pulled out the cords on the kitchen wall phone. He does the same with the others. In his haste, Kinge misses the one in the cellar.

Kinge keeps the ski mask on as he always does in a robbery. Smoking constantly, he drops ashes all over the house. He's enraged that they don't have a lot of cash because that's what he was really after. When Kinge discovers they don't even own expensive jewelry or coins, it increases his frustration to the breaking point.

Furious that he made this effort for practically nothing and excited by the sexual fantasy that has escalated since first seeing Shelby, Kinge decides to take what he can. He pulls Shelby's prom dress out of Shelby's closet and tells her to undress in the bathroom. She cries and begs him not to make her. Kinge swears at her to get off the clothes or he'll go and kill her family right then.

Once she is undressed Kinge shoves her into the master bedroom and covers the windows with towels for privacy as prison inmates do. He dresses and undresses her in the taffeta gown, tormenting and toying with her, which gets him more sexually excited. He finds a jar of Vaseline to help him sexually assault the virgin. Obsessed with not leaving behind evidence, Kinge comes prepared to protect himself. Wrapping part of the dress around her arms, he ties it to her wrists. Taking a piece of the dress he holds onto it as a ligature so he can control her while he assaults her. All she can do is scream.

Her cries are heard by the rest of the family, but are suddenly halted when her assailant stuffs a sock in her mouth. The tactic of paralyzing his victims with fear works.

Kinge keeps the sock in Shelby's mouth so he doesn't have to hear her screaming. He continues to rape and sodomize her. The torture goes on for a long time.

Kinge has taken off his ski mask as the assault continues. Now Kinge realizes he has to kill her. He can't take the chance of being identified. The gun goes off. Kinge shoots her three times in the head as she lies on her back at the top of the bed. The others don't hear the shots due to the silencer.

Afterward Kinge knows he can't leave anyone alive as witnesses. He goes into Marc's room. Tony begs him to let them go. Tony says take anything, but please don't shoot his family.

As soon as Tony finishes his sentence, Kinge walks over and stands behind Tony. He shoots Tony twice, goes around and shoots Dodie twice. Marc hears something; he turns his head and is shot twice in the face. A final shot hits his throat.

Kinge leaves the house, turning the lights off, and gets in the Harris van and drives off.

On his first trip out with the van, Kinge may have hidden the bicycle in the bushes beside Marine Midland Bank's parking lot on the corner of Judd Falls Road and Mitchell Street. No footprints were found to or from the back of the van where the bicycle would have been stored. Kinge doesn't want to abandon the bike, fearing it will be found and might be traced to him.

What Kinge did next is purely speculative. Most speculation leads to the conclusion that after thinking more about what he had left behind in the Harris home, Kinge decides to go back and destroy all the evidence.

Driving back around 4:00 A.M., it starts snowing heavily. Kinge covers his tire tracks on the Harris driveway.

Back in the house, Kinge carefully cleans off every surface, upstairs and down. He picks up all ten rounds of ammunition fragments and as many cigarette butts as he can find. When he sweeps the kitchen floor, he inadvertently kicks one cigarette butt under Tony's briefcase next to the counter. After everything is cleaned, he goes to the garage and gets a can of unleaded gasoline and another of diesel fuel.

As Kinge goes upstairs to set the fires, he drops more cigarette ashes on the steps.

First he douses Shelby's body and the bed with fuel. Then Kinge goes to Marc's room, spreads fuel over the three bodies and bed. A few minutes later, Kinge steps out into the hallway and spreads about a quart on the floor and sets the five-gallon can down next to the door. He reaches into the room and torches the fuel with his cigarette lighter. He then closes the door.

Kinge ignites the fuel in the hallway, goes back to the master bedroom, then lights the fire in there. The fires don't start right away. About twenty-five seconds after he sets his cigarette lighter to the hallway fuel, smoke begins seeping into the smoke detector down the hall in front of Shelby's bedroom and touches off the alarm system, which has an inside and outside horn. The penetrating sound fills the air as Kinge is lighting the fire next to Shelby's body. The shrill noise surprises him. In a hurry to get away, Kinge leaves the lighter on the bedroom dresser and quickly closes the door.

Panicking now, Kinge races down the stairs. During these few seconds the neighbors wake up to the alarm, but don't know where it is coming from. The Harris house is dark and the garage doors are closed.

In the next minute, Kinge runs to the garage, backs out the van in a wide arc, and tears across the lawn onto Ellis Hollow Road. When Dennis Regan looks out of the window of his house again, he sees the Harrises' garage door open. He makes his second call to the police.

The van speeds along Ellis Hollow Road until Kinge sees a vehicle coming down a driveway just beyond Game Farm Road. He slows the van. Michael curses. *Why is anybody out this early?* He sees the sedan turn left, heading toward East Hill Plaza, the direction in which he is going.

Kinge turns the van down Game Farm Road, giving the car lead-time. After the van reenters Ellis Hollow Road, Kinge sees the vehicle ahead of him going very slowly. From there, he drives straight to Ides Bowling Lanes and parks the van behind the bank next to Ides.

Kinge believes the fire will destroy the bodies of the Harris family and hopefully most of their house. But he is wrong. The doors are closed upstairs and without any air from open windows, the fires choke themselves out.

Taking the bike he has hidden, Kinge decides to meet Joanna at Ithacare before she leaves work. Time is not a problem since it is a straight ride down Mitchell Street to Ithacare. He can make the ride in less than ten minutes.

Michael Kinge gets on his bicycle around 7:00 A.M. and coasts into Ithacare's parking lot before Joanna gets off work at 7:30 A.M. He tosses the bicycle into the back of the blue Ford truck, goes to get the keys from Joanna, and then returns to the truck to wait.

Epilogue

The story that began with the brutal murders of the Harris family in Ithaca, New York, has taken so many twists and turns over the years that one wonders if the saga will ever end. First, a timely and successful investigation by Troop C of the New York State Police led to Michael Kinge as the perpetrator of the crimes. Subsequently, Kinge was fatally shot in police crossfire when he resisted arrest. Kinge's mother, Shirley Kinge, was arrested and prosecuted as an accomplice to the crime and sent to prison in January 1991. The people and police of Ithaca relaxed. The gruesome murder case had been solved and the guilty parties punished or deceased.

But this was not the ending everyone thought it was. In May 1992, newspapers in and around Ithaca ran a shocking headline that David Harding, the head crime-scene investigator in the Harris murder case, admitted to authorities he had fabricated evidence in several cases. The logical question followed: Did Harding tamper with evidence in the Harris case? The eventual answer was "yes." Harding pled guilty to crimes related to the Harris case in November 1992. The bombshell reverberated throughout Troop C, especially on the shoulders of David McElligott, who along with Karl Chandler, had conducted the Harris murder investigation. This was not good news for George Dentes, the district attorney who had successfully prosecuted Shirley Kinge. One can only imagine the shock and anger that erupted inside New York State Police headquarters. Harding had been groomed by his superiors as a rising star on the force. Now they were faced with a catastrophic situation that evolved into the worst scandal in New York State Police history.

Nelson Roth, special prosecutor appointed by Governor Mario Cuomo to investigate corruption within the state police, brought criminal charges of perjury and evidence tampering against Harding and his partner, Robert Lishansky. Both were convicted. Harding was sentenced in 1992 to serve four-to-twelve years behind bars; Lishansky was sentenced to serve six-to-eighteen years.

The criminal misconduct of Harding and Lishansky invalidated the gas can fingerprint evidence against Shirley Kinge. She was released from prison on September 29, 1992, having served a year in Tompkins County Jail and one-and-a-half years in Bedford Hills Correctional Facility in Westchester County, New York. Subsequently, the court ruled the time Kinge had served behind bars covered her stolen credit card conviction. It appeared as though justice had finally won. The bad guys were in jail, the guilty had served and the innocent freed.

With Harding and Lishansky successfully prosecuted and in prison, Roth turned to investigating David McElligott and Karl Chandler. McElligott told his friends: "I have nothing to hide. I'll tell them anything they wanta know." Someone suggested he had better hire a lawyer, but McElligott swiftly rejected the idea: "What do I need a lawyer for? I've done nothing wrong."

Harding had accused McElligott under oath, saying that evidence tampering was commonplace in Troop C, that McElligott knew and approved of it. He was just following orders. McElligott's angry reaction after hearing Harding's testimony conveyed his strong feelings. "The bastard is a liar and he knows it." McElligott willingly took a polygraph test and easily passed.

Before Roth issued his final report, Troop C's field commander (third in charge) brought McElligott and Chandler into his office. He said, "Boys, the superintendent would like you to retire."

"How come?" asked McElligott.

"I'm not at liberty to discuss this with you," the commander replied.

His face getting hot, McElligott eyeballed the boss and said, "Well, I'll be damned. This doesn't smell so good. I'd like to go and ask—"

The commander interrupted, "No, that's not possible to go over me. If you guys don't agree to take early retirement, you'll be transferred to Albany."

Both McElligott and Chandler had served thirty-five years on the force. They were nearing mandatory retirement. There was no way they were going to commute over two hours each way to desk jobs in Albany.

These savvy detectives felt sure they knew what was going on. If they agreed to retire, Nelson Roth's report would not be as highly critical of the state police. The agency would be seen as cleaning house. They were getting rid of the two investigators who the special prosecutor determined were partially liable for the rogue cops and their corrupt behavior. Roth cited McElligott for "willful blindness."

McElligott said at the time, "I told Roth the absolute truth of what happened with Harding. I said I had some uneasy feelings about 'hot shot' and warned the SOB if I found he was up to no good, there'd be hell to pay. But as I told Roth, I gave out assignments to the detectives and coordinated the investigation, but with this high-profile case there were captains, colonels and others above me checking in daily on progress we were making. The investigation was closely supervised. You have to trust people you work with or you get nowhere."

Aspects of the Roth investigation had seemed surreal to McElligott and other police officers. It was as though the special prosecutor was looking to find crime where none existed. Roth informed McElligott during their last interview that six months previous to this meeting, David Harding admitted during a jail interview that he had lied about McElligott's involvement in the evidence-tampering scandal. An incredulous McElligott asked Roth why had he hadn't mentioned this before now. Roth did not answer.

Friends of McElligott and Chandler were as furious as the two officers were over their push to early retirement. They knew the investigators were some of the best and the brightest in the Bureau of Criminal Investigation (BCI) division of the state police. Yet, these distinguished men were now caught between a rock and a hard place. They had no stomach to fight the indignity, so they retired from the force. They believed they were the fall guys to demonstrate to the public that the state police was reforming itself.

A particularly heinous pedophilia case, involving kidnapping and murder, had been on McElligott's desk to solve during and after the Harris murders. For several years he led two task forces of detectives from both New York's BCI Unit and from the Massachusetts State Police before finally bringing the perpetrator to justice. The guilty party is now serving two life sentences in New York and Massachusetts. "It's always a team effort," McElligott said, never boastful about his own role in solving cases. When McElligott and Chandler retired from the force, there were no unsolved crimes on their docket.

David McElligott is still protecting the innocent and seeking out wrongdoers. He is his own boss now, working as a private eye. Additionally, as the acting justice in the village of Watkins Glen, New York, he is often addressed as "Your Honor." He still looks around to see who that is.

Karl Chandler still lives in upstate New York and can usually be found on the golf course, weather permitting.

David Harding's life since his release on November 6, 1996, from Clinton Correctional Facility is not known with certainty. It is said he lived in Florida for a while and others claim he resumed his Waverly, New York, connections.

Robert Lishansky returned to Oneonta after being released from Hudson Correctional Facility on May 20, 1998. He is reported to be working in an educational bureau.

George Dentes, a Republican, continued to be reelected district attorney in Tompkins County, where Democrats outnumbered Republicans, three to two. Dentes got into hot water with liberal Democrats while prosecuting anti-Iraq War protesters in 2004. The "St. Pat's Four" had refused to leave an Ithaca armed-services recruiting station after splattering blood throughout the waiting room of the facility. The case was finally settled in federal court, sending the activists to prison. Gwen Wilkinson, a liberal Democrat, ran a successful campaign in 2005 to replace Dentes, having benefited from financial contributions of mainstream national women's organizations and from lesbian and gay groups. The electorate was aroused to vote for change, and she won. Wilkinson took office in January 2006. Dentes had served sixteen years as the Tompkins County district attorney.

George Dentes is currently a staff attorney for the New York Prosecutors Training Institute in Albany, New York.

Shirley Kinge, understandably embittered over the malfeasance of police officers who sent her to prison, wanted another day in court. This time she directed her lawyer, William Sullivan, to file suit against the state of New York in 1992, to prosecute Kinge's civil claims for false arrest, prosecution and conviction. Sullivan paid scant attention to Kinge's lawsuit against the state. He filed briefs so late they exceeded the statue of limitations. Years went by with no progress made or seen on the horizon.

Russell Maines, a reporter for the *Ithaca Journal*, who covered Shirley Kinge's trial in 1990, befriended Kinge after he left the newspaper and entered law school. As a full-fledged lawyer, Maines took on Kinge's beleaguered cause. In February 2002, he brought a civil action against William Sullivan to the United States District Court in New York, citing Sullivan's professional negligence. The suit asked for a judgment of $1 million. The court ruled in March 2005 that time for such a civil action had expired.

But Sullivan's troubles were not over. Assistant U. S. Attorney Miroslav Lovric obtained an indictment in October 2004 against William Sullivan in United States District Court in Binghamton for failure to file tax returns and pay taxes from 1998 through 2001. Sullivan pleaded guilty on September 29, 2005, to the federal charges. Sentencing guidelines range from six-to-twelve-months imprisonment.

William Sullivan was sentenced on June 29, 2006, to six months of home detention and two years of probation.

The testimony of Cornell University professor Dean Sutfin, during the Harris murder investigation, had been an important link to prosecuting Shirley Kinge. But later in the trial, Sutfin amended his original account when he told Karl Chandler he was sure he saw a van with a black male driver and an older black woman as a passenger in the early hours of December 23, 1989, on Ellis Hollow Road. By the end of the trial he testified he was not certain it was that day he had seen the van. He admitted it could have been another date on which he spotted the vehicle with a black driver and passenger. Since the fingerprint evidence on the gas can turned out to be fraudulent and Sutfin's testimony revealed he was uncertain of the exact date, these seemed to rule out any possibility that Shirley Kinge was near the Harris home on that fateful day.

The only legal option left for Shirley Kinge to claim money damages was to file a lawsuit in the court of claims, against the New York State Police. The court functions with one judge presiding without a jury. Its sole purpose is to handle lawsuits brought against the state and its agencies.

The one-week trial was held in January 2006 in a Syracuse, New York, courtroom. The Kinge suit charged the state police were liable, due to the professional negligence of David McElligott, arguing that McElligott showed willful blindness to Harding's unlawful acts, which led to the further Kinge argument that the state police lacked probable cause for prosecution of Shirley Kinge. The plaintiff asked for $5 million in damages.

Belinda Wagner, a New York assistant attorney general, argued on behalf of the state police, defending the professional conduct of McElligott and other officers during the 1990 Harris murder investigation.

The court's ruling is expected soon.

Shirley Kinge now lives in Atlanta, Georgia. There are those who still question her guilt or innocence.